A PROMISE TO KEEP

NATHAN C. BELTH

A PROMISE TO KEEP

A Narrative of the American Encounter with Anti-Semitism

Times
BOOKS

Illustrations included in these pages were researched and selected by Samuel Elfert, Zirel Handler and Harry Neuschafer. We gratefully acknowledge the contributions of the following photographic collections and services:

A.D.L. Picture Collection, pp. 40, 42, 62, 63, 66, 71, 85, 113, 125, 126, 132, 140, 144, 182, 190, 207, 209, 254, 266, 272, 279; American Jewish Historical Society, pp. 4, 6, 12; American Shakespeare Festival, p. 55; Collection of John Appel, pp. 24, 47, 48, 49; Beacon Press, p. 165; Bettmann Archives, p. 33; Culver Pictures, pp 90, 163; Harper & Row, Publishers, p. 168; The Jewish Encyclopedia, p. 265; Library of Congress, pp. 5, 18; Museum of Modern Art Film Library, p. 55; National Conference of Christians and Jews, p. 154; *The New York Times*, pp. 45, 100; New York Public Library Picture Collection, pp. 15, 30; U.P.I., pp. 211, 261; Frank Tames, p. 254; The White House, pp. 256, 258; Wide World, pp. 86, 104, 133, 135, 157, 159, 167, 174, 178, 201, 202; Yivo Institute for Jewish Research, p. 27.

Published by TIMES BOOKS, a division of Quadrangle/The New York Times Book Co., Inc. Three Park Avenue, New York, N. Y. 10016

Published simultaneously in Canada by Fitzhenry & Whiteside, Ltd., Toronto

Library of Congress Cataloging in Publication Data

Belth, Nathan C
  A promise to keep.

  Bibliography: p.
  Includes index.
  1. Antisemitism—United States. 2. Jews in the United States—
Politics and government. 3. United States—Politics and government.
I. Title.
DS146.U6B44 1979   301.45'19'24073   78-20680
ISBN 0-8129-0814-7

Manufactured in the United States of America

For Helen

Proclaim liberty throughout the land,
unto all the inhabitants thereof

LEVITICUS XXV: 10
(Inscription on the Liberty Bell)

Foreword

The plan for this book has been incubating for a quarter century. I first discussed it with two colleagues in, of all places, Hamburg, Germany, in 1954. We were there on invitation of the government of the Federal Republic as a study team to observe post-war German progress toward democracy and to attempt to judge what hope there might be for a revived Jewish community after the Holocaust. What we found is recorded in the report *Germany Nine Years Later*, issued by the Anti-Defamation League of B'nai B'rith which had sponsored our mission. I am still under the spell of that experience, seeking to explain, at least for myself, why America's encounter with anti-Semitism is so different from Europe's. For different it is, despite the fact that our American experience is so deeply rooted in Europe's. In these pages, I have sought to point to some answers, but primarily my purpose has been to tell the story of the American promise and to let the reader judge how it has been kept.

From time to time, the subject for this work was broached anew among the three who had first discussed it in Hamburg. The late Jacob A. Alson, head of the team that had undertaken the mission in Germany, was for a generation a distinguished leader of the League, a man of erudition, sound judgments and devotion to democratic process. Benjamin R. Epstein, then and in all the years since, national director of the League, has made major contributions to the field of human relations. It is a source of gratification to me that both have left their marks on this work. Beyond that, I find it gratifying that the writing of the book was made possible by a grant from the trustees of the Jacob A. Alson Memorial Fund and that its publication marks observance of the League's 65th Anniversary.

There are a great many people to thank: scholars whom I met only in the pages of their books; actors in the unfolding drama who shared their experiences through interviews and made private papers available to me. Nor could I have done without the splendid support, research and thinking shared generously with me by dozens of colleagues. I have endeavored to acknowledge my debt to each of them at appropriate points in text and source notes. Special thanks are due to Stanley Wexler, the League's publications director, whose editiorial skills I leaned on and whose encouragement nourished me.

Logistical problems sometimes seemed overwhelming: I might have succumbed were it not for the ministrations of Elizabeth Purnell who possesses arcane powers over such matters. She kept me on schedule and unencumbered. The assistance of Mortimer Kass, the League's information director, Florence Lummer, its librarian, and Joan Green, who coped valiantly with my scribbles in typing the manuscript, were indispensable.

To my patient, encouraging wife, Helen, I am especially grateful for her understanding of me and her insights into the subject matter of this book.

N.C.B.

New York
February, 1979

Contents

INTRODUCTION

Perception and Reality

Contemporary perceptions of anti-Semitism in America have been influenced as much by the fears as the facts of history. Reality has been distorted by the glare of mid-twentieth-century European horrors and sometimes lost in the dim shadows of the American past. The effort in these pages will be to sharpen the focus, to restate the facts of American history, to put the justifiable fears in perspective.

Anti-Semitic behavior in America has often reflected European origins, but rarely, in over three centuries of history, have anti-Semitic incidents here attained the intensity—and never have they exacted the fearful price—of European bigotry.

Because it had few ideological roots, anti-Semitism in America rarely expressed itself in outbursts of physical violence. Religiously based antipathy to Jews, cruelly expressed in all of European history, remained muted and was felt by Jews here primarily in their social and economic lives, sometimes in the curtailment of civil rights, but infrequently in violence.

At various times, American Jews were plagued by the xenophobic image of the "stranger," the prevalence of obnoxious stereotypes, the propagation of the Shylock myth, the disability of the socially rejected. Politically inspired anti-Semitism, so devasting to European Jewry in the nineteenth and twentieth centuries, gained no ground here. Even though the infection crossed the oceans in periods of its greatest virulence in Europe, the American political system and ideology provided immunity.

Such—in broad strokes—are the differences, and they in turn have dictated the strategy and tactics in the struggle against anti-Semitism. Whenever the differences have not been perceived, that struggle has suffered. Throughout the nineteenth century, American Jewry, small in numbers and showing only modest growth, felt little need for organizing self-protective efforts. Their concerns were for their brethren under attack in Europe. Their sense of security and their understanding of the American commitment was such that they did not hesitate to seek the moral and political help of their fellow citizens, and indeed of the government itself, in critical situations affecting Jews in Europe.

Jewish communal organization was principally concerned with religion, charity, and internal social and cultural affairs. Not until well past the turn of the twentieth century did an organization appear specifically formed for protective action to counter the impact of anti-Semitism at home and to make its contribution to the civil rights development of the nation. That organization was the Anti-Defamation League, formed by the leadership of B'nai B'rith in 1913, after experimenting with the format and defining the purposes for the agency since 1908.

Until that point, problems of anti-Semitism abroad were met by outstanding figures among American Jews and by the old established organizations such as B'nai B'rith and the Union of American Hebrew Congregations, often joining with parallel groups in Europe. In 1906 an important Eastern seaboard leadership group formed the American Jewish Committee, largely because of Russian attacks on Jews; but for many years it was unconcerned with the problems of anti-Semitism and the discriminations against Jews at home. In critical situations, the various organizations sought to coordinate their actions, but their efforts were pointed toward problems abroad.

Genesis for Jews in America dawned in 1654, half a century after the first white settlement at Jamestown, Virginia, and some three decades after the landing of the Pilgrims at Plymouth Rock and the Dutch at New Amsterdam. Here our story begins—recounting the high and the low moments of the history of anti-Semitism in America and of the first organization formed by American Jews specifically to deal with the problem.

A PROMISE TO KEEP

ONE

Exodus to Genesis

Particularism, not tolerance, was the hallmark of the seventeenth-century settlements in what was to become, in the fullness of time, a land built on the revolutionary idea of freedom and civil liberty. Massachusetts, where the Puritans settled to breathe the free air of the New Israel, was not a very healthy place for Quakers, Catholics, and other dissenters from the rigidities of Puritan doctrine. Maryland, where Catholics held sway, reversed the order of heresies; while Virginia, the first colony, demanded conformity with the established Anglican Church.

Historian William Lecky could speak of "Hebraic mortar" cementing "the foundations of American democracy" because of Puritan literal adherence to Hebrew Scriptures; but Judah Monis, whose Hebrew grammar was published in 1735 for use at Harvard College, was not accepted as a member of the faculty until he converted to Christianity in 1720, although Hebrew was a major subject of study at Harvard as early as 1655.

The road to freedom from the European pattern of religious intolerance in the Dutch West India Company settlement of New Amsterdam had its own peculiar twists and turns. Here the issue was forced by the appearance of the first Jewish settlers on the North American continent. Colonization by the Dutch was for purposes of trade; yet when the test came, the reaction of the New Amsterdam authorities was at first not unlike that of the English settlements because the Dutch

דִקְדוּק לְשׁוֹן עִבְרִית

N.º 271.

DICKDOOK LESHON GNEBREET.

A

GRAMMAR

OF THE

𝕳𝖊𝖇𝖗𝖊𝖜 𝕿𝖔𝖓𝖌𝖚𝖊,

BEING

An ESSAY

To bring the 𝕳𝖊𝖇𝖗𝖊𝖜 𝕲𝖗𝖆𝖒𝖒𝖆𝖗 into 𝕰𝖓𝖌𝖑𝖎𝖘𝖍,

to Facilitate the

INSTRUCTION

Of all those who are desirous of acquiring a clear Idea of this

Primitive Tongue

by their own Studies ;

In order to their more distinct Acquaintance with the SACRED ORACLES of the Old Testament, according to the Original. And Published more especially for the Use of the STUDENTS of *HARVARD-COLLEGE* at *Cambridge*, in NEW-ENGLAND.

נֶחְבַּר וְהוּגַת בְּעִיּוּן נִמְרָץ עַל יְדֵי
יְהוּדָה מוֹנִישׁ

Composed and accurately Corrected,

By JUDAH MONIS, *M. A.*

BOSTON, N.E.

Printed by JONAS GREEN, and are to be Sold by the AUTHOR at his House in *Cambridge*.   MDCCXXXV.

Reform preachers rivaled the Puritans in their intolerance for all except Calvinists.

Into this xenophobic atmosphere in 1654 came 23 Jewish settlers in flight from the Inquisition after the Portuguese had ousted the Dutch from Recife, Brazil. The ensuing confrontation was the first anti-Semitic incident in American history and its denouement the first triumph of the fight against bigotry and hatred which had been the fate of the Jewries of the Old World.

Peter Stuyvesant, the Dutch governor of New Amsterdam, mis-construed the temper of his masters in Holland, if not the position of his local population. The Netherlands, after all, had become the major haven of Jews fleeing the Spanish Inquisition, and there were Jews among the directors and investors of the Dutch West India Company. Stuyvesant's efforts to oust the Recife refugees was forestalled by his principals in Holland, and by 1657 the Jewish settlers, not without effort, acquired most of the rights of burghers of New Amsterdam and, when the English ousted the Dutch, of New York.

(Left) *Hebraic Mortar. Title page of the Hebrew grammer by Judah Monis published for the use of Harvard students in 1735.*

(Below) *The directors of the East India Company in Holland blocked Stuyvesant's move to oust the first Jewish settlers in New Amsterdam.*

The special significance of the New Amsterdam incident was not the fact that it involved the first Jewish settlers, but that it was the only incident in the colonization of America in which Jews were the prime—and not the incidental—target of xenophobic impulses grounded in the religious particularism of the dominant sect of a colony. Stuyvesant had reasoned that if he permitted Jews to stay and have freedom of worship, he would have to tolerate Lutherans and Baptists, too—as he pointed out to the West India Company board of directors. That was anathema to his Calvinist soul.

In New England and the Southern English colonies, however, Jews were the incidental victims of the prevailing intolerance. The prime targets were dissenting Christians, whether Catholic, Quaker, Baptist, or others unacceptable to the established church of a colony. Physical punishment, hangings, burnings and exile were all common for such dissenters. There is no record of Jews being physically harmed out of religious motives, and no eighteenth-century law enacted for the purpose of disabling Jews; though in 1649 Maryland passed a blasphemy law providing for the death penalty against traducers of "our Blessed Saviour." In 1658 Jacob Lumbrozo, a Jewish physician from Portugal, was charged under the law, but the court seemed unwilling to prosecute; he was never convicted or punished.

Stuyvesant surrendering to the English. Jewish settlers retained their burgher rights under the new colonial rule.

Aside from New York, Jews in the colonial period fared best in Rhode Island, to which they were specifically invited by its founder, Roger Williams, who, driven from Massachusetts for his liberal views, accepted Hebrew Scriptures as the pattern for his theory of religious freedom. To him, unlike the Puritans, it was natural to accept the Hebrews along with their Bible.

Jews found their way to Pennsylvania in 1726, considering the Quaker colony a hospitable place, even though William Penn's successors practiced their own orthodoxy and restricted voting and public officeholding to Christians. In South Carolina, the influence of John Locke, the English philosopher whose natural-rights theories infused a liberal spirit into the colony beyond the ordinary, attracted Jewish settlers early and, by 1703, Jews there exercised the right to vote for the first time in Colonial America.

Georgia, whose charter permitted only Protestant settlement, nevertheless was a haven for Jews, admitted by James Oglethorpe, the founder of the colony, on the same basis as others. He had established Georgia not as a refuge for victims of religious intolerance, but as a haven for victims of the cruel English law against debtors. In 1733 a contingent of 43 Jews from England and several months later 40 more from Portugal arrived in Savannah. Each was given a plot of land and equal rights and privileges with the other settlers. They founded a congregation almost at once. Mordecai Sheftell, the first white child born in Savannah, was of Jewish parentage. He became a leading Revolutionary War figure in his native city and state.

In the context of the time in Europe, where anti-Semitism was rife and deadly, the 250 Jews in Colonial America suffered no disabilities that were not the lot of other religious dissenters from the orthodoxies of the dominant church in each colony. They faced sporadic efforts to restrict their civil and religious rights and exclusion from some occupations, but these efforts failed on the whole, and the European medieval patterns lost their way in the American wilderness. By the time the colonies were ready to fight for independence, American experience pointed to the two great reforms that would make the United States different in the life of Jews: separation of church and state, and civil and religious equality.

These reforms—two centuries in the making—and the Jewish responses to them wrought the great change in the long and difficult history of Jewish life in the Western nations. When the great, massive anti-Semitism of the twentieth century began to grip the world,

American Jewry had developed enough stability to enable it to meet the challenges that now went far beyond religious bigotry to xenophobia heated up on a worldwide scale by political ideologies, power politics, economic competition, and racial conflict.

Logic of the Wilderness

Throughout the seventeenth century, the condition of Jewish settlers did not so much advance through direct action by the colonial governments as by failure of the ruling powers to enforce restrictions. Every settler was important for himself—his mere presence as part of the general community. By 1670 there were still only 80,000 Europeans in colonies scattered along the Atlantic coastline; even 250 Jews were a valuable asset in terms of the safety and viability of the total community. New additions to the population were more important than rigid application of the prevailing prejudices. It took a hundred years for the population of the thirteen colonies to reach 2,000,000 and the Jewish component to rise to 2,000.

The logic of the wilderness, rather than principled rejection of sectarian bigotry, led to an easing of particularist religious regulation. In New England, second-generation Puritans seemed ready to concede that there was more than one road to salvation and that dissenters from their own creed were therefore admissible to the community. In Maryland uneasy Catholics, fearing royal imposition of the Anglican Church as the establishment church, promulgated the 1649 Act of Religious Toleration to safeguard their own position and, therefore, the position of other Christians. The defensive factor in the Act no doubt also accounted for the colony's reluctance to pursue the blasphemy charge against Dr. Lumbrozo. Quaker Pennsylvania's Frame of Government and First Fundamentals in 1682-83 provided for freedom of worship, and of course Rhode Island was founded on Roger Williams' idea that "all men of whatever nation—shall have the same privileges as Englishmen, any law to the contrary notwithstanding." The thriving Jewish community of Newport assumed civic rights under this dispensation as a matter of course.

In the next half-century, the discriminatory restrictions that affected Jews became increasingly anachronistic; the disabling laws against Jews were not withdrawn, but fell into disuse as they were ignored. The growing Enlightenment in Europe and the writings of the philosophers of the movement—John Locke primarily—had begun to have a deep effect upon thought in America. With it came growing acquisition of political rights by Jews.

A climactic point arrived in the year 1740 and from a most unexpected direction—England itself. Parliament that year adopted a law providing for the naturalization of all foreigners resident in the colonies for seven years. More important, Jews were specifically exempted from taking a citizenship oath professing Christianity, although in England itself the oath retained the unacceptable phrases. As a result, Jews in America achieved an equality not reached by any in Europe. Nonetheless, Jews were still barred by Christian-professing oaths from high public office, but the concept of an established church became progressively irrelevant and the Hebrew faith achieved equality with all others. The fact that this came about without confrontation or crisis was doubly welcome.

Powered mainly by the intellectual thought of the Enlightenment and the growing resistance of the various Christian sects to the established Church of England, the separating wall between church and state continued to rise until it achieved full height with the adoption of the First Amendment of the Constitution of the United States. Nothing could have been more salutary for the position of Jews.

Unquestionably, the Church of England suffered rejection among leaders looking to American independence because the Anglican clergy were largely loyal to the Crown. Once the Revolution came, the need to dissolve the official tie of the church to state became evident to those who had accepted the logic that natural rights supersede constituted authority. Freedom of thought—especially religious belief—stood at the top of the list of essential freedoms.

Moves for Separation

The initial major move in the direction of separation came in the first colony—Virginia. In adopting its new state constitution in 1776, Virginia proclaimed "All men...entitled to the free exercise of religion according to the dictates of conscience" after James Madison had objected to a provision for mere toleration. But while the Anglican Church was thus disestablished, the effort to establish Christianity, rather than any particular sect, did not cease. In 1784 it was proposed that every citizen be taxed for the support of some Christian church.

Madison and Jefferson vigorously opposed the tax bill, Madison arguing "that the same authority which can establish Christianity to the exclusion of all other religions may establish, with the same ease, any particular sect of Christians in exclusion of all other sects." Ultimately, the act establishing religious liberty in 1786 was so phrased as to include Jews. It completely severed the state from church, expressed clearly the view that "the reason of man may be trusted with the formation of his own opinions," and declared that "matters of religion...shall in no wise diminish, enlarge or affect men's civil capacities."

With Virginia as the bellwether, other states, each in accordance with its predilections, moved in the direction of loosening the bonds that were tying the existing established churches to the political authority. Pennsylvania and New York adopted religious freedom in their new constitutions at once. The Continental Congress wrote a similar provision into the Ordinance establishing the Northwest Territory, and ultimately the United States Constitution provided for religious freedom through Article VI and the First Amendment.

Not all states acted with such alacrity and major religious disabilities for some groups dragged on well into the nineteenth century. Indeed, the Supreme Court as late as 1845 (the Permoli case) ruled that the United States Constitution did not protect citizens from invasion of their religious liberties by the states because the First Amendment applied only to the Federal government.

The disabilities of establishment persisted longest in New England, where except for Rhode Island, religious dissenters were most harried during the colonial era. There were, therefore, fewer minorities to press for separation of church and state. Thus, the last state to disestablish its official church was Massachusetts, land of the Pilgrims. Not until 1833 was the final act of separation written, and then not until after an effort had been made, as in Virginia, to establish Christianity in place of a particular sect, as the official religion.

A factor in the Congregationalists' ability to maintain themselves in their favored position in Massachusetts so long was their record of opposition to the English crown and the unquestioned adherence of their clergy to the Revolution. They did not suffer the disabilities of the Church of England hierarchy in Virginia. Also helpful to the establishment was the fact that the impact of the philosophers of the Enlightenment had led to liberalization of some of the discriminatory practices against dissenting sects. Unitarians and others could direct their taxes for religious purposes to their own institutions, and in 1808 a Boston Jew named Moses Michael Hays succeeded in having his tax applied, not to the Congregationalist Church, but to his own synagogue.

The matter of sectarian oaths of office long remained a sticking point and was unresolved in many places well after the middle of the nineteenth century. In North Carolina, the oath for legislators professing Christianity was not expunged until after the Civil War in the state constitution of 1865, even though in 1809 Jacob Henry, a Jew, was permitted to take his seat without the objectionable oath.

A major battle on the issue was fought in Maryland where there had been an uneasy shifting of power back and forth between a Catholic and an Anglican establishment since the seventeenth century. The effect was to promote, as a matter of self-defense, a policy of toleration at least for all Christian sects, though the Blasphemy Act disqualified Unitarians and Jews. Even the first Maryland state constitution of 1776 required an oath of Christian belief from officeholders. The following year Jews petitioned for relief from the requirement, but to no avail. In time, however, the issue produced one stubborn heroic figure: Thomas Kennedy, Scottish-born Presbyterian and a follower of Thomas Jefferson, who in 1817 supported a bill in the General Assembly that had been introduced by William Pinckney to eliminate the oath. The bill obtained only 40 votes and went down to defeat. Passionately committed to religious freedom, Kennedy fought hard for the bill. Justice was his cause, he said.

"There are no Jews in the country from which I come," he declared, "nor have I the slightest acquaintance with any Jew in the world. There are few in the United States; and in Maryland there are few, but if there were only one, to that one we ought to do justice."

For his pains, he was defeated at the next election, as were 15 others of the 40 who had voted for the bill. In 1823 he was again beaten in the election, but two years later, campaigning on his support of the "Jew Bill," he won; in 1826 he finally achieved his goal and the bill became law. It was a major victory on the long road to separation of church and state, as Kennedy argued, sundering "forever... the spiritual from the temporal concerns of men" and leaving behind "the insidious policy of regal governments to make an instrument of religion." Somewhat more accurately, Benjamin Franklin had commented many years earlier that "to get the bad customs of a country changed and new ones, though better introduced... is not the work of a day."

The long road to remove the "instrument of religion" from the hands of the states took a backward turn when the Supreme Court

SKETCH

OF

PROCEEDINGS IN THE

Legislature of Maryland,

DECEMBER SESSION, 1818,

ON WHAT IS COMMONLY CALLED

The Jew Bill;

CONTAINING

THE REPORT OF THE COMMITTEE

APPOINTED BY THE HOUSE OF DELEGATES

"To consider the justice and expediency of extending to those persons professing the Jewish Religion, the same privileges that are enjoyed by Christians:"

TOGETHER WITH

The Bill reported by the Committee,

AND

THE SPEECHES

OF

THOMAS KENNEDY, Esq. OF WASHINGTON COUNTY,

AND

H. M. BRACKENRIDGE, Esq. OF BALTIMORE CITY.

Baltimore:
PRINTED BY JOSEPH ROBINSON,
Circulating Library, corner of Market and Belvidere-streets.

1819

handed down the decision in the 1845 Permoli case. The court, dominated by John Marshall, on most other counts had striven to strengthen the Federal power already so thoroughly committed to disestablishment. Not so in this instance. Not until 1947, more than a century later—in *Everson v. Board of Education*, which dealt with busing for parochial school children—did the court apply the separation clause of the First Amendment to the states by invoking the Fourteenth Amendment's due-process clause. The court had worked its way up slowly to this position through a series of cases in the 1920's and 1930's. A landmark along the way was a "concurring opinion" delivered by Justice Benjamin Cardozo in 1934 in *Hamilton v. University of California*, in which he said:

> The First Amendment, if it be read into the Fourteenth makes invalid any state law "respecting an establishment of religion or prohibiting the free exercise thereof."

In the Everson case, Justice Hugo Black, speaking for the full court on the issue brought it to its logical conclusion in a definitive statement which bears repeating:

> The "establishment of religion" clause of the First Amendment means at least this: Neither a state nor the Federal Government can set up a church. Neither can pass laws which aid one religion, aid all religions, or prefer one religion over another. Neither can force nor influence a person to go to or to remain away from church against his will or force him to profess a belief or disbelief in any religion. No person can be punished for entertaining or professing religious beliefs or disbeliefs, for church attendance or nonattendance. No tax in any amount, large or small, can be levied to support any religious activities or institutions, whatever they may be called, or whatever form they may adopt to teach or practice religion. Neither a state nor the Federal Government can, openly or secretly, participate in the affairs of any religious organizations or groups and vice versa. In the words of Jefferson, the clause against establishment of religion by law was intended to erect "a wall of separation between church and State."

Specific issues involving state support or lack of it for religion have been and will continue to be contested in the courts, but as long as the separating wall stands, it will, for Jews as well as other religious

(Left) *The Maryland "Jew Bill"—A major victory in the long march toward separation of church and state.*

groups, provide the "liberty of conscience and immunities of citizenship" of which George Washington wrote in 1790 more in prophecy than out of the realities of his time. Nevertheless, the American Revolution had established the principles. Jews, perhaps for the first time in their many migrations, became citizens of a secular state and political community. But the equality achieved in consitutional law often took longer in reality; and even as progress was being made, new elements of bigotry and discrimination, both nativist and imported varieties, were entering the mainstreams of American life. However, Jews could at least bask in the warmth of Washington's pledge that "the government of the United States . . . gives to bigotry no sanction, to persecution no assistance . . ."

Catholics Bear the Brunt

The regressive strain in the American body politic was in steady retreat before the progress set in motion by the Revolution. The endemic religious bigotry was slowly, but surely giving ground—at least on the political front—when the Federalist party met in convention in Hartford, Connecticut in 1815. Angry and frustrated, the party, which had lost three Presidential elections at this oint, took a turn down a dangerous road. For the first time, there appeared at the convention an organized effort to couple, for political purposes, the prevailing religious bigotry with fear of the foreign-born which was to characterize the next century. The convention proposed to make naturalized citizens ineligible to serve in Congress. This idea and the Federalist party disappeared, but the new and powerful combinations of hatreds had come to stay on the national scene.

The xenophobic forces gained strength rapidly after 1830, even while the nation's liberal traditions grew and established the basic character of the land. Their first victims were the Masons, and though the attack was vicious, it passed quickly as Catholics—mainly immigrant Irish—became the ideal target. Jews, also immigrants and dissenters, received appropriate but minor attention. Because their numbers were few, they did not become principal targets for attack until after the 1890's with the mass immigration from Eastern Europe.

(Right) *Samuel F. B. Morse.—Inventor of the telegraph, defamer of Catholics.*

The torments suffered by the Catholic immigrants of the nineteenth century fill some of the blackest pages of American history. Violence—killings, burnings, general destruction—were commonplace. Vilification, degradation, constant political attack was their ever-present burden. From Samuel F. B. Morse, Boston-born inventor and artist in the 1830s, to Tom Watson, the Georgia demagogue, publisher and quondam senator, in the 1920's, they faced an unremitting propaganda barrage that undercut their civic and social ground and created one political movement after another dedicated to their destruction.

Morse came by his anti-Catholicism in a most traditional manner. He was born the son of a Congregationalist minister with a deep animus toward all other faiths—Catholicism most of all. Young Morse learned well. In 1829 he visited Rome, witnessed a papal procession and had an altercation with a papal guard. His experiences and observations confirmed him in his attitudes. In 1834 his book, *Foreign Conspiracy Against the Liberties of the U.S.*, appeared, showing off his inventive, if not scholarly, mind. Filled with inaccuracies and unsupportable assertions, he saw Protestantism as the protector and "Popery" as the attacker of liberty. His book received wide circulation and powered anti-Catholic movements for decades.

While Morse misconstrued and misinformed with his political writings, other literary effusions appeared pandering to the bias and prurience of the nativist turn of mind. Most notorious among these was *The Awful Disclosures of Maria Monk* and *Six Months in a Convent*. In time, a vast literature grew up which served to enthrall the gullible and therefore had its political uses.

By 1835 a political organization, anti-immigrant and anti-Catholic, calling itself the Native American Party polled nearly 40 percent of the vote in a New York City election. The party picked up where the Federalists had left off in 1815 in its attitude toward the foreign-born. It called for exclusion of all foreign-born from public office and for twenty-one years of residence of immigrants before naturalization. Indeed, under President John Adams, the Federalists had succeeded in passing an act requiring fourteen years of residence before the granting of citizenship. This was reduced to five years in the succeeding administration of Thomas Jefferson.

The strong showing of the Native American Party in New York, as it became increasingly anti-Catholic, was influenced by Catholic protest against Protestant domination of the public schools coupled with the demand that Catholic parochial schools receive assistance from school taxes paid the city by Catholic parents. Catholic leaders took especial exception to lessons which subjected their children to listen to attacks on "Popery" and the Catholic character in terms "of insult and contempt." The city fathers found these complaints "to be not wholly unfounded," but the ultimate result was a strengthening of antagonisms and an upward trend in the fortunes of the Native American Party. The strength of the party resided chiefly in the cities. It was opposed in the unsettled areas which welcomed immigrants, who were badly needed to develop the land. On the frontiers, at least, the anti-immigration policies of the nativists boomeranged.

Nevertheless, nativism cut a considerable swath in the cities during a fifteen-year period. Philadelphia, in particular, suffered devastating riots in 1844 that resulted in the destruction and burning of Catholic churches and schools and scores of homes. The rioting included many deaths and even larger numbers of wounded.

In Congress, the Native American Party pressed strongly for restrictive legislation against immigration and naturalization, without success except that for a time it enjoyed a national forum for its propaganda. Yet, the party lost ground, no doubt helped along by the very violence of thought and action it espoused. But even as the Native American Party faded, a new movement came along to take its place in the political spectrum.

Know-Nothing Successes

Popularly known as the Know-Nothings, the new organization called itself the Grand Council of the United States of North America. The Know-Nothing designation came from the fact that the council was a secret organization and its members always answered they knew nothing about it. However, the rest of the country knew soon enough. Its constitution required members to be Protestant, of Protestant parentage, and not married to a Catholic. "The object of this organization [was] to resist the insidious policy of the church of Rome...by placing in all offices...none but native-born Protestant citizens." It soon won the fervent endorsement of Samuel Morse for its anti-Catholicism and for "resisting aggression of foreign influence."

The Know-Nothings, diligent and persistent in preaching of anti-Catholicism in the streets and through widely circulated periodicals and pamphlets, showing highly developed propaganda skills, succeeded politically far beyond the levels achieved by the Native American Party. Violence became a standard tactic. Riots took place everywhere that Know-Nothing preachers appeared in the streets. In 1854, an election year, the situation became particularly tense with riots in New York, Brooklyn, Bath, Maine, Lawrence, Massachusetts, and St. Louis, Missouri. In the last city, on August 7 and 8, election time, the local papers reported, "...the military and police were unable to check...the lawlessness and crime." Some 8 or 10 people were killed, 30 seriously wounded, and scores of others hurt. In Louisville, the following year, also at election time, a two-day riot resulted in 20 deaths.

That the propaganda tactics and the incitement to riot paid off politically for the Know-Nothings soon became apparent. In the 1854 elections, the Know-Nothings elected 8 state governors, held 8 of the 62 seats in the Senate, and 104 of the 234 seats in the House. On February 5, 1855 an effort by a Pennsylvania congressman to censure the Know-Nothings as "dangerous and hostile" to the American republican form of government was defeated 103 to 78.

In June, the Know-Nothings, feeling their successes, dropped some

Know-Nothing attack—Irish immigrants bore the brunt in the Philadelphia riots of 1844.

of their secrecy and, joining in the American Party convention in Philadelphia, "demanded resistance to the aggressive policy and corrupting tendencies" of the Catholic church and, in essence, called for a policy that would bar Catholics and foreign-born from public office. The convention also called for twenty-one years of residence as prerequisite for naturalization.

Know-Nothingism crested in 1855-56 with seemingly great but actually ephemeral victories and some unhappy moments for Catholics. The avalanche of published bigotry was truly appalling. The states of New York, Massachusetts, Connecticut, and Ohio enacted laws preventing acquisition of property by Catholic churches. Baltimore was the scene of great rioting and elected a Know-Nothing mayor. The state of Maryland was captured by the American party. In January 1856, Congress engaged in a debate in which Know-Nothing congressmen had a three-day carnival of vituperation and slander. In October, again on election day, Baltimore was plagued with riots, and the American party carried the election by preventing naturalized citizens from voting. In the Presidential election, the American party polled nearly 900,000 votes for Millard Fillmore, but received only 8 electoral college votes. The crest had been reached, and now the high-water mark of anti-Catholic bigotry began slowly to recede as the nation grew increasingly enmeshed in the slavery question and came to the brink of civil war.

The Know-Nothings were still riding high when the man who was to be President of the United States during that war summed up their menace. In a letter on August 24, 1855, Abraham Lincoln wrote:

> As a nation we began by declaring that "all men are created equal." We now practically read it "all men are created equal except Negroes." When the Know-Nothings obtain control, it will read: "All men are created equal except Negroes, foreigners, and Catholics..."

Happily neither the Know-Nothings nor their spiritual heirs to the regressive strain in the American political tradition have ever in the century or more since, gained control.

The Second Exodus

The intensity of the attack upon Catholics and Irish immigrants drew some of the fire of nativism away from Jews just as the second great Jewish exodus from Europe to genesis in America began in 1830;

it would continue for half a century. In the eighteenth century, Jews had begun to come out of their ghetto confines in central Europe as the Enlightenment blossomed, but with the defeat of Napoleon, the Congress of Vienna in 1815 rescinded the reforms he had fostered benefiting German Jews, and their newfound freedoms came to an end.

The Jewish response was either to join the political opposition in the nations that made up the Congress of Vienna or to emigrate to America. With the ultimate failure of the Revolution of 1848, the emigration from the German states reached flood-tide. In the period from 1830 to 1880, the number of Jews in the United States grew from 20,000 to 300,000. Most of the German newcomers were from Bavaria. Others came from Russia, Austria, Hungary, Bohemia and Romania. To place the Jewish immigration in context, it should be noted that 5,000,000 others came from the area in the same period.

The new influx of Jewish immigrants did not so much change the character of the Jewish community as render it less fragile, and at the same time gave it greater visibility. While augmenting the communities of the Eastern seaboard, they also migrated westward, some of them as far as Texas and California. By the 1850's Cincinnati had become a major Jewish community, Galveston had a Jewish mayor, and the Gold Rush had brought hundreds of Jews to San Francisco and its environs. Jews, in fact, became a political and social factor of some consequence and at a point when a large segment of the American population was rethinking the rationalism which had so strongly influenced the American Revolution.

Two of the principal ingredients of this revaluation, largely Protestant in character, were the reactions to the excesses of the French Revolution and the difficulties of frontier life. Religious revival was sought as a replacement for rationalist theses in sustaining the assumptions of the American Enlightenment. In the process, reform of the evils of society became a "Christian duty." The movements to abolish slavery, to promote temperance, education, and other humanitarian reforms all took on a revivalist note of religious conversion. The Protestant motivation coupled to the reformist zeal was not always understandable to Jews with European experiences still fresh in memory.

The new Jewish immigrants learned slowly the values of separation of church and state and opted at first, as Catholics did, for state support of their denominational schools. Problems that were affecting Catholics such as the domination of public education by Protestant sectarian influences also affected them, and they found themselves further troubled by the revival of Sunday blue laws. After 1840 the endemic xenophobia that engulfed the Irish immigrants spilled over upon them, too, and affected the Jewish peddler or shopkeeper who did not seem to meet the standards of conformity demanded by the nativists. The unflattering stereotype became the common coin of bigotry.

How deeply it had infected the social order came as a shock during the Civil War. Jews—whose image had been that of a dissenting religious group having an accepted status and guaranteed rights— now found themselves viewed increasingly in the less acceptable image of outlanders. The major blow fell on December 17, 1862, when General Ulysses S. Grant issued General Order No. 11 expelling "Jews as a class" from the Department of the Tennessee which was under his command. The expulsion was to take place within twenty-four hours and with this most sweeping anti-Jewish regulation in American history, Grant was blaming Jews alone for trading with the "enemy," exchanging Northern suppliers for Southern cotton. That the trading led to corruption and bribery seemed evident, but whether it was entirely illicit is questionable since both Grant and General William T. Sherman had been ordered to encourage the trade. Certainly, several government agencies were working at cross-purposes in issuing permits for such commercial activity.

When news of the order reached Washington, President Lincoln directed its cancellation, but it nevertheless gave encouragement to a spate of Jew-baiting and calumny which up to then had been heard only in minor key. Now, suddenly, the Jewish peddlers and traders, mostly recent immigrants, became easy targets. Both in the North and the South, Jewish loyalties were questioned. Charges of aiding the "enemy," smuggling and money-grubbing cropped up continuously. In the tenseness of fratricidal conflict, the comparative freedom of Jews from anti-Semitic attack had become another casualty of war.

Grant never again figured in anything that would smack of anti-Semitism, but his order had mirrored the widespread bigotry of the times, if not his own feelings. By the fall of 1864, the level of attack on Jews had reached such proportions that Simon Wolf, an officer of B'nai B'rith, founded in 1843, and an eminent Jewish figure of the time, felt called upon to protest to the poet William Cullen Bryant, then recognized as dean of American newspaper editors—a man well disposed to Jews:

The War now raging has developed an insanity of malice that borders upon the darkest days of superstition and the Spanish Inquisition. Has the war now raging been inaugurated or fostered by Jews exclusively? Is the late Democratic Party composed entirely of Israelites? Are there no native Americans engaged in rebellion? No Christians running the blockade, or meek followers of Christ within the fold of Tammany?

We have been branded and outraged for four long years, until discretion has ceased to be a virtue.... Why, when the authorities arrest a criminal, telegraph immediately throughout the Union that a Jew, another Jew blockader, has been caught...? Is it, then, a crime to be born a Jew, which has to be expiated upon the altar of public opinion by a life of suffering and abuse...?

I am not now pleading the cause of the Jew, but I am defending the principle that underlies our public institutions, our private worth. Are we to go on in this uncalled-for vituperation and, sowing the wind, to reap at last the whirlwind?

The fact was that the Civil War period marked a turning point in the status of American Jews. Incidents flowing from the war added a new note of racial bigotry to anti-Jewish attitudes of a religious character, even as the Emancipation Proclamation was extending the principle of egalitarianism. True, no federal or state legislation restricted civil or political rights of Jews; no legal precedents were established to diminish their status as citizens. But, by the same token, neither legislation nor court decision attempted to curtail the new growth of discrimination that had taken root.

The decade following the war was a period of profound changes and at the same time one of turmoil, instability, and bitterness for the nation. The readmission of the Southern states into the Union came slowly. The military occupation of the South and its Reconstruction extended over long years. Not until 1878 were the last of the northern troops recalled.

Old conflicts in the North between Catholics and Protestants resumed as if there had been no war in which they had fought side by side. For a brief period during the war years, Catholics had gained some relief from the organized attacks mounted against them; they even won repeal of some local laws directed against the church. But by 1870 these attacks once more engaged Protestant zealots and nativists. Protestant groups also invested a great deal of emotional capital in their opposition to the Mormons, repelled by their espousal of polygamy. Opposition to the Mormons on moral grounds enlisted a wide range of religious groups. The effect was to draw some of the overt attacks away from both Jews and Catholics—but only for a time.

Jews came to offer a broader target—both their visibility and their numbers had grown. But compared to Catholics and Mormons, the bigotry against them was in a recessive phase until the nation, caught up in new social disorganization and economic pressures, sought a convenient scapegoat.

The 1870's was an era of industrial growth, punctuated by recession and even financial panic as in 1873. Great fortunes were made and sometimes lost, but a new social order was in the making. The old aristocracy—Yankee and Protestant—felt the pressure of a new millionaire class, which in turn was made uneasy by the stirrings and assertiveness of labor.

It was also an era of social ferment. For the newly rich, there was the need to find social recognition. If the symbols of aristocratic family were beyond their reach, they could try to substitute rich and ostentatious living. Those with the attributes of "old stock" needed to express their disdain of the new materialistic society. Both groups sought to bolster their pretensions by exclusiveness.

Describing the development, historian Oscar Handlin wrote:

> . . . . social discrimination spread back from the resorts to the cities. It also spread from the leisure-time, recreational, voluntary-service type of activity to the more serious problems that can literally be a matter of life or death. There was the development over several decades of the concept that large areas of social activity were private, in the sense that they were devoid of public interest and not subject to government interference.

Thus "Turks, Jews and Infidels" would be barred from the sacred precincts. But since Jews were the only recognizable minority among those achieving wealth and business leadership, they were the natural candidates for exclusion. The scene was therefore set for the incident in 1877 that dramatized the beginning of social anti-Semitism in the United States.

"The Second Battle of Saratoga"

Trivial in itself, the exclusion of Joseph Seligman, a banker and the most prominent American Jew of his time, from the Grand Union Hotel in Saratoga Springs, New York, then the most famous resort in the country, has historic importance. The incident, wrote historian Lee M. Friedman, gave "the starting point to articulate public expression of American anti-Semitism and an opportunity for the healthy American reaction to such antidemocratic prejudice" by some of the most notable men of the time.

In 1777 Saratoga had been the scene of the most decisive battle in the American Revolution. In 1877 it was the scene of social battle that mocked the very essence of the Revolution. It was now better known for the Saratoga trunk, Morrissey's gambling casino, and the vulgar ostentation and extravagances of the Gilded Age than for patriotic gore or the defense of Fort Ticonderoga.

For ten years Joseph Seligman had been part of the Saratoga scene. He had been a principal financier for the Union in the Civil War, helped New York City rid itself of the corrupt Tweed Ring, and been offered the post of Secretary of the Treasury in President Grant's cabinet.

But when Seligman and his family arrived at the Grand Union on June 13, 1877, he could get no accommodations. As a result of the death of its fabulously wealthy owner, A. T. Stewart, the New York retail merchant, the hotel had come under the control of his executor, Judge Henry Hilton. Judge Hilton, the hotel clerk informed Seligman "has given instructions that no Israelites shall be permitted in the future to stop at this hotel." Hilton had concluded that Jews were keeping Christian guests away.

Seligman was not one to be handled so cavalierly, and the public quarrel that ensued—ugly, bitter, and bigoted—attained national attention. Anti-Semitic notions, long suppressed or at least unspoken,

A satarist's view of the social "Battle of Saratoga."

poured out in the public prints and public discussion. Seligman was not inclined to suffer insult readily and published a sarcastic letter he had written Hilton, who was not loath to reply publicly and had no apologies for his bigotry. "I don't like this class...and don't care whether they like me or not...I believe we lose much more than we gain by their custom."

Whether he cared or not, Hilton did not go unscathed. National figures such as Mark Twain, Oliver Wendell Holmes, and notably Henry Ward Beecher, the great preacher of the day, expressed their distaste and disdain. In a widely read sermon "Jew and Gentile," the Reverend Mr. Beecher ringingly declared:

> Listen, o ye astonished people; where for fifty years North and South and East and West have come together, and have been instructed, sometimes by ministers and sometimes by Morriseys, and where every form of pleasurable vice, every sort of amusement, everything that would draw custom, has been common—there, in Saratoga, the Corinth of America, in a hotel designed to accommodate two thousand people, it seems society is so developed that it will not consent to go unless everybody that comes is fit to associate with men who made their money yesterday, or a few days ago, selling codfish.

As an aside to Seligman, Beecher commented:

> A hero may be annoyed by a mosquito; but to put on his whole armor and call on his followers to join him in making war on an insect would be beneath his dignity.

But "mosquitoes" are not easily disposed of. Hardly had the Hilton-Seligman quarrel subsided when "society" was treated to a reprise. Austin Corbin, president of the Long Island Railroad and the Manhattan Beach Company which were developing Coney Island as a fashionable shore resort, followed Hilton's lead with the public announcement that "We do not like Jews as a class...they make themselves offensive to the kind of people who principally patronize our road and hotel and I am satisfied we should be better off without than with their custom."

Hilton, Corbin, and others in similar positions of management were emboldened by reading the signs of the times. A developing thesis of the second-half-century strengthened notions that privacy—not public interest—was paramount in social activity. The tendency grew to include places of public accommodation and commercial enterprises catering to social activities. When, in the 1870's, the Supreme Court began to consider rulings under the postwar Civil Rights Act and the

Fourteenth Amendment, it supported the trend. Exclusionary practices and policies of discrimination thereby achieved a respectability
not warranted by the national commitment that "All men are created
equal."

In time, as patterns of exclusion spread, they extended far beyond
"society" at play to discrimination in most areas of human
aspiration—education, housing, business, jobs, professions and personal development. No doubt the pattern of social discrimination
dramatized by the Seligman incident was stimulated by the rise and
growing prosperity of Jews. Upward mobility was the essential
mechanism for social integration, and the Jews of the second migration had by the 1870's and 1880's reached financial and business
success to a point where they sought acceptance in prestigious circles.
The efforts to bar them—in effect, to retard their progress—generated
critical ethnic strife in the last two decades of the nineteenth century.
By this time, the third and major wave of Jewish immigration, from
Eastern Europe, was well under way.

The Third Migration

The third migration of European Jewry to America came with a rush
after 1880. The event that released the flood was the assassination of
Alexander II of Russia in 1881 by revolutionary terrorists. For a quarter
century, Alexander had ruled in a manner that had sought to ease the
worst despotism of his predecessor, Nicholas I. In 1861, when Lincoln
was contemplating his Emancipation Proclamation, Alexander acted
to free the 40,000,000 serfs in Russia. Jews cooped up in the Pale of
Settlement at times had visions that they too would achieve modest
rights of citizenship. But with the accession of Alexander III, the clock
was turned back.

Once more facing an era of suppression and perhaps violence,
Russian Jews looked for escape. As to so many other Europeans of the
period, America beckoned as a place of hope for the disfranchised and
the dispossessed. Why not an exodus to this new world? For a people
so completely insulated and isolated, emigration was not easy to
contemplate; it seemed so drastic and revolutionary a solution;
perhaps more destructive of their lives and a menace greater than the
one they lived with. But whatever hesitancy some may have had was
quashed by the bloody pogroms of 1881 and 1882. After that, many
could no longer hope for peace or safety or any kind of stability under

the new Czar's reinstituted anti-Semitic policy. The history of the next thirty years, marked by suppression and unsuccessful revolution, offered nothing to change that view. In 1903 the Kishinev massacre added to the pressure. The aborted revolt of 1905 brought new suppression.

Out of Russia, and its empire—including Poland and Romania—during these three decades came perhaps a quarter of all the Jews of Eastern Europe. Driven not only by persecution, but also by a desire to breathe free and the hope for better lives, 2,000,000 entered the United States between 1880 and 1910, and another 500,000 in the following decade despite the disruption of the World War I years. Needless to say the impact on the existing American Jewish community of 300,000 was enormous.

Contemplating this avalanche of Jewish immigrants, Irving Howe, in *World Of Our Fathers*, comments that other contemporaneous immigrations do not explain the Jewish phenomenon. For instance, "Italians came from their own independent nations.... Individual Italians might be in flight, but not the Italians as a people. Of the Jews, however, it can almost be said that a whole people was in flight."

Terror in Czarist Russia—After 1880 it led to the great wave of migration to America.

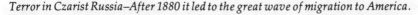

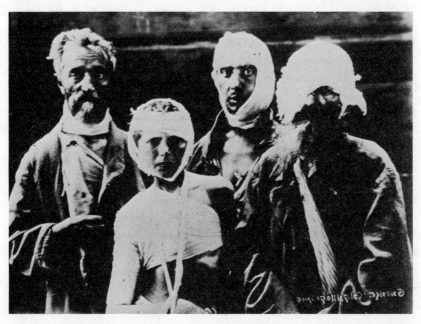

What moved the Jewish immigration was thus not identical with that ingathering of other peoples to the United States. Nearly 24,000,000 arrived on American shores between 1880 and 1920. The nation's population at the start was 50,000,000; at the close of the period it was 105,000,000. Significantly, the immigration rate almost equaled the native birthrate and was a major factor in the rancorous political efforts to close the gates to further entry of aliens. As the statistics show, Jewish immigrants were only 10 percent of the total, but anti-Semitism became a principal weapon in the arsenal of xenophobic restrictionists, even as anti-Catholicism had in the nineteenth century when the Irish immigration—one of similar dimensions—was at its peak.

The new Jewish immigrants came with stars in their eyes. "...Before I was old enough to speak, I saw all around me weary faces light up with thrilling tales of the far off 'golden country,'" wrote novelist Anzia Yezierska in *Hungry Hearts*. No group ever believed more fervently in the American mythology of freedom and equality of opportunity or came to face a more complex confluence of elements resisting their entry into the American heaven. The anti-Semitism of Eastern Europe had already isolated them from the mainstream of Western society. Most unforgivable was their religion; but also in education, manner of dress, culture, in their very occupations, they were different. Their virtues tended to antagonize; their powerful family feeling, their strain of intellectualism, their need and their willingness to work long hours to survive. In brief, they were nonconformists, no matter how much they wanted to be Americans.

(Yet, among reformers steeped in old Puritan values, a philo-Semitism developed because they saw in the immigrant Jew such desirable ethics as industriousness, sobriety, and thrift. "Even in the strange and grubby figures of the ghetto," Irving Howe wrote, "an eager Christian could find traces of the 'ancient glory' of the chosen people of the Old Testament.")

The confluent streams contributing to the intensifying anti-Semitism of the period included the religious bigotry derived from early America, the social anti-Semitism of the post–Civil War "new aristocracy," the formulations of the nativists and alienated populists given to violent expression of their xenophobia, the intellectual anti-Semitism of patricians like Henry Adams who suffered fears of being dispossessed by materialist vulgarity in his native land and having the old American virtues destroyed by the power of money, and, finally, the anti-Semitism of the new immigrants who brought with them all the accumulated hatreds and anti-Jewish attitudes of their European upbringing.

"Scientific" Subversion

Beyond all this, something new had been added to the simmering pot of social fears and conflict—an innocent-enough scientific interest in the origins of man and the development of civilization. The distinctly flawed researches of nineteenth-century scientific investigators, however—despite all of their erudition—led to the growth of ideological racism. The need to find the means for encouraging the merger of diverse population strains into a unitary nationality occupied the thoughts of many in America. Notions of the "melting pot" and of cultural pluralism were yet to be articulated in the early nineteenth century. The presence of the Negro and native Indians, the arrival of some Asians, the seemingly great differences among European immigrants, raised questions as the century progressed. Theologians held firmly to belief in biblical interpretations of the origins of man and their influence was great, but it was not strange that soon the findings of anthropology, genetics, and social science should fascinate Americans.

What of these findings? With twentieth-century hindsight, it is easy to see how they were subverted for political purposes to serve selfish interests and to foster false notions of the superiority of some races over others. The search for truth in racial matters had already entered upon evil ways in Europe by the time American investigators began their work. Among these early Americans, Dr. Samuel G. Morton of Philadelphia, a Quaker and a sincere man, developed a theory of the diverse origins of mankind, contrary to biblical notions. Dr. Josiah C. Nott of Alabama, who followed Dr. Morton's path, carried it a step further: that the races were distinct and unchangeable, and that superior and inferior races could not "live together on any other terms than that of master and slave." He had arrived at that opinion by his observation of the southern Negro.

Nott found support for his thesis in the work of the French writer Count Joseph Arthur de Gobineau whose *Essays on the Inequality of Human Races* was published in 1853. Three years later, an American edition appeared with a supplementary essay by Nott. Ultimately, Madison Grant, founder of The New York Zoological Society, popularized Gobineau's racism and applied it to immigration policy in his widely read *The Passing of The Great Race* (1916). He was a natural for the task. All his instincts led him down racist paths. Socialite, patrician, well-read, though not disciplined in the physical sciences, he fed avidly on racist theory and had no hesitancy in giving vent to the prejudices which he fixed with a special malevolence upon Jews. Significantly, a new edition of Gobineau had appeared in 1915.

"Scientific racism" found its American popularizer in Madison Grant, New York socialite and anthropologist.

It would be difficult to overstate the destructiveness in human terms of Gobineau's propagation of racist ideas—that Jews were a "mongrel race" and that "everything great, noble and fruitful in the works of man belong to one family (the Aryan)." The impact of his ideas in Europe is written large in the events of the first half of the twentieth century—in the wide acceptance of the theory of Nordic superiority, in the rise and fall of Nazism, in World War II and the Holocaust. It is marked in the distortion of scientific endeavors and philosophic ideas, in literature, the arts and in political and social thought. In America, too, it found its adherents—among intellectuals, political figures, and common men alike. Here, it faded sooner only because the democratic strain in American society was stronger. But it has not disappeared; notions of racial superiority and inferiority persist.

As will become evident in succeeding pages, the ideology of race had considerable impact on the lives of Jews in America, both immigrants and old settlers, in two areas: the prevalence of derogatory stereotypes (with its concomitant of various forms of discrimination) and the efforts to restrict immigration at a point—and in a way—that seriously affected Jewish interests.

Until the 1880's, limitations upon immigration were nonexistent. The door was open to all who came. The immigrant might find a mixed reception once he arrived, but he was not denied entry. His labor was needed. It served a national purpose. There were frontiers to be pushed back, a nation to be built. It was all a natural and essential process—resistant to both the xenophobia of the nativists and the religious bigotry which had been factors since the first half of the nineteenth century. Countering these negative factors was the tradition of America as a refuge for the oppressed of Europe.

Now, with a greatly accelerated flow of immigration, there were second thoughts. Anti-immigrant attitudes began to find public expression in many areas of society, especially as the nation passed through periods of depression and social malaise. The movement to restrict immigration ran its course over a period of forty-four years from 1880 to 1924. The ultimate battle was over the national-origins quota system which enshrined racism in federal immigration law. Not until 1966 were the last vestiges of that legalized racism eliminated.

The process of immigration restriction began slowly. In 1882 Congress passed a law excluding convicts, paupers, and mental defectives after the Supreme Court had declared state laws to the same effect unconstitutional. In 1885 Congress, responding to the pressures of organized labor, adopted the Alien Contract Labor Law, prohibiting the recruiting of labor in Europe by industry. In 1891 Congress further strengthened restrictions against immigrants who might become public charges. In 1903 President Theodore Roosevelt signed a bill to exclude anarchists, epileptics and beggars.

The crucial battle of the period—one with racial overtones drawing a line between the "superior" old immigration from Northern and Western Europe and the "inferior" new stock coming from the South and East—was the effort to pass a literacy test law. Such legislation, it was contended, would enhance selectivity; in fact, it would have merely hardened restrictions. Congress passed such a bill in 1896, but it was vetoed by President Cleveland as a "radical departure" from previous policy. President Taft vetoed a similar bill in 1913 and President Wilson in 1915. Finally the restrictionist forces passed a literacy test law over Wilson's veto in 1917.

The nativist groups which since the 1830's had engaged in anti-immigrant agitation remained an important element in the 1890's restrictionist effort, but might not have had any more legislative success without the development of agitation for such restriction among powerful East Coast and intellectual groups. While the American Protective Association played on nativist prejudice against aliens and Catholics, the Eastern restrictionists raised, for the old American stock, the specter that their dominance would be diluted and perhaps even lost to the new hordes of lesser people entering the country.

There was sufficient economic distress in the 1890's for restrictionists, whether demagogues or men of reason, to make an impact on immigration policy. The APA could invoke religious and racial bigotry in rural areas while Congregationalist minister Josiah Strong, no minor demagogue, inveighed against alien criminals and radicals in the cities. Reasoned minds could stress the economic seriousness of the immigration problem, as did Francis A. Walker, President of the Massachusetts Institute of Technology.

Many forms of civic and political organizations found their vital interests involved in immigration problems and out of these grew formidable support for legislation. Through it all ran an infectious racism and an effort to differentiate between old and new, superior and inferior immigrant stock. As already noted, in 1885 union labor succeeded in protecting its special interest with the adoption of the Alien Contract Labor Act. By 1894 the Brahmin leadership of Boston formed the Immigration Restriction League, thus conferring patrician respectability on anti-immigrant feeling. The league, through men such as Senator Henry Cabot Lodge, Prescott Bush, Charles Warren, Robert De Courcy Ward, John Fisk, and others, provided both political power and propaganda skills.

The device the league chose to achieve restriction of immigration was the literacy test. The bill of 1896, excluding adult immigrants unable to read or write their own language, was adopted by Congress by huge majorities, attesting both to the strength of public sentiment and to the effectiveness of Lodge's leadership in the Senate. Though the bill was ultimately vetoed by the President, the maneuvers in Congress revealed the ever-present danger of special attack on Jewish immigration. At one point Lodge sought to alter the text of the bill to require literacy in the language of the country from which the immi-

Henry Cabot Lodge spoke for the Brahmin-sponsored Immigration Restriction League in the Senate. He was the proponent of a tricky literacy test that would have weighed most heavily on East European Jews.

grant came and not in the tongue with which the immigrant was familiar. The sponsors thus sought to place an insuperable stumbling block in the path of Yiddish-speaking East European Jews who could not read or write Russian, Polish or Romanian. The deliberate discrimination was too crude for Congress to swallow, and it was dropped. The fact that it never again appeared in such obvious legislative form, however, did not end special disabilities faced by Jews in the administration of immigration procedures or in the general racism which influenced immigration law after 1921.

Though the efforts to adopt a literacy law were unsuccessful until Congress overrode Wilson's veto in 1917, the restrictionists laid the groundwork for all their future victories in 1907. That year, the literacy test went down to defeat only after the establishment of the Dillingham Immigration Commission. Proponents of the commission saw in it a means of deflecting some of the agitation for restrictive legislation and the Republican leadership in Congress, such as Speaker Joe Cannon and Congressman Bartholdt, who proposed the establishment of the commission, viewed the immigration question as a devisive issue hurtful to the party. President Roosevelt feared interference with his diplomatic efforts for a "gentleman's agreement" with Japan. A sound, impartial, scientific investigation of the facts relating to immigration seemed just the thing to push the problem aside for a time and perhaps even to find a just and valuable solution.

The commission consisted of three senators, three congressmen and three experts chosen by the President who would bring the proper qualities of impartiality and scientific knowledge to the matter. Four years later, after spending $1,000,000 for the services of a staff of 300, the commission published a 42-volume report crammed with questionable data that were neither impartial nor scientifically sound. The investigators began with the assumption that the "old immigration" was superior to the new and then proceeded to prove it "scientifically." In its pages are embalmed much of the insupportable notions of race and Nordic superiority so common among nineteenth-century anthropologists and geneticists. In a "Dictionary of Races" included in the 42 volumes, an effort was made to define races by categories—physically and linguistically—always to the detriment of the new immigrant as against the old, the Eastern and Southern Europeans as against the earlier Northern and Western arrivals.

Under the circumstances, it was to be expected that the report would recommend adoption of the literacy test and that Congress would act upon such legislation. On his second veto of the measure in 1917, President Wilson called it a test of opportunity, not character; but by this time, the restrictionists had enough votes to override him.

In the final analysis, however, the historic significance of the Dillingham Commission report, as historian Oscar Handlin has pointed out in a penetrating commentary, lies in the contribution it made to "the adoption of the national origins quota system...[in] American immigration legislation. By giving governmental and scientific validation to existing prejudices against new immigrants, they helped to justify the discriminations against them in the laws of 1921 and 1924."

Not to be overlooked is the indirect impact or such seemingly government-sanctioned bias. Regressive forces in the decade and more following the appearance of the report became increasingly active. Certainly racial hatreds were on the rise, and they came to be acted out more violently. In 1915 the South witnessed the obscene lynching of a Jew for the first and only time. The Ku Klux Klan in the decade of the 1920's grew in size and viciousness. The obnoxious stereotyping of Jews became a disturbing commonplace. Henry Ford's *Dearborn Independent* mounted a seven-year anti-Semitic campaign based on the fraudulent *Protocols of the Elders of Zion*. The patricians, too, seemed to respond to the temper of the times. For suddenly, in the 1920's, the Ivy League colleges became sensitive to the presence of "new" students on their doorsteps. They found the European notion of a *numerus clausus* a rather attractive idea. Thus the college quota system came into being in order to limit the entry of Jews into the precincts of higher learning.

It is questionable whether American Jews at the turn of the century fully sensed the changes in the social and political atmosphere that brought on these events. The real crisis for Jews—and indeed it was—centered in Russia and Eastern Europe. The preoccupation of America Jewry was with the bitter attacks upon their coreligionists. Their own sense of security enabled them to act with some vigor in invoking the aid of government and their fellow Americans against the European horrors.

TWO

Images in One's Head

The decade leading up to American entry into "the war to save the world for democracy" found the civil liberties traditions of the nation honored as aften in the breach as in the performance. The conditions of freedom for minorities—whether the new immigrants, as we have seen, or the racial groupings such as Negroes or Orientals—were something less than perfect.

Particularism of a secular as well as a religious character gripped the worried Old Stock to whom America "belonged." They felt invaded and besieged, and they were not about to share their heritage readily. How could they in view of the findings of "science?"

"...the Teutonic Nations," wrote political scientist John W. Burgess perfectly seriously, "are entrusted...with the mission of conducting the political civilization of the modern world.... In a state whose population is composed of a variety of nationalities, the Teutonic element, where dominant, should never surrender the balance of political power... and under certain circumstances should not even permit participation of the other elements in political power."

Such argumentation could enable the Old Stock to affirm their belief in the ideals of freedom and justice and yet deny it to the barbarian within the gates. Men like Henry Adams could melodramatically call for a *Gotterdämmerung* where "men of our kind might have some chance of being honorably killed in battle" to escape Jewish enslavement. And the racist mobs, unafraid in their frenzy, could perpetrate

1,100 lynchings of Negroes in the first seventeen years of the century.

Yet it is easy to overstate the case. While the regressive forces were destructive and oppressive, there were others that never lost sight of the national commitment and the need to share the benefits of the land with both the newcomers and the disinherited. The liberal and the reformer, aware of the changing character of the country, recognized that the burgeoning industrial society needed these elements. American ideology had to extend its beneficence to the new mix in the social order if the nation was to fulfill its destiny.

Most exciting was the reaction of the underdogs. Their life might be hard, they were frequently exploited and oppressed, but they refused to be alienated. They believed in the American mythology. They *knew* America was a better place than whence they came, and they soon enough learned how to fight for a place in this better world.

The ferment in time produced a whole crop of defense organizations to counter the attacks of bigots and the ravages of prejudice. The Niagara Conference of 1905 led the way to the establishment in 1909—with the aid of a white liberal cadre—of the National Association for the Advancement of Colored People. The American Jewish Committee organized in 1906 to join the long-established B'nai B'rith and the Union of American Hebrew Congregations to assist persecuted Jews in Europe. Within a few years it turned its attention to the home front, too. In 1908 B'nai B'rith began to work toward the development of a program of fighting anti-Semitism in America and by 1913 launched the Anti-Defamation League as a communitywide endeavor. Other ethnic and sectarian groups followed. Though their programs called for countering bigotry and discrimination practiced against themselves, their great contribution has consisted in the establishment of a new criterion. The measuring rod was not to be the affirmation of freedom and civil liberties alone, but the degree to which a minority individual was afforded the same rights of citizenship, equality of opportunity and freedom from discrimination enjoyed by the majority.

The first moves toward an organized effort to counter anti-Semitic manifestations in American life were directed at a corner of the problem: an irksome condition seemingly more wounding to personal sensibilities than the cause of basic disabilities or discrimination against Jews. It was not a universally popular approach with those who looked abroad and saw the awful problems of Jews in Eastern Europe or to those who witnessed the hardships of immigrant life in the burgeoning ghettos of New York and Boston.

The View from the Midwest

From the vantage point of a small Midwestern town such as Bloomington, Illinois, however, the denigration of Jews in the public media—in newspaper and books, on stage and in movies, in school texts and classical literature—and in common gossip—seemed not only irritating but downright dangerous. In 1908 Sigmund Livingston, a Bloomington lawyer, a man of thought and action, suggested to B'nai B'rith the development of an anti-defamation program to counter the prevalent public ridicule of Jews. There was no great bandwagon rush. It took five years of selling and testing before the Anti-Defamation League was born. One noted rabbi thought both the idea and the program ridiculous. Years later, an eminent French historian, also a Jew, looked at another corner of the problem of defamation and gave a different answer. "In the teaching of contempt," wrote Jules Isaacs, "lies the sources of anti-Semitism." Or as Walter Lippmann once pointed out, it is the picture of Jews in people's heads that determine their attitudes. Looking at the ghettos from afar, Livingston worried about those pictures in the head.

Livingston was a child of eleven when his family, emigrating from the Hessian town of Giesen, settled in Bloomington in 1883. Thus he was educated in the schools of his new American home and earned a law degree at Illinois Wesleyan University. But his education went far beyond his school books. He was an avid reader of history. As he naturally absorbed the air, traditions, and ideals of America, he seasoned his understanding with his study of the bitter history of European Jewry.

He watched the growth of Jewish immigration in the early 1900's and saw a sharpening of religious and cultural hostility toward them, often coupled with an increasing economic tension. In the light of European history, where was this likely to lead? Livingston was particularly affected by his knowledge of German anti-Semitism: the writings of William Marr who invented the term in 1879 and founded the Anti-Semitic League, the vituperations of Johann Eisenmenger's *Judaism Exposed* which for a century had been the source book for Europe's Jew haters, the proclamations of the historian Heinrich von Treitschke, who harangued Germans with the charge "Jews are our misfortune," the oratory of the Prussian Court preacher Adolf Stoecker whose career was advanced by the rabble-rousing cry, later taken up by the Nazis, "Deutschland Erwache!", the arguments of Houston Stewart Chamberlain, son-in-law of Richard Wagner, whose book, sponsored by Kaiser Wilhelm II, called Jewish existence "a crime against the holy laws of life."

The work of Gobineau, Neitzsche and other nineteenth-century intellectuals added to the evil chorus in France and England, Austria-Hungary and Russia. And then there was the vast classical literature: Chaucer's blood-libel story of Hugh of Lincoln in the *Canterbury Tales;* Marlowe's *Barrabas, Jew of Malta,* Shakespeare's Shylock, Dickens' Fagin, Gustav Freytag's Vertel Itzig, and more. Above all, Livingston wrote, "The Jew as the enemy of Christ was the easiest object lesson to be taught to the populace."

Could America escape infection? Perhaps Livingston was obsessed with fear of the evil power that resided in the false images nurtured by anti-Semites. He was certain, however, that it was prudence and not obsession which dictated that American Jews make an organized effort to counter anti-Jewish actions and attitudes. For Livingston was no hysteric, but a thoughtful, rational mind. He would see, hear, and read what was happening in the organs of American popular culture.

In 1908 Livingston succeeded in getting B'nai B'rith to take the first step on a small scale. The Midwest District Grand Lodge established a standing committee to consider the problems of defamation of Jews. Livingston was named its chairman to research and develop a method of operation. Since he had worked at length on the idea, Livingston promptly came up with a plan. "The beginning of the solution to the problem," he said, "must be publicity."

So the committee became known as the Publicity Committee and its office as the Publicity Bureau; an odd name indeed, but one grounded in the belief that once the public record was set straight, Americans would recognize slanders of Jews for what they were. The idea expressed a touching faith in the essential goodness of the American people. Despite the temper of the times, at the end of a year, Livingston was able to show that his idea might work. The burden of the evidence was that thoughtless slanders could be corrected and that certain habitual discriminations could be halted by appropriate representations.

To a company publishing a travel booklet advertising hotel and summer resorts, Livingston had written that many of the notices had contained the offensive phrase "No Jews Wanted." The president of the company promptly replied: "The matter was never given any thought... in the future we can eliminate anything of that kind... and will be glad to do so." A complaint to the Postmaster General calling his attention to postcards with "obnoxious" caricatures of Jews going through the mails brought the response that the "Post Office Department would be glad to see that proper action is taken."

Most impressive was correspondence carried on, somewhat earlier, by Adolph Kraus, president of B'nai B'rith, with Melville E. Stone, president of the Associated Press. Kraus pointed to the unhappy custom of the Associated Press identifying Jews—and only Jews—by religion in reporting a crime. If the accused is a non-Jew, Kraus wrote, we never learn "whether he is a Methodist, a Catholic or [of another] Christian denomination...is there any good reason for making such a distinction?" Stone didn't think there was and replied:

Sigmund Livingston, founder of the Anti-Defamation League.

"Your suggestion is a perfectly proper one and I see no reason on earth why we should say [the accused] was a Jew any more than we should say he was a Methodist. Based on your suggestions I will issue precisely the instructions you indicate."

What could be more encouraging? But not all such representations, Livingston soon learned, called forth positive responses. He was shocked to find that men of high moral reputation and considerable intellectual attainments would be badly infected with anti-Semitic prejudice. In 1911 he wrote to Lyman Abbot, the distinguished editor of *Outlook Magazine*.

"In your article... you state 'the widespread and long continued prejudice against the modern Jew has in part its cause in characteristics common, though by no means universal, in that race.'"

Livingston asked for a description of these "common characteristics" and Abbot, who said he counted Jews among his "warm personal friends" was not loath to do so. Even though he had "no personal prejudice" and held "in the highest honor the contributions which [Jews] have made to civilization," he could see that they "render themselves offensive" seek "the highest and best places, not always ...by the most honorable means" and are given to "ostentatious display." Livingston's reply—unlike that of Seligman to Hilton—was civil and intended to be instructive, but it was apparent to him that the eradication of prejudice against Jews, even in free and democratic America, was not going to be a simple matter.

With increasing force, it was driven home to the Publicity Committee as the months passed, that expressions of anti-Semitism were to be found everywhere—in the low comedy of the stage and screen, in the press, in intellectual circles and in the most ordinary occurrences of the day. Not the reality of the situation, but the perception of it was changing, and with it came wider support, at least within B'nai B'rith, for a nation wide effort to meet the problem head on. The die was cast in 1913.

Overcautious—Overbold

The organization efforts, starting with B'nai B'rith, soon encompassed a broad cross-section of Jewish communal leadership. By October the Anti-Defamation League had been established with a well-defined set of principles and a program clearly a product of its time. It was both overcautious and overbold, but it breathed a commitment to a humane and understanding America that was not often heard in the stressful society of 1913.

The League's "ultimate purpose," the charter read, "is to secure justice and fair treatment to all citizens alike and to put an end forever to unjust and unfair discrimination against, and ridicule of, any sect or body of citizens."

As for its "immediate object," the charter expressed a touching faith in America: the League hoped "to stop, by appeals to reason and conscience, and if necessary, by appeals to law, the defamation of the Jewish people."

When it came to program, the League added a little muscle to the approach and took the cavalier attitude toward First Amendment *caveats* on free speech and censorship prevalent at the time. The three-pronged program was to include educational endeavors, vigilance work, and legislative advocacy.

It proposed to furnish "public and university libraries . . . with lists of books . . . which tend to show the facts regarding Jewish ethics, customs, history, religion and philosophy." At the same time "the

The League charter—"Its ultimate purpose was to secure justice . . . to all citizens alike."

B'NAI B'RITH NEWS
BENEVOLENCE.   BROTHERLY LOVE   AND HARMONY

Vol. VI   OCTOBER, 1913   No. 2

Entered as second-class matter September 16, 1912, at the post office at Chicago, Illinois, under the Act of August 24, 1912.

ANTI-DEFAMATION LEAGUE

For a number of years a tendency has manifested itself in American life toward the caricaturing and defaming of Jews on the stage, in moving pictures. The effect of this on the unthinking public has been to create an untrue and injurious impression of an entire people and to expose the Jew to undeserved contempt and ridicule. The caricatures center around some idiosyncracy of the few which, by the thoughtless public, is often taken as a pivotal characteristic of the entire people.

The evidence of prejudice and discrimination has been abundant, both in social and in business circles, as well as in public life. All fair-minded citizens must regret the growth of this un-American sentiment. The prejudice thus displayed by no means reflects the attitude of the thinking, intelligent majority of our citizens, but is limited to an ignorant, unreasoning and bigoted minority. For many years the Jewish and non-Jewish citizens have failed to meet this tendency by any means save quiet criticism. But the tide has been rising until it calls for organized effort to stem it.

Regrettable as it is, this condition has gone so far as to manifest itself recently in an attempt to influence courts of law where a Jew happened to be a party to the litigation. This symptom, standing by itself, while contemptible, would not constitute a menace, but forming as it does but one incident in a continuing chain of occasions of discrimination, demands organized and systematic effort on behalf of all right-thinking Americans to put a stop to this most pernicious and un-American tendency. Prejudice is the child of ignorance. It knows no bounds, respects no individual, and violates the most sacred tenets of our democracy.

With the hope that the co-operation of both Jewish and non-Jewish citizens will be received in this effort of fair play for all people, the ANTI-DEFAMATION LEAGUE OF AMERICA has been formed under the auspices of the Order of B'nai B'rith.

OBJECT: The immediate object of the League is to stop, by appeals to reason and conscience, and if necessary, by appeals to law, the defamation of the Jewish people. Its ultimate purpose is to secure justice and fair treatment to all citizens alike and to put an end forever to unjust and unfair discrimination against and ridicule of any sect or body of citizens.

ORGANIZATION: Any reputable person, regardless of sex or creed, may become a member by signing a membership card. No membership fees nor dues shall be charged. A central office has been created in the City of Chicago, with a competent office force. All communications or complaints should be addressed to Mr. Sigmund Livingston, 722 First National Bank Bldg., Chicago, Illinois.

Stage defamation will be dealt with by enlisting the assistance and co-operation of the producers and managers of the theaters, so that investigation of proposed performances may be made before the staging of the same, thus correcting evils before any harm is done. If the co-operation of those in authority cannot be secured, then the patrons of the theater will be enlisted for active co-operation.

Newspaper and magazine defamation will be met by protest to the editor, by correcting all defamations through subsequent articles upon the same subject matter, thereby reaching the same reading public and correcting errors; and in case of willful abuse, by appealing to the patrons and advertisers for co-operation.

Defamation in textbooks which pervert the minds of children and tend to prejudice, will be met by attempts to eliminate them from the course of study.

No effort will be made by this organization to shield any malefactor. In founding this League, the Order of B'nai B'rith pledges its hearty support in the future, as it has done in the past, to the enforcement of law against all violators, Jew or non-Jew.

A committee of one hundred citizens, residents in the various cities throughout the United States, has been selected to perfect the organization and to carry out its objects.

(Signed) ADOLF KRAUS, President.
Independent Order of B'nai B'rith.

proper authorities" were to be urged to remove books "which malici-
ously and scurrilously traduce the character of the Jew" and "to place a
restriction on their use."

A "determined campaign" was to be waged to eliminate from the
educational system all textbooks which tend to pervert the mind of the
child and create prejudice and a program undertaken to "provide for
the dissemination of literature... designed to give the public a true
understanding of the Jew and Judaism."

The vigilance program the organizers of the League envisaged was
designed to monitor and counterattack discrimination and defamation. Expecting to find a strong ally in the press the League heartily
commended "certain newspapers [for] adopting the policy of
eliminating the mention of the religious denomination of malefac-
tors" and determined to "bend every energy toward making this
policy universal." The placing of Jews in a "false and unworthy light"
was not to go unchallenged or permitted with impunity.

The stage and screen especially were to be watched carefully. If it
was "apparent that a play gives an unfair or untrue portrayal of a Jew,"
the vigilance program "would endeavor to prevent its production in
its offensive form, or if already staged,... secure the elimination of the
objectionable matter."

The League's bold approach to the libels of the printed word and the
slander of the stage was bound ultimately to lead to a head-on clash
with the issue of censorship. The line between suppression of false-
hood on one hand and freedom of speech on the other is always a fine
one, and never finer than when free speech is claimed by those trading
in scurrilities. In the face of a deluge of plays and movies that mer-
cilessly lampooned Jews and ridiculed their religion and culture, it
may not have been wise, but it was altogether human, to have
appealed—as the League did—for state legislation "similar to the
statute... passed in the State of Ohio, providing for the appointment
of a Board of Censors" to prevent "the presentation in moving picture
theaters, of films which are malicious and scurrilous caricatures or are
objectionable in other respects." In time the League realized that its
proposed cure could be more baneful than the disease.

The Stereotypes in Popular Culture

Nevertheless, it is instructive to examine the anti-Semitism that
flourished in the mass culture through the eyes of these men of 1913.

Never entirely absent from the American scene, the ugly stereotyping of Jews did not seriously affect American Jewry until the turn of the century. It served the private jokester more frequently than the public scandalmonger. But after 1900, as we have seen, religious and cultural hostility to Jews was sharpened by political purpose and economic rivalry. The mass immigration had begun to change the picture. The Jewish immigrant, whatever his occupational status when he arrived, sought to improve it—and quickly. The traditional Jewish virtues of mutual aid, thrift, hard work, and study were the hallmarks of the group and they were ready to pay their dues in such coin to achieve the American goal of getting ahead.

To the bigot, watching resentfully as these industrious immigrants began to leave the workbench for commerce and the professions, each of these virtues turned into a vice. In his eyes, the Jew's strong family and group feeling became clannishness. His thrift and planning became miserliness and deceitfulness; his ambition and hopes, aggressiveness and avarice. Of such stuff are caricature and stereotypes fashioned by the purveyors of popular culture.

It was a period of tremendous growth in the country, and with it came great expansion in the instruments of communication and entertainment. Newspaper and magazine circulation climbed into the millions. The presses poured out a flood of dime novels; movie "quickies," melodramas, "dialect" comedians filled stage and screen. The vile Jewish stereotypes became standard fare. The image of the Jew stamped into the minds of Americans was that of the cheater, the arsonist, the deliberate bankrupt, the lecher, liar and miser—a man to whom a penny dishonestly earned and greedily saved was the purpose of life. As we shall see, such stereotypes were laying the groundwork for mob violence and organized hate groups.

The League attacked the problem on many fronts. Perhaps its most immediate and dramatic success was in the newspaper field. It has already been noted that many journals habitually tagged a suspected or convicted malefactor as "Jew" or "Jewish" wherever circumstances gave them an opening. "The Jew banker" or "the Jew peddler" was a common locution in the press.

One member of the League's first executive committee, Adolph S. Ochs, was particularly troubled by this tendency in the press. The

(Right) *Publisher Adolph Ochs—His memorandum offered a code for journalists.*

distinguished publisher of *The New York Times* had already addressed the problem in his own newspaper. Now he wrote for distribution by the League to editors of daily papers throughout the country a memorandum entitled "A Note on the Word 'Jew.'" The note, which included a set of "rules for guidance," reminded editors: "The word 'Jew' is a noun and should never be used as an adjective or verb. To speak of 'Jew girls' or 'Jew stores' is both objectionable and vulgar.... The use of the word 'Jew' as a verb—'to Jew down'—is a slang survival of the medieval term of opprobrium... and should be avoided altogether."

Many newspapers reproduced copies of Ochs' note and distributed them to their editorial staffs with memoranda of approval. Some editors thought the note important enough to laud in their editorial columns. A few editors disagreed. "There is such a thing," wrote *The Los Angeles Times*, "as a supersensitive person hollering before he is hurt." Livingston answered the objectors patiently:

"With the cooperation of those who have the power to form public opinion, we believe we can stop the increase of prejudice and eventually relieve the public mind of sordid antipathies so that Jews, as their fellow men, may be judged as individuals."

Within two years, in 1915, Livingston was able to report "only fifty cases" of objectionable references to Jews in the national press. Five years later, the practice had virtually stopped.

Vaudeville presented a more difficult problem, and the approach of the League was more tough-minded and brasher. The people of the popular entertainment world lacked the social consciousness implicit in journalism. What made the situation sadder was that some of the worst offenders were themselves Jews. Many of the most objectionable anti-Semitic vaudeville acts were performed by Jewish comedians, and Jewish movie producers were responsible for some of the films most damaging to the Jewish image. They were pandering to the popular taste for stereotypes. Psychologist Gordon Allport pointing out the "flavor of pathos in the self-directed humor of minority groups," has commented in his classic study of scapegoating that "if the master wants to be amused, the slave sometimes obligingly plays the clown" and in the same sense "a Jewish... comedian on the stage

(Right) *Anti-Semitic stereotypes—The fruits of popular culture.*

THE YIDDISH COMIC COW-BOY SONG NOVELTY

מזל טוב

MOZZELTOFF.

YONKLE, the COW-BOY JEW

KOSHER WORDS AND MUSIC BY

WILL J. HARRIS AND HARRY I. ROBINSON

WRITERS OF "MONTANA"

HARRY W. FIELDS

5

SUNG FEATURED WITH SUCCESS BY
HARRY W. FIELDS AND
"REDPATH'S NAPANEES"

WILL ROSSITER
MUSIC PUBLISHER

may caricature his own group to the delight of the audience" because he "is gratified by the applause."

Typical of the vaudeville turns of the time was the bearded, derby-hatted Jewish tailor calling to his son offstage, "Shakey, stop playing with matches. If you must play with matches, at least come inside and play with them." Skits like this led to complaints which piled up in the League's headquarters almost from the moment the organization was founded.

Even more widespread than the stage Jew stereotype was that of the "movie Jew." In 1913, ten million Americans were piling into movie

(Left) *"A sure winner if Bryan is elected" was the caption on this caricature of a "Jewish" pawnbroker.*

(Below) *The myth of avarice–"Zalinsky, I vant to show you I can be grateful."*

houses every day; the films that were being made to satisfy this growing market included so-called "Jew movies" which were produced at the rate of one every two weeks. Major producing companies—Universal, Keystone, Reliance, Mutual, and General Film Company—were turning out productions such as *A Stage Door Flirtation* which told the story of two "Yiddish sports" who became infatuated with a "pure and clean" dancer named Choocheata. A character named Rosenstein appeared again and again in screen plays, always as a kind of Jewish Volpone—usurious, sly, miserly. In *The Railroad Raiders*, one, Sam Lowenstein, was depicted as a jewel "fence" and member of a gang of thieves. The film gave naïve moviegoers the impression that Jews were, by trade, smugglers and robbers.

When the League's complaints to movie producers failed to elicit the quick and favorable response that had come from newspaper editors, approaches were made to film distributing companies and moviehouse owners. League members in various communities were urged to request local authorities for permission to inspect films before public exhibition and to be allowed to submit recommendations concerning them. The passage of censorship ordinances was encouraged; bulletins were put out by the League explaining to the public why certain films were considered reprehensible; an educational campaign, directed to all levels of the film industry, was launched in an attempt to win support for the League's position on the ugly stereotypes that plagued the screens from coast to coast.

A major breakthrough was achieved in 1916 when Carl Laemmle, then president of Universal, maker of a third of the annual American screen product, told the League that in the future neither his company nor any of its subsidiaries would produce films that held Jews up to ridicule or contempt. As a result of continued efforts by the League directed at the industry, by 1920 the policy enunciated by Laemmle became the general practice among movie makers.

The Preacher's aphorism in Ecclesiastes about the endless making of books applies doubly to the making of bad jokes by comedians stretching for a laugh. The motion picture industry could, after a time, forgo "Jew movies," as public taste developed for better films, but vaudeville and nightclub comics never entirely ended their use of the stereotypic or racial laugh-getter.

In periods of social tension, some restraints were observed, such as in the 1940's and 1950's, when the Hitler period and the aftermath of

World War II had created greater public sensitivity. For a time, racial jokes that stimulated prejudice were not considered funny, but as the "stand-up comic" began to invade television and was ever in greater need of "new material" the offensive stereotype returned, now coupled with the new fad of "sick humor" that often projected morbid and outrageous images of racial and ethnic groups. In one brief period in 1961, 35,000,000 television viewers of the major networks were treated to "sick humor" skits denigrating the rabbinate. The vogue passed quickly as public protest unsettled network officials. Jews were not the only victims of this new and unhappy entertainment combination, but Jewish comedians were prominent among the practitioners of pathologically "sick humor."

Stereotypes in the Classics—Shylock and Fagin

Dealing with harmful anti-Semitic stereotypes of classical literature has been a problem of a different order. Tamper with Shakespeare or Dickens, and almost as many hackles are raised as would an attempt to rewrite Holy Scriptures. Issues of censorship and of artistic integrity at once take center stage, and often the problem of human relations and the evil impact of ancient canards is lost in the controversy. It is a sticky issue and has remained so through the years with those on both sides aware that there is a good deal of merit to the position of the other.

Both Shylock and Fagin seem to have lives of their own, and under certain conditions inspire and encourage anti-Semitic myths. For Jews early in the century, the required study of *The Merchant of Venice* in high schools was particularly disturbing. Schools did not turn to other Shakespearean plays because the College Entrance Examination Board included *The Merchant* in the list of plays "required to be intensively studied as a prerequisite to admission in institutions of higher learning." In 1912 the Central Conference of American Rabbis urged the Board to lift the requirement. Soon after its formation, the League took up the problem. At the opening of the school year in 1914, the College Entrance Examination Board removed the play from the required list and with this obstacle out of the way, the League proceeded with a program of convincing school superintendents in all cities of 10,000 population or more that it was educationally desirable to replace *The Merchant* with other Shakespearean plays. In a circular letter, seven reasons were given why *The Merchant* was not fit for the classroom:

1. Because Shylock is erroneously pictured as typical of all Jews.
2. It embarrasses severely and unfairly the Jewish people.
3. It forces upon immature Jewish pupils self-defense reactions.
4. It serves to increase misunderstanding of Jews by non-Jews.
5. It intensifies prejudice and makes more difficult any friendly relationships between the groups.
6. Shylock has become an unhappy symbol of Jewish vindictiveness, malice and hatred.
7. It reacts unfavorably on group relationships.

The League enlisted the aid of other Jewish groups, Christian churches, and secular organizations with good effect. Between 1917 and 1920 many school systems discontinued study of the play, and colleges no longer required it for admission. Though not a total success, the effort was impressive. However, as time passed and the League became increasingly concerned with First Amendment rights, it questioned its own policy at least in terms of the use of the play as an educational experience. In 1950 legal efforts were made by parents in Brooklyn to compel the New York City Board of Education to remove both *Oliver Twist* and *The Merchant* from school curriculum and libraries. This time, the League opposed such action. Together with other Jewish groups, it denounced the move as an attempt at "bookburning" and found itself in accord with State Supreme Court Justice Anthony DiGiovanni, who denied the petition to ban the books, saying... "[The Board of Education has] expressly required teachers to explain to pupils that the characters described herein are not typical of any nation or race, including persons of the Jewish faith, and are not intended and are not to be regarded as reflecting discredit on any race or national group.... Public education and instruction in the home will remove religious and racial intolerance more effectively than censorship and suppression of literary works which have been accepted as works of art."

As it evolved over the years, the League's position turned upon the recognition that the medium more than the message was the critical element in dealing with the negative stereotypes of classical literature. Thus, in the school situation, it could reverse its original views on *The Merchant*—with which it had become increasingly uncomfortable—once educational guidance provided some safeguards. But the old dilemma remained when it came to public performance. At what point did criticism become censorship or protest become suppression? Over the years, these were questions which required Solomonic answers—and the answers were not always the same.

Between 1908 and 1922, *The Merchant* was produced three times as a silent movie and *Oliver Twist* at least seven times. Audiences were only too ready to accept ugly Jewish stereotypes, and the League and Jews as a group could not help but feel that these versions were an attack upon Jewish security. In 1947, only two years after World War II and the revelation of the Nazi anti-Semitic bestialities, Alec Guinness portrayed Fagin in another movie version of *Oliver Twist*. It hurt; Guinness' performance was perhaps too much of a triumph. The filmmakers had approached their project with commendable artistic fervor not matched by an equal understanding of the human-relations realities of mid-twentieth-century life. The result was that the film could not get the American Motion Picture Production Code seal of approval essential to the success of any film shown in American movie houses. Joseph Breen, director of the Production Code office, having seen an advance copy of the film script, forwarned the Rank Organization, which was producing *Oliver Twist*, of the obstacles it would face.

When at one point sketches of the settings and characters were published, the League, in friendly representations, privately pointed out to the producers the anti-Semitic pitfalls inherent in the story and advised some caution. But by this time, the League found, the filmmakers were lost in the crooked streets of their nineteenth-century stage set and in the warped world of the Cruikshank illustrations for the novel which have always been more objectionable to Jews than the Dickens text. The voices of caution bounced off an ivory tower ostentatiously labeled "artistic integrity."

Almost immediately upon release, the film ran into resistance. In Canada it was a box-office failure. In the British-controlled zone of Germany, it was met with rioting. In the United States, exhibitors at previews greeted it with devastating coolness. The subsequent efforts to obtain public exhibition of the film in the United States grew into a tangle of confused issues, aggressive press-agentry, and heated argument about the nature of censorship, freedom of speech, and artistic integrity. And of course strenuous efforts to rescue an ill-fated investment of—for the time—massive proportions.

Perhaps recalling the friendly advice offered before the project was fully underway, in 1948 the producers invited the League to a private showing—for expert opinion of the possible impact of the film in this country, perhaps to break down the resistance of reluctant American movie exhibitors. The League group that viewed the film could not relieve the producers' anxieties. They found the exhibitors' fears well-founded, but offered to sponsor, together with the producers, a scientific testing of public reaction to the film.

In view of the possible consequences to so large a project, the theatrical trade gossip mills worked overtime. Not all of it was idle gossip; some of it had the earmarks of a public relations *tour de force*, for suddenly the authoritative theater trade journal, *Variety*, published a story saying that the League did not see any harm in the film. Up to this point, the League had made no public comment; now it issued a correcting statement: it did not like the film and had told the producers why.

The issue of "artistic integrity" had failed to bring the film into the movie houses. Now the issue of censorship was to be tried. In the context, censorship was an emotional issue and it was easy to brew up a storm. But except for the motion picture industry itself, no one had interfered with the making of the film or its showing in the United States. Only the industry's own self-regulatory body had taken such overt steps by refusing its seal of approval under the Production Code clause that "no film or episode may throw ridicule on any religious faith." The American distributor of *Oliver Twist* appealed the Breen ruling to the Motion Picture Association of America. Ultimately, the seal of approval was granted after 851 feet of film suggested by Breen were eliminated.

But from the League's viewpoint, the film remained an anti-Semitic instrument to the degree that the character of Fagin projected "the stereotype which Julius Streicher and the Nazis tried to impose on the world." It rejected the charge that such public comment by a Jewish group amounted to censorship or unwarranted pressure. The wounds of the Holocaust were too fresh in memory. Jews had every right to protest the slander implicit in Guinness' interpretation of Fagin, the League insisted, but it did not go beyond voicing the outrage Jews felt.

Fifteen years later, in 1962, the League again had occasion to define its policy. The horrors of war and the images projected by Nazism were no longer as vivid in the public mind. Thus, when *The Merchant* was presented on stage in New York to a more sophisticated audience

(Right) *Classics such as* Oliver Twist *and* The Merchant of Venice *kept the myths alive.*

than reached by the movies, the League, reflecting the Jewish community, was able to take a less emotional view:

> If all people were emotionally healthy, literate, understanding and free of prejudice, *The Merchant* would be incapable of doing harm. But this is hardly the case in this imperfect world. *The Merchant* has and may continue to do harm....It is our hope that...all those involved in the present production will consider carefully their social responsibilities in its presentation....*The Merchant* is an accepted classic of world literature. As a work of great artistic quality it should not, in a free society, be subject to censorship. This has been our position for many years....

That statement has never been taken as the last word by those ready to man the barricades against any and all "censors," or for that matter by those who see greater danger in the stimulation of prejudice. Los Angeles civil libertarians rushed to the defense of a projected staging of *The Merchant* in 1966 in a public park even though no one had raised any objections, creating a one-day newspaper sensation. In 1962 the British musical comedy *Oliver*, adapted from *Oliver Twist*, was brought to Hollywood and later New York, again creating much uneasiness among Jewish organizations until they found, as one critic reported, that actor Lionel Bart played the part of Fagin "as the dottiest old dear imaginable" with little of the feared stereotype mannerisms.

The Merchant has not met with protest in recent years when played on the legitimate stage before audiences drawn to the splendors of Shakespearean drama. But in the spring of 1974, the American Broadcasting Company proposed to present a British production of *The Merchant* on its national television network. Once more the medium, more than the message, became the issue. As with the movie versions, what would be the effect on so large—and therefore largely untutored—an audience? Would they carry away with them the passion of the poetry or the portrait of Shylock, the Jew, as evil incarnate?

An interesting charade was now played out. The network sought to forestall conflict and to show concern for sound social policy by inviting Jewish groups to view the production in advance. These groups, in turn agreed to preview the film, but, conscious of the fact that they might be charged with censorship, informed the network that the decision to broadcast was its responsibility alone. The Jewish viewers were not happy with what they saw and found the production reinforced "its negative stereotype of the Jew." The network said it would arrange for Lawrence Olivier, who played Shylock, to make an opening statement on the telecast "to neutralize possible anti-Semitic fallout." Playwright Dore Schary, speaking for the League, offered the opinion that this would not "undo the damage implicit in the play" and the network could expect a storm of protest from viewers who would regard it "a disservice to Jews and good human relations."

The Merchant was broadcast on March 16, 1974. Olivier made his interpretive opening comment to little effect, for the network was hit with a barrage of listener protest, but major public controversy was avoided. The network had sought to dampen the fires of bigotry; the Jewish groups recognized that they must avoid even the semblance of censorship so violative of their own ideals, and yet were unwilling to see the continued projection of anti-Semitic images.

The conflict of views will not soon end—not as long as Shylock, Fagin, and their fictional counterparts are perceived as serving anti-Semitic ends and adherents of no-censorship-under-any-circumstances look upon them as inviolable creations of the artistic spirit. But the Shylock image is persistent and seemingly ineradicable. As late as 1975, a poll by the Louis Harris public opinion research organization found that one out of three Americans believe that "when it comes to choosing between people and money, Jews will choose money." For those with only an eighth-grade education, the figure rose to one out of two. The poll showed the belief in Jewish "clannishness" and "aggressiveness" to be equally persistent. The dilemma for Jews remains unresolved.

THREE

The Violent Decade

From 1915 to 1925, the interplay of anti-Semitic influences in the nation created for Jews the most violent decade of their American experience. An extraordinary confluence of events gave free rein to religious prejudice and nativist bigotry, racist pseudo-science and equally racist historic myths. Europe's endemic anti-Semitism spanned the ocean to further infect those intellectuals and the dominant Old Stock who, as has been shown, had already developed their own idiosyncratic responses to Jews.

The decade began with the physical horror of a lynching—the only incident of its kind in the nation's history involving a Jew. The accompanying vilification of Jews was medieval in its intensity and cruelty. The same year saw the rebirth of the Ku Klux Klan. In the new dispensation Jews joined Catholics and Negroes as prinicpal targets for nativists, and the Klan achieved heights of effectiveness and membership never reached before or since.

The Great War, which America entered in 1917, brought tirades attacking the loyalty of Jews and new myths with which to beat them. To the stereotype of Jew as grasping capitalist was added the contradictory stereotype of Jew as Bolshevik revolutionary. Soon after came that notorious import from Europe, the myth of the Jewish conspiracy to conquer the world. Halfway through the decade, the nation was startled by the sudden emergence of Henry Ford, the sage of Dearborn, as the purveyor of the most persistent anti-Semitic hoax of the century, the spurious *Protocols of the Learned Elders of Zion*.

The Old Stock and the disgruntled intellectuals struck a quieter note, but the injury was far more real and lasting. In 1917 the restrictive immigration forces in Congress succeeded in passing the literacy test law over President Wilson's veto and then went on to enshrine the national origins quota system in the laws of 1921 and 1924. Almost simultaneously, the quota system in college and university education made its appearance. President A. Lawrence Lowell of Harvard, expressing his great solicitude for Jewish students in 1922, thought that they might feel far more comfortable if not so many of them came to his institution. In their own spheres, those who controlled the large business enterprises, places of public accommodation, and the great civic enterprises similarly sought to—and did—raise restrictive walls against Jews seeking to enter the mainstream of American life.

Each of these developments deserves full analysis.

Watson and the Frank Case

Tom Watson of Georgia wrote one of the dirtiest chapters in the history of bigotry in the South. He was a creature of his time and his environment: a man of the people, a demagogue, a racist, full of frustrations that fed his hatreds, even as he fed these to his enormous following. Havoc traveled in his wake; yet when he died, full of honors, he was mourned not only by the vast throngs who had responded to his demagoguery but was memorialized by some of the most liberal spirits in the political life of the nation. Both the good and the evil in nativism responded to him. A preacher of hate in matters of race and religion, his populism made him something of a reformer in the political field. With his spellbinding personality and opportunistic proclivities, he mirrored the distorted age in which he lived.

Watson fits into our story because after a long career of organizing hate campaigns against Negroes and perpetuating the nativist anti-Catholic movements of the nineteenth century, he was responsible for the only lynching of a Jew in the nation's history. Leo Frank of Atlanta died because Watson willed it so. In the murderous, rabble-rousing campaign leading to the lynching in Marietta, Georgia, in 1915, Watson destroyed a governor of the state and compromised the state's criminal justice system.

Born in 1856 in Thomson, Georgia, Watson was raised as a Baptist. Fundamentalist and narrow in outlook, he became a teacher, but because of a talent for emotional eloquence soon turned to the law as a means of advancement. He quickly achieved considerable success as a trial lawyer. It was natural then for him to enter politics. In 1882 he was elected to the state legislature for a two-year term, and in 1891, went to Congress under the banner of the Farmers Alliance Democrats. His support of such projects as rural free mail delivery advanced him in the eyes of populists and in 1896 be became the Populist party's vice-presidential candidate. Eight years later he was the party's presidential nominee,but by that time populist votes had almost vanished.

Meanwhile, Watson had turned to journalism, hoping through newspaper ownership to obtain power and money. He achieved a considerable amount of both. Watson purchased a newspaper in Atlanta called the *People's Party Paper* in 1897 and in 1906 started both a weekly, *The Jeffersonian*, and a monthly, *Watson's Magazine*. Their principal product was sensationalized bigotry, largely anti-Catholic. Gustavus Myers, in his *History of Bigotry in the U.S.* makes the point that Watson's biographers differ on his fixation on Catholics: whether he saw it as good business to pander to popular prejudice or was merely reverting to the prejudices of his own youth. Whatever the reason, the ultimate effect was the same. Watson's publications repeated *ad nauseam* all the old tirades against Catholics, "plowing the old, worn furrows" of the evil uses of the confessional and the iniquitous doings in convents. In time he applied the same prurient interest to his anti-Semitism.

Not to burden this narrative with Watson's obsessions, it is nevertheless important to give the flavor of his diatribes.

> Not always will we tolerate the kidnapping of our children by these Romanist priests. Not always will we submit to their polluting the flower of our womanhood...Heaven above! Think of a negro priest taking the vow of chastity and then being turned loose among women who have been taught that a priest cannot sin. It is a thing to make one shudder.

There is an ironic footnote to his obsession with obscenity. Anthony Comstock, founder of the Society for the Suppression of Vice in New York and the Watch and Ward Society in Boston, defender of conventional morality, guardian of the purity of the U.S. mails, could appreciate Watson's anti-Catholicism. But his puritan soul was outraged as he read the explicit descriptions of mythical Catholic depravity in *Watson's Magazine*. The destruction of obscene literature was a passion with Comstock, and finally he could no longer resist his own inner conflict of prejudices. In 1912 Comstock sought and obtained an

indictment of Watson for the crime of sending indecent literature—
that is, *Watson's Magazine*—through the mails.

For more than three years, the case dragged through the courts in
Georgia. Watson was finally acquitted. In the meantime, Watson
made the most of his opportunities, attacking Comstock on the one
hand and Catholic priests on the other. Indeed, in fine disregard of
fact, he credited the Pope with "demanding of Congress a law to close
the mails to all such Americans" as he. In one sentence, he thus
charged the church with persecution and denied Comstock credit for a
lifetime of effort to ban obscene literature from the mails.

In 1913 Watson added yet another string—anti-Semitism—to his
nativist guitar, strumming out hymns of hate on such a hysterical
pitch as to lead to the unspeakable lynching of Leo Frank of Atlanta.
Frank, born in Texas, reared in New York and educated at Cornell
University, moved to Georgia in 1907 to become manager of a pencil
factory owned by his uncle, Moses Frank. The elder Frank had served
in the Confederate Army and the family was well regarded. Leo
quickly established himself as a young businessman of good reputation, married, and became active in community affairs as a matter of
course.

In 1913 young Frank was elected president of the Atlanta Lodge of
B'nai B'rith and as such was aware of the stirrings of anti-Semitism,
the defamatory impact of vicious anti-Jewish stereotypes in American
popular culture, and the trend to anti-Jewish prejudice among
nativists and religious fundamentalists. If he was conscious of such
matters in New York, he became even more aware of bigotry in
Atlanta. Violence, however, probably never entered his head. Only in
Russia could a frame-up such as the Mendel Beilis "blood-libel" case
take place. In the South, violence was reserved for Negroes. Such at
least is the way matters were recalled half a century later by Frank's
friend, Herman Binder, who had preceded him as president of the
B'nai B'rith lodge.

In April, however, Leo Frank was arrested and charged with the
rape and brutal murder in his factory of a fourteen-year-old girl named
Mary Phagan. Arrested with him was Jim Conley, a young Negro
janitor at the factory. Frank admitted seeing the girl and paying her
wages that day. Conley was named an accessory and sentenced to one
year on the chain gang. Frank, on little more than circumstantial
evidence, was convicted of the murder.

Binder has described the scene in the courtroom:

Mobs choked the area around the courthouse. Men with rifles stood at the open windows, some aimed at the jury, some aimed at the judge. Over and over, louder and louder the men repeated the chant "Hang the Jew, Hang the Jew."

The trial was a farce. Prosecuting attorney [Hugh] Dorsey had his case and political ambitions and didn't care how he won it. The mobs kept up their chant. I can still hear them screaming...through those open windows. And inside the courtroom, spectators were allowed to give free vent to their anti-Semitism. The jury was threatened with death unless it brought in a verdict of guilty. The judge was threatened with death if he didn't pass a sentence of hanging. No deputies tried to clear the windows or the courtroom. And sitting there, looking so small and forlorn was my friend Leo.

An old man recalling such agonizing events half a century later might have the total accuracy of his memories questioned, but no cold court record can substitute for them. Yet, as John P. Roche has pointed out in *The Quest for the Dream: The Development of Civil Rights and Human Relations in America*, "A reading of the trial record shows that

(Left) *The Leo Frank Case—Lynch Law prevailed. Frank in court with his wife seated behind him.*

(Below) *Tom Watson—"Frank died because he willed it."*

Leo Frank was the victim of circumstantial evidence which would not hold up ten minutes in a normal courtroom then or now."

In the courtroom, the issue was a man's life, but the court never really addressed that issue. When the case came to the United States Supreme Court on appeal, Justice Oliver Wendell Holmes wrote: "Mob law does not become due process of law by securing the assent of a terrorized jury...it is our duty...[to] declare lynch law as little valid when practiced by a regularly drawn jury as when administered by one elected by a mob intent on death." The high court unhappily held the case was not in the Federal jurisdiction, but Justice Charles Evans Hughes joined in Justice Holmes' dissent.

Outside the trial court, as in it, the mob not the law, prevailed; and in the wider context of the social and political order, nightmarish anti-Semitism swept all before it. Tom Watson had made justice irrelevant.

The jury had convicted Frank after a thirty-day trial that began on July 28, 1913, as a cheering, menacing, unruly mob crowded the courtroom and its environs. Judge, jury court officials, defense attorney—all concerned with the administration of justice were under constant threat: "Hang the Jew or we'll hang you." When the jury convicted, the judge pronounced sentence of death. When Frank's counsel moved to have the verdict set aside, the judge denied the motion. He was not sure of Frank's guilt, but the jury was, and that was enough for him. On appeal, the State Supreme Court with two judges dissenting confirmed the conviction. In Federal District Court a writ of *habeas corpus* was denied, yet the court declared doubt as to Frank's guilt. Finally, the appeals were exhausted when the U.S. Supreme Court ruled it lacked jurisdiction and Holmes and Hughes issued their trenchant dissent.

Throughout the twenty months this process consumed, the mills of hate were grinding on rapidly and crudely. Watson's periodical, *The Jeffersonian*, dwelled constantly on the case recounting over and over again that "Jew money" was "out to free the convicted libertine," weeping that the girl Mary Phagan "had no millionaire uncle to raise money for her." "Our little girl—ours by the eternal God!" *The Jeffersonian* ranted, "has been pursued to a hideous death by this filthy, perverted Jew of New York."

Cynically, rumors, slanders, and clarion calls to racial prejudice kept the state boiling and the mobs in a threatening mood. Elsewhere in the country, Leo Frank's sad plight did indeed call forth sympathy and offers of assistance. Congressmen, senators, and governors made appeals in his behalf. Several state legislatures passed resolutions calling for commutation of sentence or a new trial.

Herman Binder toured the country and invoked the assistance of B'nai B'rith lodges, and these in turn sought the public protest of others. The American Jewish Committtee took no organizational action in behalf of Frank, but when his appeal came before the U.S. Supreme Court, the committee's distinguished president, Louis Marshall, appeared as counsel. Marshall was recognized as one of the nation's leading constitutional lawyers. Many other prominent lawyers who analyzed the case expressed the opinion that the evidence pointed to Conley's guilt. Newspapers throughout the country came to the same conclusion and editorially denounced Georgia justice for the persecution of Frank.

The matter now rested on the desk of Governor John M. Slaton, who also had his doubts of Frank's guilt. But always behind him, as they had been behind the trial court, was the threatening mob and the vituperative Watson. Finally, Slaton acted three days before his term of office ran out. He commuted Frank's sentence to life imprisonment and had him secretly moved for protection from Atlanta to the fortresslike Milledgeville Prison Farm.

Slaton had sound reason to act as he did. Years later it came to light that he had evidence of Frank's innocence—evidence that had not come out in court, but was imparted to him by the presiding judge. Jim Conley had confessed to his attorney, William Smith, that he was guilty of the murder. Smith, bound by the client-attorney relationship, felt he could not act. Nevertheless, he finally told what he knew to Presiding Judge L. S. Roan and Judge Arthur G. Powell. Ultimately, the information was passed on to Governor Slaton.

Powell revealed much of this in his book *I Can Go Home Again* in 1943. Ten years later, Slaton told Samuel Boorstin of Atlanta, in an interview now in the files of the Anti-Defamation League, that Watson, in addition to his public attacks wrote him privately offering him a seat in the United States Senate if he would let Frank hang.

In signing the commutation order, Slaton saved his soul, but signed his own political death warrant. Troops were needed to protect him and his home from the violent mob that sought the vengeance Watson had called for. Three days later, he left office and Georgia, and a message that revealed him to be one of the few heroes of the sad affair.

"Two thousand years ago," he told his fellow Georgians, "another

governor washed his hands of the mob and turned a Jew over [to it]. For two thousand years that governor's name has been a curse. If today another Jew were lying in his grave because I had failed in my duty, I would all my life find his blood on my hands, and must consider myself an assassin through cowardice."

But the end was not yet. Slaton's act of conscience simply heightened the lynch spirit throughout the state, encouraged by Watson's continued agitation. He denounced Slaton as "King of the Jews" and charged that the governor "had been bought" by outsiders, Jews no doubt. The August 1915 issue of *Watson's Magazine* was choleric. "Once there were men in Georgia...men who caught fire from the heavens to burn a law which outraged Georgia's sense of honor and justice." The obscene atmosphere created by such calls to lynch law reached into the very prison itself. A half-demented convict slashed Frank's throat, wounding him severely. Four days later, a vigilante mob of 25 men stormed the prison, dragged the wounded man off to Marietta, near the girl's home, and there lynched him.

The nation was shocked and sickened. Groups all over the country that had sought to avert the evil day went into mourning. The press throughout the country—the South included—expressed its dismay and shame. But the *Marietta Journal* shamelessly declared: "We regard the hanging of Leo M. Frank as an act of law-abiding citizens." And Tom Watson, with cynical savagery, gloated: "A vigilante committee redeems Georgia and carries out the sentence of the law...Jew libertines take notice."

So tense had conditions in Marietta become late in June 1915 that Jewish citizens and merchants of the town feared for their lives. Vigilantes had ordered all of them to leave the county. The situation grew critical enough for Hugh M. Dorsey, the attorney general who had prosecuted the Frank case, to issue a plea to town officials to prevent the threatened expulsion. His plea helped. Watson, however, had found a valuable instrument in anti-Semitism and played on it for the responses he was evidently getting in his appeals to nativist racial prejudices:

"It is a peculiar and portentious thing," he wrote at about the time of the lynching, "that one race of men—and one only—should be able to

(Left) *Governor John M. Slaton–His act of conscience and courage ended his political career.*

convulse the world by a system of newspaper agitation and suppression, when a member of that race is convicted of a capital crime against another race." And then seemingly turning to quite another issue—immigration—that was agitating the nativists, he continued: "From all over the world, the children of Israel are flocking to this country and plans are on foot to move them from Europe *en masse* . . . to empty upon our shores the very scum and dregs of the *Parasite* Race."

Watson's double theme of anti-Semitism, added to his basic anti-Catholicism and hatred of blacks, paid off politically in a few years. In 1920 he won election to the U.S. Senate where he combined his nativist prejudices with his old populist progressivism. He emerged as an opponent of "the trusts," militarism and red-baiting until death claimed him in 1922. He was mourned by as strange a group of political personalities as ever attempted to get into a single bed.

The Ku Klux Klan sent a gigantic floral cross, records historian C. Vann Woodward, and Eugene V. Debs, the Socialist leader, called him this "heroic soul who fought the power of evil all his whole life long." Senator Harris, for his native Georgia, called him "in many ways the most remarkable man of my time in the State." Senator Thomas J. Heflin of Alabama, whose stature as a bigot grew with the years, saw in him "a great student and a great scholar." Senator Willis, perhaps exhausted by listening to all the encomia from his colleagues capped the Senate's memorial meeting with the comment: "He was a tremendous master of invective."

No doubt the tragic fate of Leo Frank is the ultimate proof of that.

Nativism Rampant—The KKK

Tom Watson was still fulminating over the Frank case when anti-Semitism attained a new institutional setting in Georgia—destined to spread widely through the nation—with the re-creation of the Ku Klux Klan in what can be called its second incarnation. Its founder was William J. Simmons, a promotor of fraternal organizations. There is some evidence that his inspiration came from Tom Watson's vision that the South needed to protect its "racial purity." Nor is there much doubt that he was moved by his own nativist bigotry and considerable hope for financial gain.

Simmons model was the Klan of the post-Civil War period whose depredations were designed to keep the newly freed slaves "in their place" and to intimidate Northern "carpetbaggers" and Southern "scalawags." Simmons replicated the original Klan in its high-handed, violent criminality and its white-sheeted regalia; its program was one of antagonism to Catholics, Jews, the foreign-born and Negroes—nativism rampant. As Simmons at one point explained:

"We exclude Jews because they do not believe in the Christian religion. We exclude Catholics because they owe allegiance to an institution that is foreign to the Government of the United States. To assure the supremacy of the white race we believe in the exclusion of the yellow race and in the disfranchisement of the Negro. By some scheme of Providence, the Negro was created as a serf."

Simmons was no great shakes as an organizer or perhaps the war interregnum hampered his organizing efforts. At any rate, from 1915 to 1920, the Klan attained a membership of only 5,000, but the framework for growth was in place. At this point, two professional promoters, Edward Young Clarke and Mrs. Elizabeth Taylor, entered the picture and struck a deal to handle the Klan's business affairs. Four years later, the Klan had reached its peak with a membership of 5,000,000.

The skill of the promoters is not to be underestimated, but circumstances played into their hands. The Klan's meteoric rise was facilitated by the economic and social crisis of the opening years of the decade. In 1920-21 there were 5,000,000 unemployed and 20,000 business failures. With such tensions affecting the nation, the Klan preached religious bigotry and racial hatred in the South, and tailored its program in the North to reflect the special problems of the cities.

Both favorable and unfavorable publicity were used to advantage. In a series of articles in 1921, the *New York Herald* described the Klan as a patriotic organization, surely with the nation's best interests at heart since it favored restrictive immigration and was violent on the subject of Bolsheviks. On the other hand, the *New York World*, in an exposé series, cited the outrages committed by masked Klansmen. Both had the effect of adding to the membership rolls, the Klan's New York director testified before a congressional committee. Only when members began to understand the internal corruption of the Klan, he believed, would membership drop. However, it was not the venality of the Klan leaders that caused its eventual downfall, but its orgies of terrorism, its criminal acts, and the public outrages.

The depredations of the Klan need not be recounted here; the record of its crimes is fully established. Its purposes were corrupt and evil from its very inception. Castigating immorality, it was itself immersed in sin; claiming to purify, it only contaminated; seeking to stabilize society, it brought only strife. In the truest sense, it was a subversive force—subversive of the law, the government and the social order. It was motivated by no ideology except a corrosive racial hatred, no purpose except greed, no instinct except masochism. It was nativism without a single redeeming feature.

The anti-Semitism of the Klan, first enunciated by Simmons, found its outlets in the boycott of Jewish merchants, vandalism against their stores, the burning of fiery crosses outside of synagogues and other Jewish institutions. Such tactics, and efforts to terrorize individual prominent Jewish citizens in many a Southern community, caused Jews, for the first time in American history, to become deeply disturbed about their place in the nation.

The Anti-Defamation League, reflecting such Jewish concern, soon was engaged in the development of a program that could rally practical opposition to the Klan. The proposals stressed the need for legislative action rather than public protests, since exposure of Klan activities had not hampered its growth. The essence of the proposal is defined in a 1922 letter by Gustavus Loevinger, a League Board menber.

"The plan is to have laws introduced prohibiting men from appearing masked on public streets and highways, also to have a law introduced to compel every secreo society to file a record of its members with the Secretary of State . . . the Ku Klux Klan members cannot afford to have their names made public as it might become unpleasant for their members if the Klan should commit any violence contrary to the laws of the State."

Some time in 1922, Simmons was "bought out" and ousted as the Imperial Wizard to be succeeded by Hiram Wesley Evans, a Texas dentist. Klan atrocities multiplied, and Evans was often directly implicated. On October 24, 1923—Klan Day in Dallas, Texas—he spoke before 75,000 on "The Menace of Modern Immigration," clearly an effort to win support from racist-oriented backers of national origins quota legislation then before Congress. "There is not a semblance of racial hate in my heart," he proclaimed, but "Jews are an unblendable element . . . alien and unassimilable . . . mercenary-minded . . . money mad." All, including Catholics and Negroes, were incapable of attaining "the Anglo-Saxon level."

Not to permit such attacks to go unchallenged, the League immediately published a "Jewish Reply to Evans" whose wide circulation was further enhanced by reprinting and favorable editorial comment in the nation's press.

Evans' tirade had the effect too of bringing into existence a National Vigilance Association to fight the Klan. It was composed of prominent public and political figures, educators, leaders of industry. Many civic and fraternal groups joined in the anti-Klan effort, and even such staunch supporters of immigration restriction as the American Legion and the American Federation of Labor—repelled by Evans' expressed bigotry—condemned the Klan. The new committee soon put forth a program such as the League already had under way.

With the League's support, Congressman George W. Lindsay of New York introduced an "Anti-Intolerance Act" in the House of Representatives in 1923, but it died in committee. However, efforts to get similar statutes through various state legislatures were successful in New York, Iowa, Minnesota, and Michigan. Klan attempts to have these laws declared unconstitutional were defeated by a U. S. Supreme Court decision in 1928.

If, at this time, attacks on the Klan were beginning to reach their

The Ku Klux Klan—An evil phoenix that rises again and again from the ashes of nativist bigotry.

mark, yet the results achieved by the Klan in state politics, North and South, were frightening. Its candidates won governorships and other state posts, congressional seats and at least one Senate seat each in Texas, Indiana, Pennsylvania and Florida. It flourished in Arkansas and Oklahoma and captured Indiana and Ohio politically. By 1924, however, the popular support of the Klan was receding rapidly. In the Presidental election that year, the three contenders for the White House all publicly condemned the Klan. Meanwhile, the criminal justice system was working its will. In Indiana, the state Klan leader was convicted and imprisoned for crimes arising from Klan operations.

To the 1925 convention of B'nai B'rith, League Secretary Leon Lewis was able to report that an ADL study of the Presidential election results foresaw the rapid decline of Klan influence. The survey covered 2,000 cities and towns and showed "that the [Klan] has been much less influential than press reports would seem to indicate and that its influence in any one community never seems to last over a very long period . . . the better element of American citizenry also seems to be withdrawing. The Klan's power for evil was stopped when it entered politics."

The dissipation of the social and economic problems troubling the country after World War I, the excesses of the Klan, the vigorous stand against it by decent citizens everywhere, combined to bring to an end the second phase of the organization. But it was to rear its hooded head again in a third incarnation.

The War Interregnum

The years during which the tragic Frank episode was played out were seemingly a prelude to the much more widespread and tenacious anti-Semitism that permeated the 1920s. The interregnum of the war years impeded this development only momentarily; then the growth of anti-Semitism came on with a rush. Charges of slackerism and war-profiteering were heard in the land against all foreigners, of course, but Jews were in for some special treatment. "The foreign born, and especially Jews," read a United States Army manual published for war recruits, "are more apt to malinger than the native-born." Thus official sanction was given to the slander which had already gained wide currency. The League in conjunction with other representative Jewish agencies entered a protest with President Wilson, who promptly ordered the manual to be recalled. This was followed up with efforts to publicize the facts about the contributions of American Jews to the war effort. There was no lack of data, but more importantly, the striving for a national unity in the war endeavor kept the lid on racial nativism until it burst forth in 1919 with the Red scare and an antiforeign nationalism.

Suddenly Jews became a principal target accused of responsibility for all of the war-born ills in the land. Jews of German origin were accused of undue influence on President Wilson and those of Russian origin were charged with coercing America into war and then unconscionably prolonging it. Frequently the two lines of charges were merged, linking German-Jewish bankers with Russian-Jewish Bolsheviks into a huge conspiracy against America. The stimulus for such anti-Semitism came from places high and low. Senator Lodge could vent his well-controlled spleen against Wilson by implying that the President's appointment to the Federal Reserve Board of Paul Warburg, a distinguished banker but recent immigrant, gave him a secret connection to Germany, and a disreputable hate sheet in Brooklyn could rail against the Jewish Bolshevist Doctrines of Morris Hillquit and Leon Trotsky. Hillquit in 1917 had run up a large vote for mayor on the Socialist ticket in New York, and Trotsky had briefly lived in the city as a refugee.

Thus was born the new double-image stereotype of the Jew which gave further evidence of the irrationality of the bigoted mind. The old stereotype pictured the Jew as the mercenary, grasping capitalist, the ruthless exploiter of the helpless worker. The new one pictured him as the dangerous Utopian Bolshevik, the subversive, the merciless persecutor of the free-enterpriser. The bland disregard of logic could be rationalized by some presumed aspect of "Jewish essence." At least nativist bigots found no difficulty in referring to Jews as "money changers" in one breath and "Bolsheviks" in the next. Similar contradictory calumnies were repeated by newspapers, magazines, and lecturers who should have known better. Ninety percent of Russian Jews were Bolsheviks; the Jews murdered the Czar and his family; Jews by nature were capitalist exploiters and proletarian bomb-throwers. Cartoonists took to portraying the Bolshevik as a bearded fellow with a Jewish physiognomy, hiding a bomb behind his back. The League traced certain journalistic distortions directly to the files of the Associated Press and entered a vehement protest. The Associated

Press took steps to "endeavor in the future...not to bring racial and religious prejudice into our reports."

Jews were only tangentially caught up in the toils of the Big Red Scare of the immediate postwar period, but the idea that they were pro-Bolshevik radicals was freely propagated. To counter this propaganda, in 1920 the League sent Isaac Don Levine, then a correspondent of the *Chicago Daily News* in Moscow, on a lecture tour of the country to refute the widespread belief that Jews had played a major role in the Russian Revolution or that it was the first step in a Jewish conspiracy to conquer the world. Levine's lectures were then distributed to 500 newspapers throughout the country and reached over 40,000 readers. In a letter of transmittal, Leon Lewis, the League's secretary, cited the articles as "a conclusive answer to the many libelous stories recently appearing in the press of the country which...charge Jews with responsibility for Bolshevism in Russia and for social and economic unrest in other countries..."

The Levine program was the first of many efforts to counter the smearing of Jews as communists. This war on Jews has had its heated as well as desultory periods depending upon the political and economic climate, it has never ended and there are still those to whom the words "Jew" and "Red" are synonymous.

As we have already noted, running concurrently through the decade of the 1920s, classic strains of anti-Semitism had been developed by the Ku Klux Klan, by Henry Ford's descent into the pit of anti-Jewish propaganda, and by the xenophobia directed toward Eastern Europeans—read "Jews." These strains entered into the legislative process that ultimately resulted in the passage of the national origins immigration quota laws.

In each of these developments, historian John Higham has pointed out there was a measure of "scientific racism that pressed downward from patrician" sources to blend "with the cruder Anglo-Saxon nativism pushing upward from the grass roots of the [rural] south and west." Certainly, that was true in the case of the Klan and the bigotry which informed much of the restrictionist forces working toward a national origins immigrations quota law. Henry Ford had little of the patrician influences working upon him. When his foray into idealistic nationalism ended up in disillusionment with the failure of his quixotic Peace Ship mission in 1915, he turned to isolationism. Somehow, he blamed "international Jewish bankers" for that fiasco. His nativist origins took over as he entered upon his seven-year war against the Jews.

Ford—The Seven-Year War

If the Klan can be said to have provided an institutional structure for anti-Semitism in the 1920s, Henry Ford can as readily be said to have built a production line for anti-Semitic propaganda. Together, they represented the ultimate flowering of nativist bigotry against Jews. The noted historian Allen Nevins, who was Ford's biographer, seeking the sources of his "spasm of violent anti-Semitism" finds them in his populist background, his rural upbringing, in his ignorance and misinformation and "not (in) any deepseated bigotry or vein of malice." To credit Ford's hatreds largely to his nativist beginnings is an act of generosity on the part of so astute an observer. The reasons are far more complex and both bigotry and malice played a part in Ford's seven-year war against Jews.

To prosecute that war, Ford converted the weekly newspaper he owned— the *Dearborn Independent*—into a virtual propaganda factory, providing munitions for the hatemongers of the world. "It would have been better had Ford never entered journalism," Nevins wrote. To which one can only say "Amen."

Ford's reputation as an intuitive thinker is evident in his own field, but once he left the automobile business that renowned intuition turned to sheer prejudice, because it was supported neither by knowledge nor by training. When he turned to political questions, he had the support only of his own intellectual arrogance. He had a quick and intricate mind, but it was uninformed and undisciplined in almost everything except his special skill. He felt books were things that cluttered the mind; it is questionable whether he was ever able to think through a political problem on the basis of logic or fact. His adventure with the Peace Ship and his anti-Semitic campaign offer convincing evidence of this. Only a man who could call all history "bunk," would have so readily accepted the conspiracy theory of history inherent in the *Protocols of the Elders of Zion* hoax, or sponsored a journalistic project such as the *International Jew*.

More important than to determine why Ford carried on as he did is the need to understand why he succeeded for so long in winning attention for his anti-Semitic campaign. We need to know more about

American reaction to one so clearly engaged in aberrational behavior. Seemingly, one reason for the response to Ford was the fact that anti-Semitism was in the air. In 1920 there was a distinct anti-Jewish bias accepted by large numbers and in many areas of the social order. Ford was recognized as a genius in his field; genius in the popular mind was transferable. His views were listened to with respect even in fields where he was utterly ignorant and, as Norman Hapgood phrased it, where he exhibited "the mind of a child." True, his Peace Ship demarche in 1915 was a debacle, but that happened he could say, because the leaders of the Great War would not listen to his wisdom. But now that Ford had "uncovered" a long-term conspiracy by Jews to rule the world there were many, at least in the nativist segment of the population, ready to believe. Finally, there was the capacity for mischief which a truly wealthy man could exercise; it didn't matter to Ford that during the years the *Dearborn Independent* was published, he covered losses of nearly $5,000,000.

The *Independent* fired its first salvo against the Jews on May 22, 1920, and kept up the barrage for 91 issues. Before that happened, however, E. G. Pipp, the editor of the *Independent*, resigned. A liberal Catholic, Pipp had resisted the trends that were leading the paper down the anti-Semitic trail. The production of the articles had been placed in the hands of W. J. Cameron, who assumed the task at first reluctantly, but in time threw principle to the winds and engaged in his project as a malevolent work of art. When Pipp quit, Cameron stepped in as editor. While Cameron supplied the "art," Ernest Liebold, Ford's secretary, provided the poison. It was his function to provide the ammunition for the *Dearborn Independent's* anti-Semitic barrage. "When we get through with the Jews," he was once quoted in court, "there won't be one of them who will dare raise his head in public."

Liebold organized an investigative bureau in New York to gather information on the private lives of prominent Jews and soon became known as a ready buyer of any anti-Semitic matter that would feed the Ford machine. It was inevitable that the most notorious anti-Semitic hoax of the century, the *Protocols of the Learned Elders of Zion*, would find its way into his hands. Evidently Liebold knew nothing of the history of the *Protocols*; but if he did, it would not have mattered, because it exactly suited his needs. As Keith Sward, author of *The Legend of Henry Ford*, put it succinctly: "no manual on Jew-baiting had more to offer." Cameron, he continued, "improved on the forgery so skillfully that, in modern dress it became one of the foremost existing brochures on anti-Semitism. The...Ford version...stands to this day as one of the world's most widely read standard editions."

How thoroughly Cameron—a onetime preacher—had thrown off all the inhibitions of principle is shown by his assertion that Jesus was not a Jew, "as commonly conceived."

Activities such as Liebold's could not long go unnoticed. The Anti-Defamation League was aware of the imminent publication of the *Protocols* in the *Dearborn Independent* months before the first article in the series appeared. The *B'nai B'rith News* spoke of steps being taken to reduce the damage likely to be done. This was the first hint the American public got of what was to come; and when it came, its implications of danger were greater than anyone could have foreseen.

But shocked as American Jews may have been, Henry Ford was no less so by Jewish reaction to the opening shot of his anti-Semitism campaign. Somehow, he had nurtured the idea that the "good Jews" of the country would support him in his crusade against the iniquitous "international" Jew. The first one he seems to have heard from and in the most telling way was a man whom he considered a "good Jew." Dr. Leo M. Franklin, long an intimate and neighbor of Ford's, was one of the few Jews Ford really knew. He was Detroit's most distinguished rabbi, a member of the Anti-Defamation League's first executive committee in 1913, and its spokesman in Detroit in the years since. Ford had made a practice of presenting the rabbi with a new custom-built car each year as a mark of friendship.

Saddened by the sudden turn to anti-Semitism of the *Dearborn Independent*, Dr. Franklin took the most dramatic way of expressing his displeasure. When shortly after the first articles appeared, the new season's car was driven to his home, he asked that it be taken back. E. G. Pipp reported Ford's reaction of astonishment. In a few days, Ford called to ask, "What's wrong, Dr. Franklin? Has something come between us?"

Up to that point, Ford perhaps had not talked about his campaign to anyone but his inner group led by Liebold and Cameron, but he was soon deluged with protests and complaints by the thousands. However, in Dr. Franklin's view, as reported to the League's Executive Committee in June, his interview with Ford "showed all too clearly that the ordinary methods of appeals to reason and justice would be of no avail."

To a Detroit newspaper, Franklin said, "Few thinking men have given any credence to the charges offered against Jews. But his publications have besmirched the name of the Jews in the eyes of the great majority, and especially in the small towns of the country, where Ford's word was taken as gospel. He has also fed the flames of anti-Semitism throughout the world."

The extent to which the *International Jew* articles and subsequent pamphlets were to fuel the fires of world anti-Semitism was to become evident in future years—and to the discomfort of Henry Ford himself. In the meantime, there was reason to take Ford's anti-Semitic drive with the utmost seriousness. *The Protocols* first appeared in 1901, written by a Russian fanatic named Sergius Nilus and probably drawn from the hack novels of a German writer Herman Goedsche and a French political polemicist Maurice Joly, who had aimed his barbs at the regime of Napoleon III. *The Protocols* stimulated the savage Russian pogroms during the period 1903-19. The notorious "Black Hundreds," a quasi-official Russian group fostered by the Czar, used the early versions of *The Protocols* to incite its members to murder and the pillage of entire Jewish communities. A second edition of *The Protocols* was published officially by the Czar's government immediately after the abortive 1905 revolt in Russia. Later editions were apparently responsible for the mass slaughter of Ukrainian Jews, both by pro- and anti-Bolsheviks during the Russian Revolution. Cameron's literary doctoring and modernizing of the translation obtained by Liebold from Boris Brasol, a white Russian émigré, however, soon produced the Ford version of *The Protocols* that was to become the standard.

American Jews—horrified but not intimidated—held a special conference in September 1920 to plan strategy to meet the threat. The Central Conference of American Rabbis, the National Council of Jewish Women and the B'nai B'rith asked the Anti-Defamation League to undertake a program of counteraction. In November another meeting was held that included the American Jewish Committee, the American Jewish Congress, and the United Synagogue of America. In December nine of the organizations joined efforts to issue jointly a pamphlet exposing *The Protocols*. It was called *The Protocols, Bolshevism and the Jews*.

In the meantime, the League was giving wide circulation to a pamphlet by Sigmund Livingston, *The Protocols–A Spurious Document* and another *The Poison Pen* targeted on the *Dearborn Independent*, the men behind the *International Jew* articles and Henry Ford's attacks on Jews.

In the face of such a counterattack, Ford nevertheless held to his line. After all, the protests were coming from Jews, and though he had hoped for a better reaction from "the good Jews," he continued unperturbed until he was shocked by a statement—defending Jews and denying the authenticity of the *Protocols*—signed by 116 distinguished public figures. The names were led by those of President Woodrow Wilson, and former Presidents William Howard Taft and Theodore Roosevelt and included such men and women as Jane Addams, Charles A. Beard, W. E. B. DuBois, Clarence Darrow, Robert Frost, Edward Everett Hale, Edwin Markham, Ida Tarbell, and even so eminent a Bible Belt figure as William Jennings Bryan.

The statement, *The Perils of Racial Prejudice*, which had been written and circulated at his own initiative by John Spargo, a well-known writer of the time, said in part:

> These publications [i.e., Ford's avalanche of newsprint] are introducing into our national political life a new and dangerous spirit, one that is wholly at variance with our traditions and ideals, and subversive of our system of government.... The logical outcome of the success of such a campaign must necessarily be the division of our citizens along racial and religious lines, and ultimately, the introduction of religious tests and qualifications to determine citizenship. We call upon all those who are molders of public opinion—the clergy and ministers of all Christian churches, publicists, teachers, editors and statesmen—to strike at this un-American and un-Christian agitation.

John Spargo touched a nerve that brought an unprecedented response to his evocation of the American ideal among those whose spirits had been beaten down by the difficulties of the times and the constant barrage of nativist bigotry. On top of the Tom Watsons, on top of the Klan, the voice of Ford and his minions was just too much. Churchmen, editors, public opinion molders responded to the leadership of the group that signed Spargo's statement. Native-born liberals suddenly found their voices, often muted when the Old Stock expressed racist notions.

Yet Ford was no doubt shocked to see among his critics some establishment names from whom he might have expected support. He may have even believed that his criticism of Jews was not unlike that expressed among those now critical of him. But then he probably never understood the difference between raucous bigotry and polite bias; nor that the lack of intellectual underpinning in his attitudes could only evoke the same kind of responses among such men as these as the antics of the Ku Klux Klan.

Nor was his cause helped by the bunk the *Dearborn Independent* passed out as history, and cited here at random: Queen Isabella, the

Catholic, was a "Jewish front," and the money for Columbus' voyages was raised by three "secret Jews"; Benedict Arnold, the Revolutionary War traitor, was a "front" for Jewish bankers; all of "economics, conservative, radical, capitalistic and anarchistic, is of Jewish origin." Jews were infiltrating both the Masons and the Jesuits. With such nuggets of "fact" it became hard to differentiate between the Ford's and the Klan's publications except by the difference in size of the bankrolls available to them.

It seemed safe enough to garble history, to invoke the names of long-dead heroes and villains and to invent fictitious "history" for the promotion of anti-Semitism. What that called forth were cries of indignation and a good deal of ridicule. But in April 1924 the *Dearborn Independent* began a series of anti-Semitic attacks that accused Aaron Sapiro, a distinguished Chicago lawyer active in the farm cooperative movement, and a group of Jewish bankers and merchants of seeking to control the nation's wheat farming.

"This whole Kahn-Baruch-Lasker-Rosenwald-Sapiro program," the articles declared at one point, "is carefully planned to turn over to an organized international interest the entire agricultural interest of the Republic... between the lines one reads the story of the Jewish communist movement in America, which seeks to make the United States what it had already made of Russia."

For the *Dearborn Independent*, the series proved a fatal mistake; for Henry Ford it was a debacle. The articles continued into 1925, but Sapiro promptly sued for defamation of character, and the case came to trial in 1927 in Detroit. As Nevins has pointed out, the attacks on Sapiro and on the eminent Jewish bankers and merchants whose names had been dragged in "were as offensive as they were ill-founded."

The suit was directed personally against Ford and his responsibility for the libel, but Cameron testified for five days, taking upon himself sole responsibility and asserting that Ford never discussed articles on Jews with him. Of course, the defense supported Cameron's position. Credulity was stretched to the breaking point with the assertion by Ford's attorney that his client had never even heard of Sapiro. It snapped when Sapiro's counsel brought to the stand a former *Dearborn Independent* employee, James M. Miller, who swore that Ford had told him he intended to expose Sapiro.

Ford himself dreaded nothing as much as having to take the witness stand, having once had an excruciating experience in a case against the *Chicago Tribune*. The efforts to keep Ford from having to testify in open court read like the account of a military campaign. Finally he was served with a subpoena, but just before his turn came to take the stand, Ford was injured in an auto accident. He was not seriously hurt, but it gave him a respite. In the meantime, a most unusual series of events took place. Ford operatives filed charges of jury tampering by the plaintiff. In reply to a question, an outraged woman juror had spoken to a news reporter. The court thus was forced to declare a mistrial, but expressly cleared Sapiro or the jurors of any misconduct.

Ford had escaped having to take the stand. He now had another six months' respite, and he used it to assert the purity of his motives, quite in the way a major corporation might agree to settlement of an antitrust suit without admitting any prior wrongdoing.

Public statements, legal settlements, apologies to individuals and the Jews as a group, now came contritely trooping. Ford's emissaries to the Jewish community were E. J. Davis of Detroit and Joseph A. Palma, a former U.S. Secret Service agent about to acquire a Ford dealership in New York. Their approach was to Louis Marshall and Nathan D. Perlman with an offer from Ford "to repair the damage" of the *Dearborn Independent* articles "as far as I can." When the Jewish leaders expressed their receptiveness, Ford wrote his letter of apology on June 30, 1927, to Davis, who then made it public through Arthur Brisbane, the Hearst editor who was friendly to Ford but highly critical of his attacks on Jews. A copy was sent to Marshall. In this tortuous manner did the world get word of Ford's change of heart. None was more surprised than W. J. Cameron, the editor of the *Dearborn Independent*; Ford had kept him completely in the dark about his intentions. Ford wrote:

For some time past, I have given consideration to the series of articles concerning Jews which since 1920 have appeared in *The Dearborn Independent*. Some of them have been reprinted in pamphlet form under the title *The International Jew*. Although both publications are my property, it goes without saying that in the multitude of my activities it has been impossible for me to devote my personal attention to their management or to keep informed as to their contents. It has therefore inevitably followed that the conduct and policies of these publications had to be delegated to men whom I placed in charge of them and upon whom I relied implicitly.

To my great regret I have learned that Jews generally, and particularly those of this country, not only resent these publications as promoting anti-Semitism, but regard me as their enemy. Trusted friends with whom

I have conferred recently have assured me in all sincerity that in their opinion the character of the charges and insinuations made against the Jews, both individually and collectively, contained in many of the articles which have been circulated periodically in *The Dearborn Independent* and have been reprinted in the pamphlets mentioned, justifies the righteous indignation entertained by Jews everywhere toward me because of the mental anguish occasioned by the unprovoked reflections made upon them.

This has led me to direct my personal attention to this subject in order to ascertain the exact nature of these articles. As a result of this survey I confess that I am deeply mortified that this journal which is intended to be constructive and not destructive, has been made the medium for resurrecting exploded fictions, for giving currency to the so-called *Protocols of the Wise Men of Zion*, which have been demonstrated, as I learn, to be gross forgeries, and for contending that the Jews have been engaged in a conspiracy to control the capital and the industries of the world, besides laying at their door many offenses against decency, public order and good morals.

Had I appreciated even the general nature, to say nothing of the details, of these utterances, I would have forbidden their circulation without a moment's hesitation, because I am fully aware of the virtues of the Jewish people as a whole, of what they and their ancestors have done for civilization and for mankind toward the development of commerce and industry, of their sobriety and diligence, their benevolence and their unselfish interest in the public welfare.

Of course there are black sheep in every flock, as there are among men of all races, creeds and nationalities who are at times evildoers. It is wrong, however, to judge a people by a few individuals, and I therefore join in condemning unreservedly all wholesale denunciations and attacks.

Those who know me can bear witness that it is not in my nature to inflict insult upon and to occasion pain to anybody, and that it has been my effort to free myself from prejudice. Because of that I frankly confess that I have been greatly shocked as a result of my study and examination of the files of *The Dearborn Independent* and of the pamphlets entitled *The International Jew*.

I deem it to be my duty as an honorable man to make amends for the wrong done to the Jews as fellow-men and brothers, by asking their forgiveness for the harm I have unintentionally committed, by retracting so far as lies within my power the offensive charges laid at their door by these publications, and by giving them the unqualified assurance that henceforth they may look to me for friendship and goodwill.

Finally, let me add that this statement is made on my own initiative and wholly in the interest of right and justice and in accordance with what I regard as my solemn duty as a man and as a citizen.

After seven years of calumny, it was only natural that the Ford explanation was received with some skepticism among Jews—no matter how much they wanted to believe. But the skepticism was not limited to Jews alone.

"Nobody but Mr. Ford," the *New York Herald Tribune* commented ironically, "could be ignorant of a major policy of his publication. Nobody but Mr. Ford could be unaware of the national and international repercussions of this policy of anti-Semitism. Nobody but Mr. Ford could say that he did not appreciate even the general nature, to say nothing of the details, of these utterances by his own editor."

The New York Times found incredible the fact that Ford could phrase "his statement as if his attention had recently been drawn to the grievous wrong which he had done." The fact is, of course, that for several years, he has had the matter brought to his notice, both privately and publicly. It did not take too much foresight, the *Times* predicted, to see that Ford's change of heart "will not at once undo the damage which his violent and unfounded attacks have caused."

Once having cast the die, Ford moved ahead quickly and held to the line he had projected in his letter to Davis. On July 16, 1927, an out-of-court settlement of the Sapiro suit was announced. Sapiro received an explanation and a check reported to be $140,000. Two weeks later, the *Dearborn Independent* published a statement which declared:

> It has since been found that inaccuracies of fact were present in the articles and that erroneous conclusions were drawn. As a result of this, Mr. Sapiro may have been injured and reflections cast upon him unjustly. Such statements as may have reflected upon Mr. Sapiro's honor or integrity, impugned his motives, or challenged the propriety of his personal or professional actions are withdrawn. Likewise, the charge that there was a Jewish ring which sought to exploit the American farmer through cooperative associations is withdrawn.
>
> Mr. Henry Ford did not participate personally in the publication of the articles and has no personal knowledge of what was said in them. He of course, deprecates greatly that any facts that were published in a periodical so closely connected with his name in the minds of the public should be untrue...

At about the same time, Ford wrote to Herman Bernstein, a well-known Jewish editor later to become American Ambassador to Albania in the Hoover Administration. Bernstein had been on the Peace Ship in 1915 and it was to him that Ford had attributed the statement that there was a Jewish conspiracy to control the world. Once again Ford apologized and offered restitution. At the close of the year, the *Dearborn Independent* abruptly ceased publication.

Like *The New York Times*, Bernstein and his attorney, Samuel Unter-
myer, pointed out to Ford he could not undo all of the damages with
his retractions alone. In November of 1927, Ford had written the
anti-Semitic German publisher Theodore Fritsch to cease publishing
The International Jew which he had translated into German. It was to no
avail. *The Protocols* and *The International Jew* continued to circulate
throughout the world under the Ford imprimatur in the 1930's and to
the present day, even though officials ostensibly had ordered all
existing copies destroyed. The evidence is that the campaign against
Jews simply went underground. W. J. Cameron was retained in the
Ford hierarchy and became nationally known to millions as the company's spokesman on the *Ford Sunday Evening Hour* radio broadcasts.
Subsequently, Cameron organized the Anglo-Saxon Federation
which continued distribution of *The Protocols* and arranged speaking
tours for anti-Semitic clergymen.

American entry into World War II must have set Ford's teeth on edge
once more in the matter of *The Protocols* which had become a staple of
Nazi propaganda. It was an association he did not enjoy. Shortly after
the attack on Pearl Harbor, Richard Gutstadt, national director of the
Anti-Defamation League, received a call from Harry H. Bennett, chief
of the Ford company's personnel department. Mr. Ford was disturbed
by the continued use of his name by anti-Semitic elements and
"highly indignant" over the renewed charges against him. Could
something be done? The two men worked at a new effort to halt the
circulation of the anti-Semitic materials and Ford wrote to Sigmund
Livingston, the League's national chairman, on January 2, 1942:

> In our present national and international emergency, I consider it of
> importance that I clarify some general misconceptions concerning my
> attitude toward my fellow citizens of Jewish faith. I do not subscribe to or
> support, directly or indirectly, any agitation which would promote an-
> tagonism against my Jewish fellow citizens. I consider that the hate
> mongering prevalent for some time against the Jew is of distinct disser-
> vice to our country, and to the peace and welfare of humanity.
>
> At the time of the retraction by me of certain publications concerning
> the Jewish people, in pursuance of which I ceased the publication of the
> *Dearborn Independent*, I destroyed copies of literature prepared by certain
> persons connected with its publication. Since that time I have given no

(Right) *Ford to Livingston—The ultimate affirmation of his change of heart.*

Ford Motor Company

ROUGE PLANT

DEARBORN, MICHIGAN

January 7 1942

Mr Sigmund Livingston
160 North LaSalle Street
Chicago, Illinois

Dear Sir:

In our present national and international emergency,
I consider it of importance that I clarify some general misconceptions
concerning my attitude toward my fellow-citizens of Jewish faith. I
do not subscribe to or support, directly or indirectly, any agitation
which would promote antagonism against my Jewish fellow-citizens. I
consider that the hate-mongering prevalent for some time in this
country against the Jew, is of distinct disservice to our country, and
to the peace and welfare of humanity.

At the time of the retraction by me of certain publications concerning the Jewish people, in pursuance of which I ceased the
publication of "The Dearborn Independent," I destroyed copies of
literature prepared by certain persons connected with its publication.
Since that time I have given no permission or sanction to anyone to use
my name as sponsoring any such publication, or being the accredited
author thereof.

I am convinced that there is no greater dereliction
among the Jews than there is among any other class of citizens. I am
convinced, further, that agitation for the creation of hate against
the Jew or any other racial or religious group, has been utilized to
divide our American community and to weaken our national unity.

I strongly urge all my fellow-citizens to give no aid
to any movement whose purpose it is to arouse hatred against any group.
It is my sincere hope that now in this country and throughout the
world, when this war is finished and peace once more established,
hatred of the Jew, commonly known as anti-Semitism, and hatred against
any other racial or religious group, shall cease for all time.

Sincerely yours,

Henry Ford

k

permission or sanction to anyone to use my name as sponsoring any such publication, or being the accredited agent thereof.

I am convinced that there is no greater dereliction among the Jews than there is among any other class of citizens. I am convinced, further, that agitation for the creation of hate against the Jew or any other racial or religious group, has been utilized to divide our American community and to weaken our national unity.

I strongly urge all my fellow citizens to give no aid to any movement whose purpose is to arouse hatred against any group. It is my sincere hope that now in this country and throughout the world, when this war is finished and peace once more established, hatred of the Jew, commonly known as anti-Semitism, and hatred against any other racial or religious group, shall cease for all time.

It was the clearest, most unequivocal—indeed, most unimpeachable—statement repudiating the past and affirming his change of heart Ford had ever made. And it was accompanied by a vigorous effort to end the distribution of the offending propaganda here and abroad. But as in the Greek legend, the evil that escaped from Ford's Pandora's box has never been totally imprisoned again.

Henry Ford—He could not bring himself to reject a Hitler government decoration

FOUR

Panic Among the Nordics

In the 1920's, the Old Anglo-Saxon Stock, ever mindful of its breeding and manners, could take no comfort in the violent tactics of the nativists or the national aberration that was the Ku Klux Klan. Ford's manufactured anti-Semitism even moved many of them to join out-spoken liberal spirits in expressions of disapproval and protest. This was not the America they wanted.

But they looked out on the ferment of the postwar world and felt American civilization, as they understood it, threatened by all those non-Nordic racial strains that had invaded the nation. Half a century of racist "scientific" thinking had created a siege mentality among many of the Old Stock. They recognized their own power, but it was possible they could be overwhelmed!

Henry Adams had long ago sounded that note of panic with his plea that the civilization he cherished go down fighting against the invad-ing barbarian. In the 1920's, intellectuals among the Old Stock impro-vised on that theme, until the idea had become an obsession. Madison Grant, the dilettante synthesizer of American scientific racism, raised, in the very title of his book, *The Passing of the Great Race*, the ultimate fear of the Old Stock. Among patrician intellectuals at the universities, among some of the notable literary figures of the day, this fear for the culture, the language, the very basic traditions of the nation was repeated in its many variations.

On such a note of panic for Nordic survival, novelist Gertrude

Atherton, who swallowed Madison Grant whole, could cry out that "the enormous influx of European plebeians" was spreading "the poison of democracy," as if democracy was indeed an interloper, unknown and unrecognized in the American heritage. She found American "society, like literature... suffering from the democratic flu" caught from the "Alpine round-heads" whom "nature denied ...the creative spark." And in a recounting of the races in Europe, she suggested—perhaps with some intuitive vision of the then not-too-distant future—that the Nordics "so far... are too enlightened to sterilize such groups and exterminate them."

Such emotionally charged fear had to find its political and social expression. In self-defense, the activists among the Old Stock felt they had to deny entry into the American heaven to all but their own. Leaning on scientific racism, they pressed on the political front for the ultimate in restrictive immigration laws. On the social level, they changed the sense of the word "discrimination" from an act of distinctive taste to one of selective bigotry by a pattern of social, economic, and education barriers that was perhaps more hurtful to Jews than any of the outright violence of the time.

Even among the patricians, the process did not go entirely unchallenged. In Harry Starr's elegant phrasing, there were still those "in that manner peculiar to New England, [who] revered the democratic ideal while not relaxing faith in the destiny of [their] own kind."

Racism and Immigration—The Final Act

By 1917 American immigration policy had traveled a long way from that enunciated by George Washington. In his Presidential proclamation of Thanksgiving Day, 1795, Washington urged the nation "to beseech the kind author of these blessings... to render this country more and more a safe and propitious asylum for the unfortunate of other countries." It was not an idle admonition to his countrymen. The restrictionist spirit was already abroad in the land. There were those who believed the country was at that point fully settled. In 1797 it was argued in Congress, contrary to Washington's expressed hope, that the times called for a cessation of immigration. With a population of 2,000,000, the nation could no longer afford a liberal policy; that was fine when the country was still new.

The argument, of course, could not be maintained and restrictionism made little headway. When it did, it was pushed back—even as the frontier was pushed back—until in 1882 the Chinese Exclusion Act was adopted. With that, the long march toward a national origins quota system of immigration—conceived in racism and nurtured in xenophobia—was begun. The literacy test law, first passed by Congress in 1897 and successively vetoed by President Grover Cleveland, William Taft and Woodrow Wilson, finally was enacted twenty years later when a second veto by Wilson was overridden. The tensions of the Great War had given the restrictionists the proper climate for their victory and they were at last ready for the final act.

The restrictionists flourished in the post–World War I atmosphere and they confidently pushed ahead to achieve a numerical limit to immigration. Whatever the motives of particular groups among them, the general fear that the uprooted of war-torn Europe would descend in their millions upon the country swept away the traditional ideal of asylum. In 1920 the House of Representatives passed a bill to suspend all immigration. Besieged by those who cared about the asylum principle and the great number concerned with the fate of those seeking entry to the country, the Senate rejected the House action as too great a turnabout.

In its place, the 1921 quota law was adopted and signed by President Warren G. Harding as a stopgap measure. With its enactment, the asylum principle that had governed American attitudes went out the window and a race-conscious national origins policy came in a side door. The 1921 law limited immigration to 3 percent of each European nationality resident in the United States in 1910, with a maximum of 357,000 immigrants from all sources annually. The effect was to admit more Northern and Western Europeans than Southern and Eastern immigrants. This was the national origins quota in embryo, to be developed fully under a law that would supersede it after fourteen months.

It is this development which is of interest to our chronicle of the anti-Semitism and racist ideology that gained ground so rapidly during the 1920's. Reading the record of the public and congressional debates leading to the establishment of the national origins quota system in its evolution from 1921 through 1929, one finds ethnic considerations and therefore also the anti-Semitic quotient—as perhaps the primary motivation of the restrictionists. After 1921, economic interests, such as organized labor, found their purposes largely fulfilled by the severe limits on the total number of immigrants to be admitted. It was chiefly those concerned with maintaining their

dominant position as a governing class or obsessed with notions of what an "American race" should be like, who pressed for the closing of the gates against the "clamoring horde."

Throughout these years, Jewish leadership—probably the most effective minority-group spokesmen against the succession of ever-growing restrictions—had a dual concern. The principle of asylum was vital to them. The need for refuge among Jews in Europe was great, especially among those in the newly independent Eastern European nations carved out of the Russian and Austro-Hungarian empires. With the closing of the gates to the United States, the problem was compounded. The racial quotient that entered into the national origins provisions and its accompanying xenophobic debate was equally a source of anxiety; the fallout was bound to affect all American Jews whether newcomers or not.

Jews recognized quickly enough after 1921 that the battle against restriction had been lost. They would continue to hold to their position against restriction, but they could hope only to limit the damage and minimize obnoxious ethnic characterizations and discriminatory immigration regulations.

The restrictionists, riding high and tasting victory, rediscovered Madison Grant and Lothrop Stoddard. Their books and "scientific" theories, ignored in the war years, suddenly excited new interest among patriotic societies, the popular press, and the Nordic beneficiaries of their theories who feared for their place. The *Saturday Evening Post*, most widely read of the weekly journals, published a series of articles in 1920 and 1921 by Kenneth Roberts, later known for his historical novels of early America, that foresaw a rising tide of immigration that would inundate the country with undesirables. Editorially, the *Post* looked upon free immigration as a destructive force and a threat to the nation.

Taking up the cry in a tone of crisis and hysteria in the years that followed were many daily newspaper editorialists and such organs as the *American Legion Weekly* and *World's Work*. The latter, in 1923 and 1924, ran a series of articles whose message was a now-familiar amalgam of superpatriotism and racist theory in the best Grant manner. The basic assertion was that the United States, founded by a racially

(Left) *Chinese Exclusion–Race riots such as here depicted in Denver led to the immigrant restriction act of 1882.*

homogeneous group of Anglo-Saxon peoples which flowered into the "American race," was fully formed by the 1890's. Subsequent immigrations challenged the spiritual unity that was the solid base of the nation. To permit further immigration would destroy the republic. Ironically, the articles were written by one Gino Speranza, a Chicago lawyer of Italian descent, obviously not compatible with his argument of the need for homogeneity.

With some feeling of confidence, writers could keep hammering away on the subject of the racist horrors that could befall the nation because there were a sufficient number of social scientists to feed their fears and support their misconceptions. Carl Brigham, a Princeton psychologist of high repute, published *A Study of American Intelligence* in 1923 on the basis of wartime Army mental tests, which proclaimed that "American intelligence is declining, and will proceed with an accelerating rate as the racial mixture becomes more and more extensive." William MacDougall, eminent Harvard psychologist, not given to quite such extremes, nevertheless asserted that the more aggressive temperament of Nordics permitted them to play a more dominant role in history than others. Harry Laughlin, the geneticist who had figured prominently in the writing of the Dillingham Commission report and remained as the eugenics expert of the House summed up in 1922: "The recent immigrants, on the whole, present a higher percentage of inborn socially inadequate qualities than does the older stock."

From the perspective of the present day, such views are no longer acceptable either as science or public policy. In a post-Hitler world they can be met only with outrage or weary disillusionment, but in 1924 the Congress of the United States, eager to get on with the business of closing the gates to immigration, found in "scientific" racism the answer to its heart's desire. The April 1924 debate in the House addressed itself to "racial purity" as the means of the nation's salvation. The melting-pot idea to which the country had been committed was now labeled a dangerous belief. "The trouble grows out of a country composed of intermingled and mongrelized people. "(Its) stability . . . depends upon the homogeneity of population," said one congressman. Another called for "one race, one country, one destiny."

The keynote for the national origins advocates had been sounded by the report of the House Immigration Committee: "It is hoped to guarantee, as best we can at this late date, racial homogeneity in the United States." Even democracy and the capacity for self-government were labeled racial traits which belonged to the Nordics. "If, therefore, the principle of individual liberty, guarded by a constitutional government... is to endure, the basic strain of our population must be maintained," the report declared.

Not all restrictionists were so convinced of their own arguments as to fail to recognize that they were advocating undemocratic concepts. Defensively, they argued it was not racial prejudice but concern for the national welfare that motivated them. In a way this was an answer to Congressman Adolph Sabath of Illinois who led the opponents of restriction in the House and wrote the minority report of the House Immigration Committee. He had been a leader in the Anti-Defamation League since 1913, and one of its founders.

Of the impending bill, Sabath said, "It would be the first instance in modern legislation for writing into our laws the hateful doctrine of inequality between the various component parts of our population." He saw restrictive legislation as a nationally divisive and disruptive rather than a unifying factor.

So did others. Opponents of restriction ceaselessly pointed to the bill's conflict with democratic ideals and its manifest discrimination. Rhode Island Senator LeBaron Colt asserted that racially grounded discrimination was "entirely un-American." Defensively, Senator Oscar Underwood of Alabama, who stood for restriction on economic grounds, deplored the emphasis on racial considerations. "... instead of standing for the great principles of human rights and human liberty and freedom of conscience," he said, "we are going to tear down our standard and yield our cause to passion and to prejudice."

The Immigration Act of 1921 had ended unrestricted immigration and discarded the asylum ideal. The Act of 1924, keeping the earlier law intact, adopted racist theory and substituted the goal of racial homogeneity for faith in America's democratic tradition. The principle of regarding each prospective immigrant on his merit as an individual was replaced with criteria wherein merit was judged by an immigrant's ethnic, racial, or national origins. Thus rejecting the basic democratic concepts of American society, Senator David Reed of Pennsylvania, leader of the restrictionists in the Senate, proposed that the Act of 1924 be looked upon as "the second Declaration of Independence."

Of course, Senator Reed felt a bit Jeffersonian because he was the author of the national origins quota provision. Despite the power of the restrictionists in the House, Congressman Sabath had succeeded in having this provision eliminated in the House version of the bill that went to conference. Reed succeeded in having it added to the Senate bill, and it was retained in the final conference version. When the bill came back to the House for a final vote, the provision stayed in with only two members dissenting; Sabath and Samuel Dickstein of New York.

The final version of the Immigration Act of 1924 passed in the House 323 to 76 and in the Senate by 62 to 6. It was a vote cast on strictly ethnic lines; party affiliation seemed to be no factor. Only in the Northeast, where there was a considerable population stemming from Southern and Eastern Europe, did opponents of the bill get a three-vote edge in the House. The restrictionists had won hands down. The Act set a quota of 150,000 for Europe based on the census of 1890, which was then to be replaced in 1927 with the national origins quota plan based on the census of 1920.

The three-year delay before placing the national origins clause in operation was designed to enable the government to calculate the quotas for each country. Under the aegis of a Cabinet Committee consisting of the Secretaries of State, Commerce, and Labor, a board of six statisticians from these departments went to work. When they completed their task in December 1926, the irrationality of the national origins approach at last hit home to the very groups that had been loud in its support. Suddenly the restrictionist front split apart in anger, and one group hurled charges of racism against the other—the very charges which up to then had been voiced only by opponents of restriction.

So difficult had been the problem of determining national origins on a statistical base that the group of experts voiced their own dissatisfaction with the results. The Cabinet Committee, in turn, refused to take responsibility because "the statistical and historical information available raises grave doubts as to the whole value of these computations... for the purposes intended." President Calvin Coolidge just passed it all on to the Congress. The issue was thus back in the political arena and there it stayed for two rancorous years of debate and recrimination.

It is easy to see why. The so-called Nordic and Anglo-Saxon elements of the population had jointly expected to benefit from further curtailment of immigration out of Southern and Eastern Europe. The statistics could not support such expectations. Instead, the calculations enormously increased the quota for Great Britain (from 34,000 to

73,000) at the expense of other Northern and Western Europeans. The German quota figures dropped from 51,000 to 23,000; the Irish from 28,000 to 14,000; the Scandinavians by nearly two-thirds. Quite unexpectedly, the Italian, Polish and Russian figures all rose but their joint total was still only about 16,000.

Now vigorous campaigns were mounted by onetime adherents of national origin quotas. Congress found itself bombarded by the new contending elements. German and Irish spokesmen warned against the "Anglicization of these United States at a feverish pace." Dire predictions were voiced by once-jubilant restrictionists that the country was being divided along racial lines. The German-American League petitioned the House Immigration Committee stating its "firm conviction that the modus employed in figuring these quotas is a gross violation of the admitted intent of the new law to further the immigration of the Nordic races while lowering the number of newcomers of less desirable races." The Scandinavian groups impressed their unhappiness upon their representatives in Congress.

One of these was Chairman Albert Johnson of the House Immigration Committee who responded in February 1927 by reporting out a bill to repeal the national origins quota provision in the Act of 1924. "The pressure is very great," he said, "not only from members of the Committee, but from members of the House generally, who respond to group demands." That was sufficient reason for the committee to sponsor repeal in its report, stating that "it seems far better to have immigration quotas for purposes of restriction fixed in such manner as to be easily explained and easily understood by all."

Subjected to the same pressures, the Senate opted for postponement for a year, hoping things could be worked out in that time and passed such a bill readily. The debate in the House that followed was heated and acrimonious but the postponement bill passed there, too, when Midwestern congressmen broke away from the restrictionist line to join antirestrictionists of the Northeast. For the moment, therefore, the restrictionist forces were thoroughly split.

When public debate on the issue resumed in the winter of 1928, it was evident the patriotic societies that largely represented Anglo-Saxon Old Stock had organized to defend the national origins quota. They mounted a most effective lobby, organized an immigration conference in Washington and countered the efforts of their erstwhile ethnic associates. Prominent in the coalition of patriotic societies were the Junior Order of United American Mechanics, The Sons of the

American Revolution, the Patriotic Order Sons of America, and the Daughters of America. On the opposite side, the German, Scandinavian, and Irish groups picked up where they had left off the year before and the combatants made the most of their opportunities since this was a Presidential election year. The politicians squirmed and looked for a way out, at least until after the elections. Both the Senate and the House once more took the path of postponement—the former without debate, the latter without a record vote after much acrimony.

During the Presidential compaign, both major-party candidates tread gingerly on the issue. In his acceptance speech at the Republican convention, Herbert Hoover clearly stated his opposition to the national origins quota because it was impossible to determine quotas "accurately and without hardship." But he never again spoke on the issue in the campaign. Alfred E. Smith, the Democratic candidate, ran an ambivalent course: critical of the 1890 base at one point, generally favorable to some restrictions at another.

After the election, the opponents of the national origins quota seemed to lose ground though they kept up their efforts. On the other hand, the patriotic societies developed a lobbying steamroller. Their number had become greatly augmented, better organized, and better led. The public debate and the representations to Congress covered all the old ground with all the old phrases and arguments. The tired old Seventieth Congress at its final sessions in February 1929 was in no mood to make a decision. The House voted another postponement; the Senate failed to act at all before the clock ran out on the session.

The newly inaugurated President now found himself in the unhappy position of having to act under the 1924 law to establish the national origins quotas by April 7 to take effect on July 1, even though he was opposed to them. Mr. Hoover took the mandatory action, but called for an immediate special session of the new Congress for a repeal of the plan. The Senate thereupon tabled the bill and voted down a parliamentary maneuver to discharge its Immigration Committee from further consideration of the repeal. The victory belonged to the patriotic societies. It took forty years to write racism into the immigration law; it would now take another forty years to expunge it.

Discrimination—The College Quota System

The long-term movement toward restrictive immigration had a parallel exclusionary trend throughout the society. That startling event of the 1870's when Joseph Seligman could not find acceptance in a Saratoga resort hotel had, in the 1920's, become a commonplace pattern of discrimination in business, social institutions, public accommodations, even as in public affairs and where one might live. The exclusions were not absolute; there seemed to be minimal acceptable quotas. Sometimes an incident would surface and there would be a bit of a fuss. But then things would quiet down, and the exclusionary gates would close again.

In just such a manner did the pattern of limiting enrollment in the colleges develop and spread until it had become a well-established and generally recognized quota system of admissions. The quota system was clearly aimed against Jews, who more than any other group of recent immigrant origin, were pressing upon those institutions in which the Old Stock had invested its upper-class values and elitist notions.

Why the college quota system flourished has no single and simple explanation. Certainly, there was, in the Old Stock, a sense of invasion of the sacred precincts by "foreign" elements. The racial prejudice factor and social discrimination played their roles. The college educational establishment could not shake off the effects of anti-Semitic attitudes and propaganda that were so pervasive at the time. Finally, there was a clash of goals. For the sons of the Old Stock, college years were meant to develop one's talents for life as members of the leisure class. The "gentleman's C" was adequate, if not preferred as an academic rating. As Thorstein Veblen put it, "... scholarship [was] ... made subordinate to genteel dissipation," and "to grounding in those methods of conspicious consumption that should engage the thought and energies of a well-to-do man of the world."

The stress of the Jewish students was, as a matter of course, upon scholarship, intellectual pursuits, academic achievement. Coming largely from a lower economic stratum they were not inclined—and were mostly incapable—of playing the social game. Their goal was the practical one of advancement through education. In that sense their presence was a challenge to the student establishment.

Except in terms of this conflict in values and interests, this resistance to the "invader," there was no logical argument for quota restrictions. The colleges were expanding, and the qualifications for admission called for minimal academic credentials. A student could get into Harvard in the 1920's with a diploma from an acceptable high school and a not overly challenging entrance examination. Average intellect and application to his studies would carry him through.

The elitist colleges were not the only ones that played the restrictive game. Criticism of Jewish students took on a pejorative note whenever their numbers grew to a point where they began to be noticed. Always it struck at their social characteristics—often cruelly so—as if they were untrained creatures of a lower order. They didn't fit. Of recent alien origin, they should wait a generation or two before knocking at the door of the colleges, else they might pollute American civilization. The argument was an extension to the second generation of the one used to close the gates to their immigrant fathers.

Statistical data on college restrictions in the 1920's and earlier are hard to come by, but the operation of the informal system was clear. It had its roots seemingly in the student body itself. At the elitist schools, Jewish students were barred by the honor societies, the eating clubs, and fraternity houses. Even at publicly operated City College of New York in 1913, a fraternity dropped its affiliate because too many Jews had been "pledged." These incidents took place though they were rarely discussed. But a dean at New York University, explaining a sudden drop in the number of Jewish students in 1922, remarked that "whenever the student body is found to contain elements from any source in such proportions as to threaten our capacity for assimilating them, we...restore the balance."

Columbia University, a prestige school within New York City, finding that its Jewish enrollment in 1920 stood at 40 percent, took steps to cut it to 22 percent within two years. Syracuse had its little internal battle in 1923, when about 15 percent of the student body was Jewish. Except for Harvard, the number of Jews at the Ivy League schools were minimal and the records vague, though the situation was quite clear. In 1930, Rutgers, still a prestige small college, and many years from its transformation into a state university, limited its admissions to 33 Jewish students, to "equalize the proportion."

What emerges is an informal but determined system of bias, almost untouchable as long as it retained its surreptitious character, but increasingly harmful to the ambitions and goals of larger and larger numbers of young Jews seeking to find their way into mainstream America. Suddenly, and in the most unexpected way, in June 1922, it all came out in the open. The cover of secrecy, as the contemporary phrase has it, "was blown." College admissions quotas became a topic of public discussion, the subterfuges subject to exposure, their reform a matter of political agitation. At the center of the storm stood President A. Lawrence Lowell and Harvard University, probably the least culpable of all the elitist schools.

On June 1, 1922, Harvard abruptly issued an announcement stating that since "the great increase in the number of students at Harvard College," and because of a lack of enough classroom and dormitory space and related problems "it is natural . . . there should be talk about the proportion of Jews at the college."

The very bluntness of the statement sent shock waves around the country. Lowell seemed determined to bring the whole subject out in the open. Whether it was candor, naïveté, prejudice or sheer assurance of his patrician place that moved him, he was not going to pursue a quota policy of admissions—if it came to that—surreptitiously. Year by year, the proportion of Jews at the college had grown until it stood at 20 percent.

"To shut the eyes to an actual problem of this kind and ignore its existence," he said in his commencement address a few days later, "or to refuse to grapple with it courageously would be unworthy of a university."

And shortly afterward, Lowell expressed the thought to an alumnus that it would be to the benefit of Jews themselves if not so many of them came to Harvard.

A reading of the record reveals that it was probably neither excessive candor nor academic statesmanship nor a courageous decision not to play the game by the old rules, that motivated Lowell. In a sense, his hand was pushed. The subject of quota restrictions had been under discussion among Jewish and Christian students and faculty for some months—discussions on an intellectual and controlled level. Soon, however, it began to appear in garbled form in Boston newspapers, and it was obvious to so practiced a hand as Lowell that the matter would become a political football at the State House.

The events of that week in June were so startling and the flavor of the discussions so significant in the context of the social conflict, that it is valuable to replay the record here. On June 7, 1922, Alfred A. Benesch, a Cleveland lawyer, an officer of both B'nai B'rith and the Anti-Defamation League, having read Lowell's announcement, wrote to him:

> In common with other Jewish graduates of Harvard, I was astounded at the official statement issued last week with reference to the restriction of enrollment. Even had the statement made no special mention of students of the Jewish race, it would have been objectionable because of the

undoubted implication. Containing, as it did, however, particular reference to the Jews, io is tenfold more objectionable because of the direct suggestion made to those who might not otherwise perceive its purpose.

It is utterly impossible for me to comprehend how an institution of learning which has throughout its history received contributions from men of all religious faiths, and which has enjoyed an enviable reputation for non-sectarianism, can even contemplate the adoption of a regulation obviously designed to discriminate against the Jews. The late Jacob H. Schiff for years maintained a deep interest in Harvard and was loyal to Harvard's traditions. Do you think that he would remain silent were he alive today, in the face of such action on the part of the university authorities?

Felix Warburg and other eminent Jews of New York City and elsewhere were liberal contributors to the Harvard Endowment Fund. Are their feelings not to be considered?

I am a graduate of more than twenty years standing. I have contributed

The Benesch–Lowell correspondence–The New York Times published it on page 1, unabridged and without interpolation.

to the Endowment Fund and am contributing now annually to the scholarship fund established by my class, the class of 1900. You would criticize
me with poor grace, were I to withhold any further contributions under
the existing circumstances.

Shortly after my graduation I wrote an article entitled, "The Jew at
Harvard" in which, I think, I successfully combated the notion then
prevalent that Harvard was anti-Semitic. I hope that I shall not be under
the necessity of writing a similar article with a changed point of view. I
hope, too, that the regulation which has unhappily stirred up so much
unpleasant publicity for Harvard does not find its origin in the fact that
Jewish students numbering perhaps 10 percent of the student population
at Harvard, are the successful contestants for perhaps 50 percent of the
prizes and scholarships.

Students of the Jewish faith neither demand nor expect any favors at the
hands of the university, but they do expect, and have a right to demand,
that they be admitted upon equal terms with students of other faiths, and
that scholarship and character be the only standards for admission.

I am still hopeful that the newspaper reports are not based entirely
upon fact, and that I may hear from you soon a true statement of the
situation.

Lowell replied:

There is no need of cautioning you not to believe all that you see in the
newspapers. As a colleague said to me yesterday, there is perhaps no
body of men in the United States, mostly Gentiles, with so little anti-
Semitic feeling as the instructing staff of Harvard University. But the
problem that confronts this country and its educational institutions is a
difficult one, and one about which I should very much like to talk with
you. It is one that involves the best interests both of the college and of the
Jews, for I should feel very badly to think that these did not coincide.

There is, most unfortunately, a rapidly growing anti-Semitic feeling in
this country, causing—and no doubt in part caused by—a strong race
feeling on the part of the Jews themselves. In many cities of the country
Gentile clubs are excluding Jews altogether, who are forming separate
clubs of their own. Private schools are excluding Jews, I believe, and so,
we know, are hotels. All this seems to me fraught with very great evils for
the Jews, and very great perils for the community. The question did not
originate here, but has been brought over from Europe—especially from
those countries where it has existed for centuries.

The question for those of us who deplore such a state of things is how it
can be combated, and especially for those of us who are connected with
colleges, how it can be combated there—how we can cause the Jews to feel
and be regarded as an integral part of the student body. The anti-Semitic
feeling among the students is increasing, and it grows in proportion to
the increase in the number of Jews.

If their number should become 40 percent of the student body, the race
feeling would become intense. When, on the other hand, the number of

Jews was small, the race antagonism was small also. Any such race feeling among the students tends to prevent the personal intimacies on which we must rely to soften anti-Semitic feeling.

If every college in the country would take a limited proportion of Jews, I suspect we should go a long way toward eliminating race feeling among the students, and, as these students passed out into the world, eliminating it in the community.

This question is with us. We cannot solve it by forgetting or ignoring it. If we do nothing about the matter, the prejudice is likely to increase. Some colleges appear to have met the question by indirect methods, which we do not want to adopt. It cannot be solved except by a cooperation between the college authorities and the Jews themselves. Would not the Jews be willing to help us in finding the steps best adapted for preventing the growth of race feeling among our students, and hence in the world?

The first thing to recognize is that there is a problem—a new problem, which we have never had to face before, but which has come over with the immigration from the Old World. After the nature of that problem is fairly understood, the next question is how to solve it in the interest of the Jews, as well as of every one else.

In answer to this, Benesch wrote:

I find myself in complete harmony with some of the statements in your letter of June 9, but in complete disagreement with others.

I hope and believe it is true that the instructing staff of Harvard University is not anti-Semitic at heart. I am apprehensive, however, that the wave of anti-Semitism which has been inundating the country during the last year or more has not left the members of the staff untouched. I am apprehensive, too, that some members of the Harvard alumni have not been inactive in expressing and making felt their anti-Jewish and unsocial proclivities.

Although I agree with you that, unhappily, there is a rapidly growing anti-Semitic feeling in this country, I must take issue with you upon the proposition that this feeling is caused in part by a strong race feeling on the part of the Jews. Is not the strong race feeling on the part of the Jews the result rather than the cause? In other words, has not the strong race feeling been developed as a measure of self-defense?

You throw out the suggestion that "if every college in the country would take a limited proportion of Jews, I suspect that we should go a long way toward eliminating race feeling among the students, and, as the students passed out into the world, eliminating it in the community."

Carrying your suggestion to its logical conclusion would inevitably mean that a complete prohibition against Jewish students in the colleges would solve the problem of anti-Semitism. Moreover, it might lead to the establishment of a distinctively Jewish university, a consummation most sincerely to be deplored.

If it be true—and I have no doubt that it is true—that the anti-Semitic feeling among the students is increasing, should it not be the function of an institution of learning to discourage rather than to encourage such a spirit? If certain members of the alumni and certain members of the student body foster so un-American a spirit, Harvard University, which has always stood for true democracy and liberalism, should be the first to condemn such a spirit, and exert every effort to prevent its growth.

If it is at all possible for you to call a meeting of a group of Jewish graduates, together with the members of the corporation and such other graduates or undergraduates as are interested in this vital problem, such meeting to be called within the next ten days or two weeks, I shall be very glad personally to make the sacrifice of time and money to attend such meeting. I believe, as do you, that a matter of this character can best be discussed by word of mouth.

Lowell's final letter to Benesch said:

You are quite right—it is the function of an institution of learning to discourage anti-Semitic feeling and the question is how is it to be done? It does not seem to me that we shall reach such a result by ignoring the problem of race. It exists in the Old World and it is rapidly coming here. The first step, it seems to me, is to recognize that it is a problem and then try to discover what its causes and its cures may be. It is just the result that you point out that I wish to avoid—that of distinctly Jewish and distinctly Gentile universities. We want exactly the opposite. We want to have both Gentiles and Jews in all our colleges and universities and strive to bring the two races together.

A committee to consider this subject will be appointed in a few days, and one of their first duties will be to get into communication with the thoughtful Jews in this country.

The New York Times was so impressed with this correspondence that it devoted a goodly portion of its first page of June 17 to reprinting it without comment.

Meanwhile, back on the Harvard campus, the drama was being played out by students, faculty, and administration. Once the news was out, Lowell quickly went up Beacon Hill to the State House to confer with the Speaker of the House when a member of the legislature offered a bill to investigate Harvard. Lowell failed to forestall the discussions, but the Speaker issued a press statement that "Harvard would remain as in the past, a great university for all the people...." The other legislators remained unimpressed. It was proposed that Harvard's tax exemption be reviewed and that references to the university be stricken from the state constitution. The governor named a committee to investigate discrimination at the school, and the Boston City Council condemned the university's administration. Of course, this may have all been sheer political opportunism, but it indicated that ethnic and racial prejudice had become an emotional and sensitive matter in a state such as Massachusetts.

The State House politicos and the Boston press fed upon each others sensational responses to the "troubles" at Harvard, adding little to the verities. Lowell's statements, frank and open though they were, did not alleviate greatly the disquiet felt by Jews and others concerned with race discrimination at what was accepted as the nation's leading university. What did happen on the Harvard campus in the months prior to the June 1 statement? For a sober, often poignant, sometimes troubled, answer we have the testimony of Harry Starr, then president of the Harvard Menorah Society and a prime mover in the student discussions in the preceding months.

Certainly, the fact of a growing prejudice against Jews was on the minds of many students and faculty members in the spring of 1922. The number of Jewish students had grown year by year, slowly but steadily until they now formed 20 percent of the student body. That seemed to be a catalytic number setting off chemical reactions among the young Brahmins and vibrations among thoughtful Jewish students. Out of casual conversation came the idea for an informal conference. The idea was approached cautiously; faculty advisers were

President A. Lawrence Lowell—He expressed the view that a Jewish quota would benefit Jews at Harvard.

consulted. Finally, five leading Christian students and five from among the Jewish undergraduates met on April 12. Present, too, was a distinguished and highly regarded faculty member. The stress was on the informality of the discussion, on its unofficial character; yet there was the feeling that the exchange might have great weight with the administration.

"We went into the conference," wrote Starr subsequently in the *Menorah Journal*, "determined to stand with dignity upon the unqualified right of Jews to be at the college regardless of the disciplinary infractions of some or the willingness of others to sacrifice extracurricular glory for academic distinction."

The Jewish students refused to recognize a "Jewish problem." "He is a problem only to those who make him so . . . [he] can not look upon himself as a problem." Nor could a "self-respecting Jew allow any talk which would cast a shadow" over him "as an American with the right to domicile not only on the soil but in the institutions arising from that soil . . . you cannot disguise intolerance by talking of expediency or of balancing 'racial interests.'"

Thus frankly, did the Jewish young men state their basic position. The Gentile conferees were equally open. They did not "consider it wrong to keep Jews segregated in a dormitory." It seemed to them natural for Jews to want to be together even as they did themselves, but "in the same breath talked about Jews segregating themselves." They did not flinch admitting that in any competitive situation they "could not help but keep in mind that the man before him was a Jew" yet they "tried to keep that item as small as possible."

In turn, the Jewish students expressed the view that "both Jews and non-Jews suffered from a peculiar self-consciousness that caused the Gentile to fear his own judgment always being mistaken for anti-Semitism and the Jew to believe that the slightest attack on him was inspired by Jew-hatred."

With such admirable frankness and remarkable maturity for men so young did these student leaders discuss their relationships. The things they had talked and complained about only among themselves, they now said to each other to clear the air, perhaps to find solutions. After this first meeting, the Jewish students consulted with the dean of the college in hope of finding statistical data on discriminatory practices in the college's social and extracurricular life. Dean Chester Noyes Greenough promised his help and then admitted "how puzzled he had been to find a way of allaying a growing undergraduate feeling that there were too many Jews."

"That was perhaps the most illuminating thing about the discussions," wrote Starr. "While we entered them believing that the existant feeling came from the dislike of certain Jews, we learned that it was *numbers* that mattered; bad or good, *too many* Jews were not liked. Rich or poor, brilliant or dull, polished or crude—*too many Jews ...*" is what was feared and what mattered.

The two sets of student conferees resumed their discussion on May 8 to consider ways of improving relationships on campus. The talk quickly came back to the underlying issue. Wrote Starr:

> There would be no question of improved relations if the Jews were willing to accept limitations; but if not—there could be no improved relations, the Jews being always a marked group ... they were not concerned with our intense desire ... to make [Jews] the finest specimens of Harvard men possible.
>
>   It was the natural thing for these kindly mannered men, who bore not the slightest trace of malice to admit that a few good Jews were quite delightful at the club, or the hotel—but they must "not for their own sake" accumulate, even though the accumulation be induced by the worthy feeling that Harvard was the best place in the world ...

Here was an echo of Lowell's own position. He was concerned with the presence of too many Jews at Harvard for "their own sake." But he had not yet given public expression to that thought. Was it then a long-held view and the consensus of the patrician class—or a large part of it?

An ironic thought occurred to Starr. He was reminded of "that English Lord in Beerbohm's *Zuleika Dobson* who exclaims: 'Certainly, the Americans have a right to exist—but I wish they wouldn't exercise that right at Oxford.'"

While the student group was meeting, Harvard's faculty, too, was considering the so-called Jewish problem. Hope was expressed that the Jewish students "might consent to some limitations." Once again the Jewish undergraduates sought out Dean Greenough to express their opinion that "the vast majority of self-respecting Jews stood on their absolute right to be at Harvard; that as the character of America had changed, so the essential character of Harvard, if necessary, must change along with it ... the whole lesson of American democracy was lost if it taught" Jews to be servile and non-Jews to "coddle a prejudice instead of tearing it out of their hearts."

The Jewish student conferees then pressed home their position on advice of philosopher Harry Wolfson, their advisor, in a formal letter to Dean Greenough. It made two major points:

Any limitation of the number of Jewish students whether direct or indirect, whether based on any theory of racial differences, or on arguments of expediency, we must consider unjustifiable on any ground. As Americans, we should view such a step as a direct contradiction of a philosophy of Americanism predicated on the theory that no distinction shall be drawn between men on the basis of race, color, or previous condition of servitude. As Harvard men, we must regard it as a disillusioning commentary on traditional Harvard liberalism. And as Jews, we should feel humiliated at this apparently unprecedented expression of racial discrimination in the United States, against a group that has been taught to consider itself an integral part of the larger American life. The implication in such a step that, somehow or other, the Jews are an element whose presence brings problems to be studied from a different angle than the problems of non-Jewish Americans, is fraught with danger to any attempts at creating a richer American life.

Nor can we allow the assumption that there exists any group of undesirable as against desirable Jews, no matter how the line of demarcation be drawn. That members of the Jewish faith may have their black sheep is no more astonishing than that members of other religious groups have their undesirable specimens. And, if there are at the University such Jewish students as tend to bring discomfort to the general moral or social sense of the student body, then as Harvard men, we should be anxious to remove from our midst such undesirable citizens. But we must stress again that it would be only an unfair misapprehension of racial values that would allow a classification of Jewish students into groups—whether by the geographical origins of their parents, length of residence in this country, or social status.

The five who signed the letter were Harry Starr, Max Frederick Goldberg, Paul Harmel, David Soffer, and Richard J. Mack, declaring it "to be the honest convictions of a large majority of Jewish students."

The storm raised by the Harvard announcement, Lowell's commencement address, and the sudden public awareness of the discussions that had been going on at the university subsided with an announcement by the Harvard Board of Overseers that the matter had been placed in the hands of a faculty committee. No changes in admissions procedures would be made until the committee had completed its work.

Ten months later, the committee reported its findings. No doubt it had taken cognizance of the strong feelings called forth by the possibility that Harvard might slip into the ways of racial bias practiced at other colleges. The concern of an active Jewish alumni and student body, the presence of distinguished Jewish scholars on the faculty, and an eminent Jewish leader, Judge Julian W. Mack, on the Board of Overseers unquestionably had their impact. Nor could public criticism of the university and indeed the position of liberal spirits associated with Harvard, such as Professor David Gordon Lyon, be readily put aside. More was expected of Harvard.

More was forthcoming. The committee found that a quota system would run counter to the Harvard tradition of "equal opportunity for all regardless of race and religion." Like Caesar's wife, Harvard had to be above suspicion so that "even so rational a method as a personal conference or an intelligence test, if now adopted...as a means of selection, would inevitably be regarded as a covert device to eliminate those deemed racially or socially undesirable..."

On another facet of admissions policy, the committee did recommend that the university seek a wider regional representation for its student body. For an institution such as Harvard, there was merit to such a proposal, yet it had been used by other Eastern schools— notably Columbia University in New York—to restrict the number of students from the heavily concentrated Jewish population in the East. With somewhat eased admissions standards for students from small cities and towns, there soon was a perceptible effect on enrollment of Jews. By 1931 the ratio of Jewish students dropped from 20 percent when Lowell first voiced his views to 10 percent. Lowell retired in 1933 to be succeeded by James Bryant Conant. In 1940 the proportion of Jewish students had risen again to 25 percent. Conant had redefined Harvard's mission:

"The primary concern of American education...is not the development of the good life in young gentlemen born to the purple....Our purpose is to cultivate in the largest possible number of our future citizens an appreciation of both the responsibilities and the benefits which come to them because they are Americans and are free."

The affair at Harvard is central to this narrative on several counts. It dramatized for Jews the critical importance of maintaining merit as the principal criterion for educational advancement, which in turn provided the pathway into the mainstream of American life. For the first time, too, Jews were able to grapple with the secretive—often denied—quota system of admissions practiced by colleges, universities, professional schools, and other institutions to a greater or lesser degree all through the nation. Nicholas Murray Butler could invoke a Jewish quota at Columbia simply by never acknowledging it; Lowell, as we have seen, because of his own character and that of Harvard, could not or would not follow a similar tactic. But elsewhere the secretive approach persisted, and the quota system became an emotion-laden issue for Jews. Not until after World War II did the educational establishment hit the sawdust trail—admitting its transgressions and taking steps to reform its procedures. Leaders in this movement were the American Council on Education and the Anti-Defamation League. Their collaboration will be discussed in a later chapter.

The Harvard episode also served as a reminder that not all of the Old Stock was lost to the democratic tradition. If the depressing spirit of Henry Adams and the racism of the eugenicists hovered over and sometimes panicked a large proportion of the patrician class, it is equally true that the American dream of an earlier Adams and the democratic spirit of a Ralph Waldo Emerson gripped many among the patricians who did not fear for America or their own destiny.

In the clash between the best and the worst in the New England tradition, Lowell stood at the center. Torn by his upper-class loyalties, he sometimes gave way to the prejudices of the establishment. But he could not easily shunt aside the tradition upheld at Harvard for forty years by Charles W. Eliot. A Brahmin among Brahmins, Eliot fought the regressive trends pressed by the scientific racists during his long life.

In a brilliant summing-up at the age of eighty, when he had already retired as president of Harvard, Eliot wrote to Charles Francis Adams in 1914:

> You and I are about the same age and began life with much the same set of ideas about freedom and democracy. But you have seen reason to abandon the principles and doctrines of your youth, while I have not. So far as I know, my fundamental beliefs are about the same as they were when I was twenty; but I imagine the grounds of my belief to be more solid now than they were then. My fate in this respect seems to me happier than yours; and to my thinking fate is not the right word for it. Your changed beliefs are the outcome of your experience in life, and my unchanged beliefs are the outcome of my experience and observations in life.

With these beliefs Eliot had turned Harvard from "a provincial and patrician college into a cosmopolitan and democratic university." The Harvard that Eliot built and nurtured made it possible for Jewish scholars to find their way onto its faculty and Jewish youth into its classrooms. They did so during Lowell's tenure as president, which began in 1909, until the events of 1922, when the social pressures against them grew as we have seen. In the Eliot tradition, Lowell might have acted differently, but it would not have been in character.

As a member of the patrician establishment, Lowell, ever loyal to his class, could join the Immigration Restriction League and even serve for a time as its vice-president; Eliot became its most eminent foe and scoffed at the notion that the "American race" was being over-whelmed by immigrants. In the great controversy over the nomina-tion of Louis D. Brandeis to the U.S. Supreme Court by President Wilson, Lowell found himself comfortable joining in the Boston Brahmin petition against the appointment. Eliot strongly backed Brandeis, whom he would even have welcomed as his successor at Harvard. "It would please me to be followed by a Jew," he once told Norman Hapgood, who had brought up the name of Brandeis.

In the Sacco-Vanzetti case—that great *cause célèbre* of the late 1920s—Lowell, troubled by the question whether the trial had been fairly conducted, served as the chairman of the governor's committee of inquiry, but in the final analysis found the trial fair. Harold Laski, who had reason to appreciate Lowell, commented after the decision: "I agree fully with all Felix [Frankfurter] says of Lowell in this case. Loyalty to his class transcends his ideas of logic and justice." Herbert B. Ehrmann, a defense counsel in the case, and many years later president of the American Jewish Committee, wrote: "Mr. Lowell acted as chairman, or rather, as it appeared to us, as prosecutor."

Commenting on another occasion, Laski explained much about Lowell at Harvard. He saw him as "a competent man of the world, not very profound, a tiny bit of a snob and self-conscious of it, yet on the whole a thoroughly good fellow who cared deeply about America without any great grasp of what it meant."

Indeed, the contradictions in Lowell served to demonstrate how difficult it might be, for those whose forebears had given substance to the nation's democratic ideals, to regain faith in the American Dream.

Discrimination—Social and Economic

In the prospering 1920's, economic factors added a sense of urgency for higher education among working-class as well as middle-class Jews. Education and professional training was the admission ticket into the new world of the corporate-managerial society that was re-placing, on a fluid national scale, the older, rigid locally based patrician order. This new order, like the old, however, was dominated by the Old Stock. Entry into it depended on one's origins. If family association was somewhat less recognizable, on this national scale, it was replaced by such factors as coming from the right school, belonging to the right church, being acceptable in the better country club, and living in the approved suburb.

Jews did not enjoy these attributes, so that during the decade of the 1920's, they were largely closed out from those industrial companies which controlled more than half of corporate wealth and perhaps 35 to 45 percent of total business wealth. Nor were they readily admitted to such basic sectors of the economy as commercial banking, insurance, and public utilities. They were left to practice free enterprise, if they could, in soft goods, retail trade, the amusement industry, communications, and some marginal industries with large risk factors. Even in the retail field, the local store might be Jewish-owned; the chain store was not.

Jewish entrepreneurial skills in the fields that were open to them, nevertheless, produced successes that in time created a considerable economic upper class and a prosperous middle class. Yet, the growing concentration of industry in large corporate enterprises depressed the employment opportunities of young Jewish men and women to whom even low-level clerical jobs were closed off. Looking at discrimination practiced by elite management of corporate enterprise, a contemporary observer, Dr. I. M. Rubinow, then secretary of B'nai B'rith, pointed out, "They have been shifting [the ground for anti-Semitism] from religion to biology and from both to economics."

In an analysis called *The Economic and Industrial Status of American Jewry* at the end of the decade, Dr. Rubinow, an authority in the field, bemoaned the paucity of statistics, but asserted that the visible evidence showed "the economic future of the mass of American Jewry is decidedly uncertain, perhaps more uncertain from the point of view of human satisfactions than from that of the comparatively simple task of securing . . . some sort of living." Hope for personal fulfillment, even when coupled with considerable talent, could not be expected to open careers in the field of one's aspirations.

For all the lack of statistics, a mass of empirical evidence pointed to the difficulty Jews faced in getting even the lowliest jobs in the corporate world. The want-ad sections of newspapers in cities such as New York and Philadelphia frankly acknowledged the resistance to Jewish job seekers. Even when newspapers refused to print the blunt phrasing "No Jews need apply," applicants could be asked to "state race and religion" or be denied consideration when interviewed.

Often prospective employers sought to avoid the need to act directly by the use of employment agencies, most of which were not averse to assuming the task of screening out Jews. Heywood Broun and George Britt delved into the subject at the close of the decade and reported their findings in *Christians Only: A Study in Prejudice*. Their description of the many devices used to establish a veritable boycott of Jews in commercial and white-collar employment is now a familiar story. In the decades since the beginning of the 1930's, the same tactics have been used against other minority groups.

But in 1929, an employment agency which displayed the sign "No Jewish applicants until further notice" on its walls blamed this on the fact that some employers frankly asked it not to send Jewish applicants, and others said they maintained a quota for Jews, already filled. Employers, on the other hand, would disclaim personal prejudice, but assert that they they lost business because their customers did not like to deal with Jewish employees. Others offered the even lamer excuse that their personnel wanted to work in a homogeneous group, and Jews just did not fit in.

A survey of 23 commercial employment agencies in June 1929 by the Bureau of Jewish Social Research came up with some telling figures. One refused to register Jews and another said it could place no Jews. Eight were discouraging because they thought their efforts would be an exercise in futility. Seven were willing to chance an effort to place Jewish clerical workers, and only six said that they could find jobs for Jewish girls.

The Vocational Service for Juniors, a New York East Side voluntary agency seeking jobs for young people, reviewing ten years of effort, reported finding 12,000 jobs for its 27,000 applicants. Half of these applicants were Catholic, 10 percent Protestant, and 38 percent Jewish. Thus, 44 percent of all applicants were placed, but only 20 percent of the Jewish applicants found employment, even though they were often educationally better qualified.

At a higher level of job seeking, Broun and Britt reported figures from the alumni employment agency of a major university, where 15 percent of the graduating class was Jewish. Three months after commencement, as a routine matter, those without jobs were referred to the bureau. Of those still unplaced, 40 percent were Jews.

The conventional wisdom of the time was that nine out of ten jobs in the white-collar occupation in the major cities were closed to Jewish applicants. Those chiefly discriminated against were the children of immigrants, straining to make the leap from the ghettos and the ghetto occupations of their fathers into the professions and new industries. They were seeking to break out of the working class into the more secure and better-situated American middle class. The obstacles they encountered often left indelible marks on their lives. Many who encountered prejudice in their efforts to secure employment, training,

Help Wanted—A typical employment agency advertisement in the 1930's,
The intent was clearly stated.

and advancement in their chosen fields, after a time, tended to retreat into "safe" areas of employment—and to retreat into themselves as well.

With the Crash of 1929 that led to the Great Depression, this burden of discrimination brought the realization to Jewish communal leadership that a worrisome situation had turned into a critical one. In December 1929 the Anti-Defamation League, which had been charting the discriminatory patterns throughtout the decade, called a special conference to confront the problem and followed through with a second meeting a year later in January 1931. The result of these two meetings was the formation of a National Conference on Jewish Employment in which the League joined forces with B'nai B'rith, the American Jewish Congress, the Fraternal Order of B'rith Abraham, the National Jewish Welfare Board, the National Council of Jewish Women, and the United Hebrew Trades of New York.

The effort was to develop practical programs for opening job opportunities and countering discriminatory practices. By the later 1930's, B'nai B'rith had developed an effective vocational service. The new unit and the League worked diligently on the problem. Statistics and evidence of prejudice now began to pile up; solutions and changes in the practices, however, came slowly. Decades were to pass before the barriers came down to a point where Jews entering the labor market could feel that they would not automatically have to face discrimination in certain industries.

Economic discrimination remained critical to the welfare of American Jews throughout the Great Depression. But it became a secondary consideration as the 1930's, arriving with a rush of political problems, soon brought with it the new menace of an imported anti-Semitism from Nazi Germany and a home-grown lunatic fringe only too ready to accept its favors and adopt its ways.

And, as so often before, the eyes of American Jewry turned abroad in an all-consuming concern for European Jews who were directly under the Nazi guns when Hitler rode into power in 1933.

FIVE

Depression and Invasion

As so many in the nation, American Jews found the stressful decade of the 1930's an age of desperate despair tinged by exhilarating hope. They shared the despair with all those who suffered the effects of the Great Depression and the national miasma that spread in its wake. Their hope was stirred by a feeling that, as never before, they were gaining admittance to the promised new world; the American mainstream was opening up to them. And this feeling they shared with all the minority groups that had paid the price of alienation from the old order.

As always, Jews had their special anxieties. Of increasing concern was the rising Nazi tide with its immediate threat to the very lives of European Jews and its attacks upon the security of Jews everywhere. American Jews watched these developments with dread. The ordeal of the 1920's, however, gave them an unexpected strength and consider-able tactical skill in dealing with overt attacks. It had been a period that produced the worst spate of anti-Semitism in American history. The nation had traveled the low road of tribalism and bigotry. Yet Ameri-can Jews, looking back with some relief that those years were behind them, recognized there had been developments they could view with satisfaction.

But these worrisome facts remained: though the 1920's had on the whole been a period of economic stability, the Ku Klux Klan had run its vicious course. The immigration gates had been slammed shut

with a law that clearly labeled Jews, among other Eastern and Southern Europeans, as racial inferiors. Henry Ford had employed his
millions to carry on a seven-year anti-Semitic campaign. The Old
Stock establishment had accepted and manipulated the theories of
scientific racism as an instrument for the exclusion of Jews from
mainstream America. True, the Klan and Ford's campaign had faded
out, but if a period of stability nurtured the anti-Semitic drives of the
1920's, what lay ahead could be viewed only with trepidation.

The 1930's ushered in a collapse of faith in the business establishment. The efforts of business-dominated society to extricate the nation from its crisis failed dismally; and government, equally dominated by business, seemed to have no answers.

To a large part of the patrician class, it had seemed ordained that
business rule government and that government serve as the instrument for preserving business. President Coolidge once had stated that
succinctly: "The business of the United States is business." Now one
of their own, Franklin D. Roosevelt, more patrician than Coolidge, but
a different kind of man, was suggesting that "government by organized money is just as dangerous as government by organized
mob."

The old order that dominated the business establishment had heard
such sentiments before from members of its own class and listened
indulgently. The comments normally came from reformers and
philosophers, "dilettantes" who fervently believed in the ideology of
the American Revolution, which so much of the Old Stock had long
ago forsaken for racist notions and a drive for the preservation of class
privileges. But now these sentiments came from a charismatic political
leader at a moment when business had lost control in its own house.

When Roosevelt swept into office as President in 1932, the reforms
his comment implied restructured not only much of the government,
but broadened the political establishment to include the participation
of the *de facto* disinherited groups. During the course of the decade,
the nation was to become a government-dominated rather than a
business-dominated society. If Roosevelt was "a traitor to his class,"
as the Old Stock which controlled business and had governed so long
considered him, he nevertheless brought into his Administration
some of its finest minds—men committed to the best in American
tradition. At the same time, he rallied around him the many groups
whose ancestors had not arrived on the *Mayflower*, members of racial
and ethnic minorities and social and economic classes, still fighting

the battle for their share in the American promise. That Jews were one of the ethnic groups to flock wholeheartedly to the Roosevelt banner is a distinctive fact of the history of the period. The Roosevelt coalition had created a new establishment that admitted them to membership and reflected their aspirations. They entered this new adventure joyfully as Roosevelt "encouraged a process of social reconciliation" from which the nation was to emerge "united as never before."

Roosevelt mobilized the new political coalition for social change within the framework of the American system, a fact not readily accepted by the old business establishment and opposed by leftist movements not interested in reform but in revolutionary change. Not clearly understood—and therefore frightening to the Jewish observer—was the significance of the proliferation of extremist organizations and their apparent successes. No doubt the most massive of these extremist organizations were those of Senator Huey Long and Father Charles Coughlin, who came to prominence as the radio priest of Detroit. Both capitalized on the nation's economic ills and attacked big business. Long's constituency was drawn largely from the hinterlands, Coughlin's from the urban discontented. They did not, however, follow the classic patterns of nativist bigotry. Huey Long's Share-the-Wealth movement never displayed anti-Semitic tendencies. Indeed, for years Jews had been prominent among his Louisiana political associates. But Long's movement after his assassination in 1935 was inherited by Gerald L. K. Smith, who was to become one of the nation's most persistent anti-Semites.

Father Coughlin began his political-propaganda career as a New Dealer, soon broke with Roosevelt, and ended up as the anti-Semitic leader of a profascist movement. Yet, though probably a closet anti-Semite all his life, he did not let his prejudice show overtly till 1938, near the apex of his public career. In retrospect, Long's rejection of anti-Semitism and Coughlin's early reluctance to make use of it had a significance that went largely unrecognized by American Jews at the time. For the moment, at least, anti-Semitism had lost the political values that it possessed in the 1920's. In the depths of the Great Depression, neither the old nativist virtues nor their bigotries could be invoked successfully with those suffering from the blight of the economic and political system that had nurtured them. It was generally recognized that the ethnic and racial groups had had little power in the 1920's, and therefore little responsibility for the troubles that followed in the 1930's. In a period of such economic stress, Jews might have been subject to at least some degree of scapegoating. This did not develop because industry, banking, and the establishment were perceived as the indisputable culprits. That was the view not only of the average citizen, but as already noted, of the extremists such as Long and Coughlin. Old establishment critics of the New Deal, too, dwelt upon ideological argument and eschewed racialist criticism.

A contributing factor may have been that in the 1930's, the intellectual community, including the anthropologists, psychologists, and sociologists, had begun to travel down the long road away from the scientific racism that had peaked in the 1920's. The whole style of thinking about minority problems turned, and they were recognized as "not so much racial as cultural."

If American racism was thus receding, it was soon replaced by a foreign invasion that galvanized the Jewish community into a defensive stance such as it had never adopted before. American Jews watched the growth of National Socialism in Germany with concern that turned to fear for the fate of German Jewry when Hitler rode into power in 1933. Efforts at rescue was the primary task undertaken, but it was recognized that Nazi anti-Semitism was a product for export as well, with America regarded as a prime market.

The first evidence of this was the organization of the Teutonia Society as early as 1924. It became the basis for the Friends of the New Germany in 1933 and ultimately the German–American Bund. The Bund, in turn, was the infection point for the scores of lunatic-fringe organizations that proliferated throughout the country—noisy, venal peddlers of bigotry, some organizations in name only, some merely a letterhead or a single individual, but all engaged in the subversion of American principles and the sale of scurrilous pamphlets and periodicals. Until World War II, they carried on a turbulent activity that was a constant threat to public order.

The significance of some of these groups will be examined at greater length. Most of them called for no fundamental changes in the social order and were therefore of no political importance. Neither did they exhibit any economic strength or elitist support. Nearly all of the 121 organizations recorded during the 1930's came into being in hope of Nazi handouts and disappeared when those handouts ceased and income from dues and the sale of anti-Semitic literature fell off. The description "lunatic fringe" for these groups, if not wholly accurate, is nonetheless fitting; for their unstable, alienated members were motivated more by their hates than their loyalties. The leaders, usually messianic personalities in whom paranoia alternated with the euphoria of great expectations, were verbally facile and often even eloquent, but rarely exhibited organizing or administrative ability. Their ultimate impact in the public arena was thus antisocial and aberrational.

Jews dealt with the problems raised by these avowedly anti-Semitic groups with far more self-confidence than in the 1920's. Their concern was perhaps even greater, but their experience in the earlier decade had given them a sense of place in the social order that strengthened their feelings of security. Indicative of this was the establishment of a fact-finding and research program by the Anti-Defamation League that watched and recorded the activities of the extremist groups. Jews revealed a perception of the perils inherent in these fringe organizations that was far more acute than that of other Americans, due largely to their greater awareness of the menacing events in Nazi Germany and to their own experiences of the past.

The fact-finding program was begun by Richard E. Gutstadt, a Californian who in 1931 had succeeded Leon Lewis as the League's executive director. It consisted simply of diligent and unremitting researches in which several thousand volunteers all over the country participated. (Lewis himself, now in retirement, assumed the leadership in what proved a particularly active area of Nazi infiltration: California.) Anything that appeared in print—in newspapers, pamphlets, and public records—or was heard on radio, at public meetings or in court proceedings was funneled to the League's offices in Chicago. There the reports were codified, analyzed, and developed into coherent pictures of the various extremist organizations and their interlocking activities. Of especial interest to the League was the degree to which these groups lent themselves to Nazi German efforts to penetrate the American scene and the financial benefits they gained from such cooperation. As a result, the files acquired a spectacularly beneficial additional value to the U.S. Government. Public agencies soon became the greatest users of the accumulated information, and when war broke out, the Government found the League's source material a means for quickly identifying many Nazi agents and their associates.

But it was soon recognized that the League's fact-finding program attacked only half the problem. The constant scrutiny of Nazi and nativist anti-Semitic activity revealed the enormous quantities of propaganda reaching the American public. Where were the answers to come from? Sigmund Livingston believed that "unless Jews themselves educate the public, it will go on in its ignorance and accept every vile fiction and distortion." Unhappily, most Jews were unprepared to meet the onslaught of anti-Semitic lies and distortions, too. That problem had to be solved first. The League thereupon organized study groups, published a series of information pamphlets and books on Jewish history, practices, and beliefs, and equipped thousands of Jews to meet problems that might arise in their home communities from the actions of the organized anti-Semitic movement. In the mid-1930s, as many as two thousand "Fireside Discussion Groups" were functioning in communities and colleges, providing a program to counteract the propaganda. These cadres built confidence among Jews and understanding among friendly fellow citizens.

A further development of similar purpose was the establishment of a speakers bureau with a prestigious panel of Christian clergymen, rabbis, university professors, and public figures who addressed both community and leadership groups throughout the country. By 1937 they were delivering a thousand addresses a year to general audiences with salutary effect. Gutstadt's personal brilliance as an orator added immeasurably to this effort.

The McCormack Committee

Jews, of course, were not alone in their concern with Nazi propaganda. By the time Hitler rose to power, churchmen, political liberals, labor leaders, and the intellectual community were aware that the Nazi attack upon Jews was only a forewarning of the attacks upon those groups, ideals, and institutions in which they had invested their lives. In Congress there were men who looked with troubled eye upon the export of Nazi propaganda to this country and upon the readiness with which it was being received by extremist groups. Among these was Representative John McCormack of Massachusetts, who was later to become Speaker of the House.

McCormack, a Catholic, was sensitive to the suffering of his coreligionists from nativist bigotry; and nativist groups seemed the most susceptible to Nazi infiltration. Representative Samuel Dickstein of New York, chairman of the House Committee on Immigration and Naturalization, understood Jewish fears. McCormack and Dickstein were among the earliest proponents of a congressional investigation of Nazi activities. To support his viewpoint, Dickstein was able to turn to the files of the League, and he found additional support in the cooperative efforts of a number of Jewish defense organizations.

The country had not yet arrived at the point, however, where it recognized Nazism as the most dangerous ideological import. Fear of communism was pervasive. To win support for their resolution to investigate Nazi propaganda, they therefore broadened the terms of their proposal to include "the diffusion within the United States of subversive propaganda from [other] foreign countries"—that is, communist and fascist. The special investigative committee was voted into being on March 20, 1934. Speaker Henry T. Rainey named McCormack its chairman, and Dickstein became vice-chairman. In a year of operation, the McCormack Committee held 7 public hearings, 24 executive sessions, and recorded 4,320 pages of testimony from several hundred witnesses.

The net effect was to place into the official records the efforts at subversion by the Nazi apparatus in this country and the racist activities and petty racketeering of its American nativist allies. These facts may already have been generally known, but the congressional inquiry served to convince doubters and raised warning signals for many Americans. It did not, however, greatly inhibit the lunatic-fringe organizations. They continued their activities just so long as there was a dollar to be gained.

McCormack himself made this point in his report to the House:

"Because this Committee has seen the true purpose behind these various groups, it will lump them together and characterize them as un-American, as unworthy of support and created and operated for the financial welfare of those who guide them and do not hesitate to stoop to racial and religious intolerance in order to achieve their selfish purpose."

The McCormack Committee was particularly effective in unmasking covert propaganda actions of the Nazi Government. The committee "found indisputable evidence" that German diplomatic personnel "engaged in vicious and un-American propaganda activities, paying for it in cash in the hope that it could not be traced." American public relations firms, ostensibly retained by industry for promotion of trade, "dealt with public and political questions" and prepared reports "intended to be relayed to the German government."

The public relations firm of Carl Byoir and Associates represented the German Tourist Bureau and Ivy Lee–T. G. Ross counseled I. G. Farben Industries, the chemical combine. The two American firms were leaders in their field. Their services, the committee found, "were largely of a propaganda nature." That these services were for the benefit of and paid for by the Nazi Government was clearly established by testimony from George Sylvester Viereck, Ivy Lee, and others engaged in these operations.

German steamship lines became an important factor in the propaganda operations. They invariably came in with tons of Nazi literature—some then smuggled in and some sent through customs legally. At the request of the German ambassador in Washington, the steamship lines provided free junkets for writers and lecturers "in the interest of the state," and Nazi indoctrination "socials" were held on board ship while in port. These propaganda activities continued far beyond the period covered by the McCormack Committee hearings. They seemed to achieve little response from the 20,000,000 Americans of German origin. But they nurtured the largely alien group which joined the Friends of the New Germany, its successor, the German-American Bund and the lunatic-fringe nativists who saw profit and political advantage in their Nazi association.

In its various incarnations and name changes, the Bund was clearly an extension of the Nazi party and responsive to orders and controls emanating from party officials in Germany. Rudolf Hess, Hitler's assistant fuehrer, could order the dissolution of Nazi groups here and be obeyed. Offices of the original Friends of Germany formed in 1933 were on the same floor as the German consulate in New York. Within the year, this group dissolved and urged its members to join a coordinate group called Friends of the New Germany. In 1936 the name was changed again to the German–American Bund.

In the meantime, a series of "fuehrers" had come and gone. The first was Heinz Spanknoebel, who entered the country claiming to be a clergyman. He strong-armed his way into leadership because he seemed to enjoy support and financial help from Germany. But that was also his undoing. He was soon indicted by a Federal grand jury for failing to register as a foreign agent, and he skipped the country. The mantle now fell to Fritz Gissible, also an alien and once a leader of the Teutonia Society. Gissible gave way to one Reinhold Walter, a naturalized citizen, who shortly was replaced by Herman Schmuch, who had been president of Teutonia. Gissible, however, remained in power as the kingmaker, and used the others as "fronts" because they had American citizenship. (Gissible had been warned to drop his membership in the "Friends" by the German counsul-general in New

York because it was incompatible with his membership in the Nazi party.) Meanwhile, internal conflicts had burst into the open as the combatants for leadership accused each other of terrorism and misappropriation of funds. Finally, Fritz J. Kuhn appeared on the scene in 1935 dominating the renamed German–American Bund until the end of 1939, when he was sentenced to serve two and one-half to five years in prison for embezzling Bund funds.

The Rise and Fall of Fritz Kuhn

The further antics of the German–American Bund have been recounted in the reports of the Dies Committee, which picked up the threads of the unfolding story as the successor to the McCormack Committee. The Bund in New York was subjected to additional thoroughgoing investigation by a state legislative committee headed by Senator John J. McNaboe. The two investigations came up with essentially the same conclusions: the Bund was an extension into this country of Nazi purpose and program. Its function was to promote Nazi ideology and propaganda. Thousands of pages of testimony bore witness to these conclusions in exhaustive and exhausting detail.

"Testimony before the committee," Chairman Martin Dies reported to the Congress, "both from friendly and hostile witnesses, established conclusively that the German–American Bund received its inspiration, program and direction through the various propaganda organizations which have been set up by...[the Nazi] government and...functions under the control and supervision of the Nazi Ministry of Propaganda..." The Bund's "program and activities" were found to be "similar to Nazi organizations in Germany and other countries."

Senator McNaboe found that the Bund "came into existence with explicit instructions from Germany to carry on propaganda without antagonizing the whole country" as the Friends of the New Germany had done "chiefly through the stupidity of its leaders."

Kuhn was the wrong man for such an assignment. He was incapable of *not* outraging American sensibilities. Nor was the Bund and its membership capable of changing character. Subtle propaganda was not their style. If they could not express their hatreds and strut in their uniforms, they simply could not function.

The proof of this was revealed most obviously at a massive Bund rally in New York to mark Washington's Birthday, February 20, 1939.

Washington and the American flag were now to become the Bund symbols. The Brown Shirt uniforms were to be replaced by American trappings. To obtain the use of Madison Square Garden, the Bund had to pledge it would not indulge in anti-Semitism. To give further evidence of this change in image, the Nazi Government had disowned the Bund five months earlier.

But despite all this, the picture did not change either visually or in its sound effects when a frightening 19,000 people jammed the sports arena. The American flag was on display, but surrounded by swastika banners. The Bund Storm Troopers affected a gray uniform, supposedly modeled after the American Legion. Still, they looked like Storm Troopers whose shirts had fallen into the wrong dye vat. Nor had the manners of the crowd or the tone of the speakers changed. Despite the pledge to authorities, no speaker left unsaid the vilest of anti-Semitic threats and charges. Hitler and Mussolini were cheered; Roosevelt and democracy "cudgelled and derided."

The attendance at the rally was not so much an indicator of the size of the Bund's membership as the attraction it had for American fringe groups. The crowd was augmented too by many vigorously opposed to Nazism. No reliable figures on Bund membership were ever established. Kuhn testified to a figure of 20,000 to 25,000, but half that number was probably closer to the truth. The Bund sought to keep its membership lists and sources of its funds secret, but was constantly infiltrated. Kuhn's personal chauffeur kept the Anti-Defamation League informed on both counts.

Criminality was not uncommon in the Bund as conflicts within the ranks and the records of arrests attest. The charges run from embezzlement to assault to indecent exposure. Kuhn himself was the biggest fish to get caught in the criminal net. Twice in his career he served prison terms. At least on one other occasion, he escaped punishment because a forgiving victim did not press charges and instead helped him to emigrate from Germany to Mexico. In 1921 Kuhn was sentenced to four months in jail in Munich for rifling the pockets of fellow students at the university. When he was released from jail, he was employed by a Jewish family friend in his warehouse. Caught stealing merchandise valued at 2,000 marks, he was discharged. Pleading parents persuaded his employer to help him leave for Mexico. Kuhn worked as a chemist in Mexico from 1923 to 1927, then entered the United States where he obtained employment at the Ford hospital laboratory in Detroit and later at the Ford River Rouge plant. He

became an American citizen in 1933 and then promptly joined the
Friends of the New Germany. He was successively leader of the
Detroit local, the Midwest District, and ultimately the national leader.
The Washington's Birthday rally was the high point of achievement,
but he did not survive it long as leader. In December 1939 he was
convicted and sentenced on the embezzlement charge in a New York
court. After serving half his sentence, Kuhn applied for parole but he
was judged "a hazard to the public peace and security" and denied
release. After World War II broke out, the U.S. Justice Department
announced that if he were released from jail he would face denaturalization and internment as an enemy alien.

After Kuhn's fall, the Bund encountered increasingly rough going.
The constant exposure by investigating committees, and the ongoing
efforts of anti-Nazi groups, coupled with the noisy actions of the Bund
itself stiffened public opposition and stimulated government authorities to curb its activities. Over the years, the Bund had operated
camps for purposes of indoctrinations, military drill, and large rallies.
One of the most notorious of these was Camp Nordland at Andover,

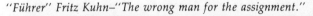

"Führer" Fritz Kuhn—"The wrong man for the assignment."

New Jersey. In August 1940 citizens of the area were startled by the burning of a forty-foot cross, the massed display of swastika flags, and the strident sound of Nazi songs on loud speakers. The Ku Klux Klan had come to celebrate "Americanism" with their friends in the Bund. For the New Jersey authorities, this was the last straw. Revolted by the display and worried about the effects upon its youth, residents of the area asked for relief under a state law against the operation of a "public nuisance." In June 1941, Camp Nordland was shut down by state order.

It was now late in the day for the Bund and Gerhardt Wilhelm Kunze, a Philadelphia chauffeur, who had succeeded Kuhn as its leader. Other states also took action. Florida enacted a law against all Bund activities. Federal authorities dogged the steps of the leaders. Immediately upon Hitler's declaration of war on the United States, on December 11, 1941, the Bund newspaper, the *Free American and Deutscher Weckruf and Beobachter* was shut down, and the Bund offices taken over by U.S. Treasury agents.

With the nation at war, the Justice Department now took seriously the frequent boasts of Bund leaders that their first loyalty belonged to Hitler's Germany whether they held American citizenship or not. On

The American Nazi Bund—Playing the "patriotic game" at a Bund camp in New Jersey.

March 25, 1942, the Attorney General announced that he would seek the denaturalization of a considerable number of Bund members, Kuhn among them. Most dramatic was the action of the FBI in June in arresting two groups of saboteurs. It created a sensation. The men had landed on Long Island, New York, with cases of explosives and orders to sabotage factories and military establishments. Former members of the Bund, they had gone back to Germany to be trained for just such a mission. A military court convicted eight of the group. Two were sentenced to long prison terms and six were executed.

With equal vigor, though on lesser charges, the Federal authorities prosecuted a long list of Bund leaders. Kunze was indicted at about this time in Hartford, Connecticut, as a member of a spy ring passing military information to Germany and Japan and again in New York for obstructing the operation of the Selective Service System. Brought back from Mexico to which he had fled, he was sentenced to fifteen years on the first charge and five on the second.

The Silver Shirt Syndrome

William Dudley Pelley offers the classical case of the frustrated personality who turned to the practice of anti-Semitism as a profession. He was a man of great ambitions and only modest talents, embittered because the world had not recognized his worth and left unrewarded his pursuit of fame and fortune.

Pelley was very good at writing advertisements for himself. Such talents as he had were those of a writer, but as always in such instances, it is difficult to separate fact from fiction. He was born in 1885 in Lynn, Massachusetts, the son of an itinerant Methodist preacher and felt burdened throughout his youth by his father's religious fanaticism. As a young man, he joined his father in a paper-manufacturing business. He then turned to journalism, worked on a variety of small-town newspapers, wrote fiction, contributed to national magazines, and landed in Hollywood in the 1920's where he had a little success in the film industry, but had finally to earn a living selling real estate.

Pelley never seemed quite good enough for success, and it infuriated him. As he himself has written, he suddenly found release in spiritualism. Indeed, he found in it not only an escape from reality and personal woes, but turned it into a publishing enterprise, establishing a spiritualist magazine, *Liberation*, and a pamphlet press in Asheville, North Carolina. But success escaped him here, too.

By the close of 1932, Pelley, now forty-eight years old, once more was in serious financial straits. To save himself, he turned to politics and bigotry. In January 1933, one day after the Nazis took power in Germany, Pelley announced formation of the Silver Shirt Legion and offered himself to the nation as the American Hitler. To lend a bit of color to the enterprise, he styled himself, Chief Pelley, as a variant on the German term *Fuehrer*. His appeal was to the nativist bigot, the onetime Klansman, the Protestant fundamentalist, though it pleased him to talk from time to time of "the thousands of fine Catholic boys in our ranks." His hope was to tap the Nazi purse and to find the success that had escaped him all his life.

What manner of man was this who had organized the archetype of the 121 lunatic fringe nativist groups capitalizing on the Nazi cause investigated by the McCormack Committee? Donald Strong found

the psychological implications obvious. Spiritualism did not provide adequate expression for Pelley's desires. Anti-Semitism, on the other hand, salved his feelings of inadequacy by offering delusions of grandeur. He would lead a nationwide movement of Silver Shirted men to drive the Jews and revolutionaries from power! He would be the savior of his country! Here was a channel not only for externalizing his aggressions, but also for releasing the bitterness generated by years of frustration.

This has merit as psychological analysis, but Pelley had more venal motives too. He was desperately in need of money and, as the McCormack Committee reported, he was in persistent pursuit of Nazi groups and Nazi leaders for the financial support they were able to give him. Within a year, the Silver Shirts, picking up adherents from the disintegrated Klan, reached a membership of 15,000. Pelley was selling huge quantities of anti-Semitic literature and had augmented the circulation of his onetime spiritualist magazine, *Liberation*, which he had turned into an anti-Semitic organ. Financial success, however, continued to elude him. In April 1934 Pelley had to suspend publication of *Liberation* until August because his publishing enterprise, the Galahad Press, had fallen into bankruptcy. Ultimately, this led to Pelley's conviction for the fraudulent sale of stock and a suspended jail sentence.

Such setbacks did not faze Pelley. Indeed, he forged ahead in order to maintain his delusions of power. Within the year, he organized the Christian party as the means for "smashing Jewish communism in the United States and the disenfranchising of the Jew from further political and economic mischief" at the new Presidential election. As always, with Pelley, the word was equivalent to the deed. The Christian party, he told the readers of *Pelley's Weekly*, had become a power "in the impoverished United States," created "suddenly and dauntlessly" by Pelley himself the "pioneer in the strictly American movement to smash the megalomaniac clutch of apostate Jewry on our Christian institutions." Pelley himself, of course, ran as the party's Presidential candidate, but it achieved a place on the ballot only in the state of Washington. He received 1,598 votes out of 700,000 cast in the state.

By now Pelley had begun to make money both from the publishing and sale of anti-Semitic literature and from substantial gifts from men of means. But, as always, his financial manipulations brought unwanted attentions. The courts in North Carolina opened hearings of revocation of his parole in the Galahad case; and while he was able to stave off imprisonment for a time, the Superior Court in Asheville sentenced him to a two- to three-year term in January 1942. With the nation at war, in March, the Post Office Department stopped the mailing of his publication, now known as the *Galilean*, and in April he was arrested by Justice Department agents as part of the crack down on seditionists that had also affected the German-American Bund. Pelley was accused of violating the Espionage Act by making false statements in the *Galilean* that interfered with the military forces. He was tried in Indianapolis, where the paper was published, convicted of promoting Axis propaganda, and sentenced to fifteen years in prison. He served for seven years until his parole in 1950.

While Pelley's ultimate fall turned on his seditious activity, which might imply some high ideological commitment on his part, no such exalted motives can be attributed to him or to the others who, during the 1930's, operated on the fringes of the political movements of the nation. He was simply, as the Dies Committee summed up, a "typical case" of a "racketeer engaged in mulcting thousands of dollars annually from his fanatical and misled followers." From the documentary evidence, the committee found that conclusion "inescapable." Also to the point was the statement from the bench by Superior Court Judge Zeb Nettles in the North Carolina conviction of Pelley: "... for three weeks I have sat here... and helped unravel a course in crooked dealing, thievery and stealing sufficient to damn any man, much less this contemptible seeker after notoriety."

The Silver Shirt organization was a prototype for the many groups, which, with varying degrees of success, sought to capitalize on racial and religious bigotry as a petty racket. The Defenders of the Christian

Faith began in 1925 as a "mailing list" fundamentalist organization opposed to modernism in religion, but its founder, Gerald B. Winrod of Wichita, Kansas, in 1933 discovered "Jewish Bolshevism" at about the same time that Pelley did. He built a gigantic publishing business, a magazine of large circulation, and became a prime distributor of anti-Semitic tracts, pamphlets, and books produced by others. He remained for decades in the lucrative business of disseminating hate materials, but never built a membership organization.

Robert Edward Edmondson, a newspaper man and financial writer, went into the anti-Semitic propaganda business in 1934. His gimmick was a reporting service. Again there was no membership organization, but the Edmondson Economic Service flourished as a distributor of anti-Jewish tirades, either by mail or through other fringe groups. James B. True, Jr., was in the same business as Edmondson—only he charged more for his newsletter, *Industrial Control Report*. He was a free-lance writer when Roosevelt was first elected. The New Deal became the principal target of his fanatical hatred, but he soon turned to anti-Semitism. As described by the Reverend L. M. Birkhead, director of the Friends of Democracy, True was a neurotic and an unmitigated sadist, inventor of a hip-pocket club he called the "Kike Killer." True could be irrationally violent in his talk, but he was a paper tiger. Harry Jung's speciality was "patriotism" and "secrecy," his training that of an antilabor agent provocateur. Anti-Semitism was only part of his racket, but it became the major business of his American Vigilant Intelligence Federation.

To this brief listing could be added—picked at random—such "patriotic" organizations as the Order of '76, the Paul Reveres, the American Christian Defenders and names like Colonel Eugene Nelson Sanctuary, Colonel Edward Marshall Hadley, George Deatheage, and Mrs. Albert W. Dilling. It still would remain only a sampling of the men and what passed for organizations in the lunatic fringe of the 1930's. The total list is far too long and undifferentiated to make a detailed accounting here. It is sufficient to know that though they had their hatreds in common, they rarely could submerge their rivalries to work cooperatively. Such disunity was their only contribution to democracy.

The Coughlin Phenomenon

As the most spectacularly successful leader of an anti-Semitic movement in the 1930's, Father Charles Coughlin might have gone even further if he had not been a priest. For all their drawing power, his charismatic personality and voice could not overcome the anti-Catholic prejudices of that large body of nativist Protestants who were the reservoir from which other anti-Semitic groups drew their members. Coughlin's following was therefore very largely Catholic, principally urban rather than rural, and more likely to be blue-collar workers than white-collar middle class. Their educational level was commensurately lower, and they were more readily manipulated.

Coughlin, of course, was a genius at manipulation of people, propaganda, and, despite his "funny money" ideas, of the purse. If he had been equally adept at politics, and not burdened by his priestly frock, he and not Gerald L. K. Smith might have assumed Huey Long's mantle and successfully carried forward Long's vision of empire. Nevertheless, his shrewdness and skill developed a three-faceted power base that shook the nation for a decade. His radio program—begun as an effort to build up a local church, the Shrine of the Little Flower in Royal Oak, Michigan—was turned into a national platform for his ever-shifting cause. His periodical *Social Justice* became a source of personal income, an extension of his radio voice, and an action program to boot, as a million copies were hawked in the streets by his supporters. The Christian Front grew to be his political-action arm, for which he accepted full responsibility when it suited his needs and disclaimed when the street violence it promoted became embarrassing to him. Coughlin knew how to dissemble as well as to preach, but he had no acceptable program to offer. Indeed, as so many demagogues of the Roosevelt era, he misjudged America. He turned to fascism and anti-Semitism just as the country—watching the events in Nazi Germany—was recoiling from these ideologies of hate. When war came, Father Coughlin was finally silenced by his church.

Coughlin turned to overt anti-Semitism in the aftermath of the 1936 Presidential election, for Roosevelt's remarkable sweep at the polls was a complete repudiation of Coughlin's panacea for the nation's ills—a protofascist system of "social justice" that was to replace democracy and capitalism. For two years, Coughlin had been haranguing the nation with his mellifluous radio voice that "capitalism is doomed and not worth saving" and promoting a "state capitalism," which, though only vaguely defined, had the outlines of an embryonic fascist program. In 1934 he had formed the National Union for Social Justice to promote this program, and by 1935 he had broken completely with the New Deal which he had once warmly supported.

In 1936 Coughlin was knee-deep in partisan politics pushing his schemes for government ownership of banks, a variety of populist economic notions, isolationism, anticommunism and control of labor strikes. In March of that year Coughlin began publishing *Social Justice*, attacking the two-party system as a "sham." In June he endorsed William Lemke, a North Dakota congressman, for President on a National Union party ticket. The new party's platform could hardly be differentiated from Coughlin's own program. Lemke and his running mate, Thomas A. O'Brien of Massachusetts, quickly won endorsement from Gerald L. K. Smith, inheritor of Huey Long's Share-the-Wealth movement, and Dr. Francis Townsend's Old Age movement. At this point, Coughlin, evidently in a euphoric state, counted up the potential votes for Lemke. Smith claimed a following of 3,000,000; Coughlin's estimate of his National Union membership was 5,000,000. A Gallup poll in June predicted that 7 percent of the electorate would vote for a Coughlin-backed candidate and perhaps 10 percent for one backed by Townsend. With the figures dancing in his head, Coughlin predicted that the Lemke–O'Brien ticket would roll up 9,000,000 votes. So sure was he of the result that he offered to close

Peddling Jocial Justice in 1936–At this point the principal target was FDR.

down his national radio program if that figure was not attained.

On November 7 Coughlin told his radio audience he was going off the air. Lemke had received only 882,000 votes. Roosevelt had scored the most spectacular election victory in the nation's history. He had received 27,753,000 votes and carried every state of the Union except Maine and Vermont, which ended up in Republican Alfred Landon's column. Landon's popular vote was 16,675,000.

Obviously, Father Coughlin was not the only one who had misjudged events. In political scientist John P. Roche's analysis "what had occurred was an almost unbelievable loss of contact" by both

Gerald L. K. Smith, Father Charles E. Couglin, and Dr. Francis E. Townsend— Their right wing coalition attacked the two party system in 1936 and went down to defeat with their candidate, William Lemke.

extremists and respectable Roosevelt opponents "with the temper of the American people." Throughout his first term "...Roosevelt had convinced the great majority of the American people that, however difficult the times...the government was an instrument of succor which was concerned with the well-being of all strata in Society."

As the election returns proved "...the more the [ultra-conservative] Liberty League denounced Roosevelt's 'statism,' the more Coughlin attached his 'Bolshevik-plutocratic' tendencies, the more the Communists and Socialists assaulted his lack of planning, the more the G.O.P. inveighed against his drive for 'dictatorship,' the more the American people decided F.D.R. was 'their man.'"

Neither the press nor the polls seemed to measure the depth of this faith of the people in Roosevelt. Indeed, the voters were "strangely silent" until election day. Like so many other politicians, Father Coughlin was left in shock, but it took only a brief time for him to recover. Then he was back on the air with the announcement that his big mistake in 1936 had been to believe that democracy could work when all along he should have known that the Jewish conspiracy behind communism and New Deal "plutocracy" made that impossible. The closet anti-Semite now mounted his radio pulpit in full fascist regalia.

After a respite of less than three months, Coughlin's radio broadcasts were reinstituted on January 24, 1937, on an expanded network. Within a few months, he moved to establish his *Social Justice* councils from which all non-Christians were excluded. In March 1938, his fascist program took on more definite form. Proposing a Corporate State of America, he suggested abolition of political parties because most politicians were communists. Members of Congress in the Coughlin "state" would be elected by corporate groups with common interests and the President by the members of Congress. As he painted himself into his fascist corner with words of praise for Mussolini and support for Hitler's irredentist ambitions, he evidently saw the need for a supporting organization in the Nazi tradition. He thus created the Christian Front, avowedly fascist and anti-Semitic, admittedly ready to take to the streets in bully-boy fashion.

All reserve in Coughlin's anti-Semitism now dropped away. In the summer of 1938, *The Protocols of the Elders of Zion* began to appear in the pages of *Social Justice*. The new twist, as Coughlin phrased it, was that he was "not interested in the authenticity of the *Protocols*" but "in their factuality." As a further explanation, *Social Justice* declared under

the pseudonym "Ben Marcin": "No one is interested in the identity of
the author, whereas everyone is interested in the contents of the
book...."

Such locutions may have gone down with the readers of *Social
Justice*, but they brought forth devastating critiques from respectable
sources. However, once the die was cast, Coughlin could not be
deflected from his anti-Semitic drives. In the issue of *Social Justice* of
July 25, 1938, Coughlin pulled out all the stops of anti-Semitic theology
from the charge of deicide, to the Shylock image of Jews as unscrupu-
lous money-lenders and controllers of international banking, to their
alleged responsibility for the success of the Communist revolution in
Russia. After that all was merely commentary—persistent, fallacious,
uninhibited by facts or the repudiation of his fellow churchmen.

Coughlin's approach to anti-Semitic propaganda was in the classic
mold of invention of facts, exploitation of old and exploded canards,
claims to having unearthed hitherto-neglected historic events, and

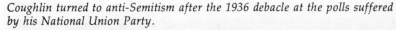

*Coughlin turned to anti-Semitism after the 1936 debacle at the polls suffered
by his National Union Party.*

bold repetitions of the diatribes of other anti-Semites. His use of *The Protocols* is a case in point, but only the most obvious one, since their authenticity had been so widely discredited. Yet Coughlin boldly asserted that two Polish rabbis had vouched for their accuracy and provided their names. The chief rabbi of Vilna, however, denied the existence of these men. Hitting on another favorite theme—Jewish responsibility for Russian communism—Coughlin in his November 27 broadcast quoted another nonexistent authority:

"The chief document treating of the financing of the Russian revolution is one drawn by the American Secret Service and transmitted by the French High Commissioner to his government. It was published by the *Documentation Catholique* of Paris on March 6, 1920, and was preceded by the following remarks, namely, 'the authenticity of this document is guaranteed to us. With regards to its exactness, the exactness of the information it contains, the American Secret Service takes responsibility.'" The United States Secret Service would do no such thing. Following the broadcast, its chief, Frank J. Wilson denied that any "such report was ever made" by his government agency.

Another classic invention of fact appeared in *Social Justice* in 1940. The Civil War, it was asserted, was fought not over slavery; the issue was freedom from the Jewish international bankers. To prove the point, *Social Justice* quoted British Prime Minister Disraeli at a Rothschild family gathering:

"Under this roof are the heads of the family of Rothschild—a name famous in every capital of Europe and every division of the globe. If you like, we shall divide the United States into two parts, one for you, James, and one for you, Lionel. Napoleon will do exactly and all that I shall advise him."

The source of the quotation was a book called *The Rothschilds* by John Reeves published in 1887. Of course, it was out of print and not readily available. But an energetic newsman of the *Chicago Daily News* did find the volume and the quotation. It read:

"Under this roof are the heads of the family of Rothschild—a name famous in every capital of Europe and every division of the globe—a family not more regarded for its riches than esteemed for its honor, virtues and public spirit."

No one at *Social Justice* seemed embarrassed by the exposure; but then, by 1940, they had become hardened to such matters. The most flagrant of episodes had occurred on December 5, 1938, when Coughlin published under his own signature, an article entitled

Background for Persecution, a blatant adoption of the Nazi propaganda line, many passages taken verbatim from a bitter attack on Jews delivered by Dr. Joseph Goebbels at the Seventh Nazi Congress in 1935.

Coughlin's method of dealing with such exposure and with direct challenges to his veracity was to ignore them. As long as he was not silenced by his bishop, he could afford to practice the Hitlerian tactic of the Big Lie with impunity and to ignore the criticism of his fellow churchmen who found the use of his priestly status an abomination and his program a perversion of church doctrine. That he rejected such criticism was apparent not only by his continued activity but in the blunt statement published in *Social Justice* on November 14, 1938: "The only source of unbiased truth is Father Coughlin."

Within the month, Cardinal Mundelein, the leading prelate in the Middle West, though not Coughlin's immediate superior, declared that "As an American citizen, Father Coughlin has the right to express his personal views on current events, but he is not authorized to speak for the Catholic church, nor does he represent the doctrines or sentiments of the church." The statement did not deflect Coughlin, nor did it stimulate Bishop Michael Gallagher of Detroit—who had the power to do so—to order him to desist. Coughlin thus had his bishop's silent assent.

Before turning further to the counterattack of Coughlin's critics, Catholic, Protestant, and Jewish, it would be well to sketch in greater detail the role and activities of the third element in Coughlin's propaganda apparatus—the Christian Front. It was the device that converted his following, developed by the radio network and *Social Justice*, into a cohesive organization at least in Eastern cities such as New York—that could function as an activist and political instrument. That it became primarily a street gang was due to the character of its adherents.

The original *Social Justice* councils evidently did not fulfill Coughlin's need for a membership base. Unable to draw upon a general Christian following and needing greater institutional support, he sought an activist Christian Front. Even if that were a misnomer, it yet enabled him to penetrate certain Catholic institutions and gain the backing of a number of like-minded priests.

Perhaps Coughlin took a leaf out of the Communist party organizing manual—or, for that matter, from Nazi tactics. At any rate, on May 23, 1938, *Social Justice* suggested the formation of cells of "no more than 25 members" and to let these cells—or platoons, as *Social Justice* referred to them—proliferate. Within a few weeks, Coughlin announced in a "message to platoons" that "you and your people are affiliated directly to me."

New York City became the primary base of the Christian Front and one of the original platoons, established by a priest of the Paulist Fathers, met at their rectory. When this arrangement became patently embarrassing to the Paulists, meadquarters were moved to a beer hall, for as the Christian Front grew, it turned toward violence that inevitably drew the attention of law-enforcement agencies. By the spring of 1939, 50 to 75 rallies were being held every week. They frequently became problems for the police as their violence of speech turned to physical attack on the streets of the city. Court records show 233 arrests at such rallies in 1939. In at least one instance, a city magistrate, himself a Catholic, found the anti-Jewish threats so chilling that he sent two Christian Fronters to the workhouse for seventy-five days. "These people," he said, "who call themselves the Christian Front and Christian Mobilizers are dragging Christianity through the dust. They do not speak for Christianity."

Coughlin at the same time preached "the Franco way" and his *Social Justice* readers understood this at least as a qualified appeal to violence, to "meet force with force as a last resort." John F. Cassidy, leader of the Christian Front in New York at the time, took it as license to organize what he euphemistically dubbed "sportsclubs" to go into the streets "to protect their rights by force." "We are prepared to say to the Communists that they lay down their arms or we will meet their arms with our arms—firearms," Cassidy declared. Seventeen of Cassidy's "sportsclub" members were picked up on January 13, 1940, by the FBI, and a considerable cache of arms found in their homes was confiscated. J. Edgar Hoover explained the FBI action by charging that they had planned to kill Jews and communists, "knock off about a dozen Congressmen," and take over a number of Federal buildings.

Coughlin's capacity for dissembling now stood him in good stead. He promptly repudiated the conspirators in a statement to the Associated Press, though they were clearly the very cream of the Christian Front in New York. Two weeks later, in *Social Justice*, he had a change of heart. "... we are not running out on the fine body of New York Christians who make up the membership of the Christian Front...," he said. "...I freely choose to be identified as a friend of the accused. It matters not whether they be guilty or innocent... my place is by their side until they are released or convicted."

That the Christian Front, so largely Catholic and Irish in its membership, was an embarrassment to liberal church and Catholic leadership is borne out by the constant criticism emanating from these sources. This discomfort was augmented by the fact that the Christian Front attracted a larger number of men with criminal records than any of the nativist organizations. Its penchant for violence was no doubt the magnet that drew these hostile and unstable personalities. To enumerate all of the violence and criminality at this late date would serve little purpose.

Countering Coughlin

The weapons in the hands of Coughlin's critics with which to counter his anti-Semitic diatribes seemed no match for his airborne attacks. They had a sense of outrage, a moral stance, and the facts with which to refute his Big Lies. But he had the superior delivery system in a propaganda war. In the 1930's, the country still had much to learn about the manipulation by demagogues of its commitment to freedom of speech and press. After the first two anti-Semitic broadcasts, so astute a journalistic observer as Heywood Broun commented:

"The race between the truth and misstatements is quite similar to the famous match of the tortoise and the hare. The truth is mighty and will prevail, but often it gets away badly from the barrier.... Apparently thousands of persons are still unaware that the picture set up by his eminence of Royal Oak has been punctured full of holes."

Broun was ruminating thus on the network broadcast in which Coughlin had charged that the Bolshevik Revolution had been led by Jews and financed by American Jewish bankers. At least in New York, the broadcast had ended Coughlin's relationship with Station WMCA, and the station and its advertising clients in turn became the scene of mass picketing by the Christian Front and Coughlin followers of a variety of stripes.

Coughlin may have calculated and decided to endure the charges that would be hurled at him by Jews, but criticism from church sources was harder to take, for it undermined his pretensions that he was the source of Catholic truth. The most devastating critique from a prelate of the initial broadcasts came from Monsignor John A. Ryan, then professor of sociology at Catholic University, in an article in *Commonweal*. He soberly demolished Coughlin's concocted facts with authoritative scholarship, accused him of expressing his sympathy for the Jews of Germany "in such terms as to suggest [they] deserved

...the cruel injuries which they have suffered," and expressed his own feeling that Coughlin was "eager, or at least willing, to promote anti-Semitism in the United States."

In a telling admonition, at the conclusion, Monsignor Ryan reminded Coughlin that Catholics had been urged "in particular to refrain from encouraging [his] campaign of anti-Semitism from fear that the same methods and the same psychology will be used against them when the next anti-Catholic movement gets under way." But, he declared, "the first two commandments provide infinitely higher motive and an immeasurably more effective one. From every point of

Coughlin adherents in New York picketing radio station WMCA's advertisers. The station dropped his broadcasts in 1938 when he failed to clear in advance the speech that opened his anti-Semitic campaign.

view Catholics should refrain from fostering by speech, action or silence anti-Semitism in the United States."

Monsignor Ryan was not alone among Catholics in reminding Coughlin of his priestly commitments. Alfred E. Smith, the leading Catholic figure of the time, spoke out:

> When a man presumes to address so great a number of listeners as Father Coughlin reaches, particularly if he is a priest, he assumes the responsibility of not misleading them by false statements or poisoning their judgements with baseless slanders. From boyhood I was taught that a Catholic priest was under the divine injunction to "teach the nations" the word of God. That includes the divine commandment "Thou shalt not bear false witness against thy neighbor."

That statement was carried as a preface in a monograph *Father Coughlin: His "Facts" and Arguments* published in 1939 by a coalition of Jewish organizations, the General Jewish Council, in which the Anti-Defamation League, the American Jewish Committee, the American Jewish Congress, and the Jewish Labor Committee joined forces to meet the crisis of the times. The League and the Committee, leaders in the field, had as a matter of policy and tactics been inclined to maintain low profiles in public. Against the background of the Nazi persecutions, the activities of a Coughlin, the German–American Bund and the various fringe organizations seemed more menacing than anything American Jews had experienced before. Whether this was a valid assumption or not, pressure to act vigorously and publicly came from Jewish communities throughout the nation. Joint action seemed called for, and a broad, direct counterattack was mounted against Coughlin. The monograph—the most incisive analysis of Coughlin's propaganda line and thoroughgoing refutation of his anti-Semitic charges to appear—was a first step in that effort. A most dramatic element in the pamphlet was the printing in parallel columns of the 1938 article "Background for Persecution" by Coughlin—heretofore referred to—and its verbatim source in a speech by Dr. Goebbels in 1935. Ever since, this has been one of the most damning bits of evidence of Coughlin's turning to Nazism.

Jointly and individually, the Jewish agencies, using the Council as a clearinghouse, pursued their program, each in the area where its greatest strengths lay, meantime picking up allies beyond their most optimistic hopes from other sectors of the public.

Protestant church organizations, watching Coughlin and his satellite organizations, were quick to deny that their programs in any way

reflected the Christian position. "No organization or groups of individuals fostering such evil propaganda...has the moral right to call
itself Christian," declared the Brooklyn Church and Mission Federation, warning Protestants to steer clear of the Christian Front. In the
same vein, 273 Protestant clergymen in New York decried "the
rise...of organizations which...exist merely and mainly to foster
anti-Semitism" and considered it a "blasphemous effrontery to represent themselves as Christian." Methodist, Episcopalian, and other
major church councils joined with similar statements. Numerous
Catholic clergymen, Catholic laymen, and Catholic publications such
as *Commonweal* joined in the criticism and the opposition to
Coughlin—unhappily waiting for the Bishop of Detroit to act.

Coughlin, of course, was of particular concern to religious leaders
and their official groups felt it necessary to speak out against what they
felt to be a subversion of Christian morality. Civic and political leaders
and the intellectual community saw Coughlin as only one element in
the wide attack upon basic American ideology and the democratic
system. Their focus, in terms of Nazism, was political. Would the
United States eventually become involved in war? Anti-Semitism—
except to Jews—was not as salient an issue as neutrality or intervention in the affairs of Europe. As time passed, revulsion against the
kind of anti-Semitism, overt and promoted, represented by the Christian Front, the German–American Bund or the Silver Shirts, moved
forward in the public consciousness and grew in proportion to the
country's rejection and abhorrence for Hitlerism.

The shock of *Kristallnacht* in November 1938, when the Nazis destroyed the German Jewish community in brutal glee, left even the
most eloquent at a loss for words. President Roosevelt could only say
that he "could scarcely believe that such a thing could happen in a
twentieth-century civilization." But America's shock was clear in a
poll taken at the time, showing that 88 percent of all Americans
disapproved of Nazi treatment of Jews. Coughlin took this moment to
declare his anti-Semitism. Within two weeks, he made his first radio
attack. He misread America, as did the others in his camp. For all his
tumult and shouting, he never really affected the mind of America or
tore away its sense of decency in the political arena. Here at least—if
not in terms of social or economic discrimination—the Jewish counterattack against the purveyors of strident anti-Semitism won out.

In September, 1940, a month before Coughlin permanently gave up
his radio program, *Social Justice* endorsed Wendell L. Willkie for

President against Roosevelt, who was running for his third term. Willkie's reply to the endorsement was a kind of summing up for America:

> I am not interested in the support of anybody...who is in support of any foreign economic or political philosophy in this country....If I understand what his [Coughlin's] beliefs are, I am not interested in his support—I don't want it...he is opposed to certain people because of their race or religion. I have no place in my philosophy for such beliefs. There is no hedge clause about that...I don't have to be President of the United States, but I do have to...live with myself. I am not interested in being President of the United States to compromise with my fundamental beliefs.

At the Point of War

The anti-Semitism of the 1930's wrote a new page in the American experience. The domestic crisis of the Great Depression revealed that the movements of the 1920's were a burnt-out case and could not rise to the classic opportunities presented by the troubled economy. The stimulus for an organized anti-Semitism had to come from the outside. The rise of Nazism and the threat of war stirred an anti-Semitic response, but almost entirely from the marginal areas already reviewed. Most Americans responded negatively, and as the years went by, their recognition of the dangers inherent in the Hitler régime reached the critical point where they were ready to support the Allied cause up to the point of war. The Nazi persecution of Jews was viewed with abhorrence and the activities of the Bund and its imitators with distaste by the generality of Americans—and opposition by the democratically committed.

Not all Americans were committed to Hitler's defeat or convinced of the grave danger he represented to a democratic world, America included. Isolationists believed that staying out of Europe's war was of far greater moment. Here, at least, respectable circles might have looked upon Jews as possibly working toward American involvement in war.

If an elitist group could have given respectability to an anti-Semitic movement under such pretenses, it was the America First Committee, and from its rank might have come the necessary man-on-horseback that the fringe groups could not produce. Colonel Charles A. Lindbergh could have been that man. After having visited Germany and accepting a decoration from Hitler, he was convinced that the

Nazis could not be stopped. For America to back the Allies seemed
folly to him. He said as much at an America First rally in Des Moines
on September 11, 1941, and then warned: "The three most important
groups who have been pressing this country toward war are the
British, the Jewish, and the Roosevelt Administration." To these he
added Anglophiles, intellectuals, and capitalists who believed "the
future of mankind depends upon the domination of the British Empire." He then sought to soften his reference to Jews with the comment
that "it is not difficult to understand why Jewish people desire the
overthrow of Nazi Germany" and that "no person with a sense of
dignity of mankind can condone the persecution the Jews suffered in
Germany."

For all his status as a national hero, Lindbergh's Des Moines address
was largely viewed as wrongheaded and politically inept. In 1941 such
statements placing the onus of imminent war upon the shoulders of
Jews were regarded as incitement of anti-Semitism. The resentment it

Colonel Charles A. Lindbergh addressing an America First Committee rally—
"Wrong-headed and politically inept."

raised among Jews was echoed even in the ranks of the America First Committee and the isolationist press. John T. Flynn and Alfred E. Smith, two of the leading voices in the committee, repudiated Lindbergh's views and worried that the committee would once more be invaded—as it had been from time to time—by the disreputable extremist groups. How Americans as a whole viewed the matter was shown in a poll taken a month after Lindbergh's address. In response to the question "What persons or groups do you think are most active in trying to get us into the war?" only 6 percent answered "Jews."

Jewish organizations such as the Anti-Defamation League viewed that answer as evidence of their success. They had found allies among the democratically minded and developed a strategy that effectively countered Nazi infiltrations and the excesses of nativist extremists. America had listened at a time of great crisis and understood that anti-Semitism was unacceptable because it violated its deepest commitments. Indeed, in the mind of America, crude, overt anti-Semitism had suddenly acquired a disreputable character it could never again quite shed.

For Lindbergh, the ultimate irony was that three months to the day after his Des Moines speech—and four days after the attack on Pearl Harbor—Hitler declared war on the United States.

SIX

World War II– Anomalies of Prejudice

The emotional shock to the nation of the Pearl Harbor attack was as traumatic as the physical damage to the Pacific fleet. Anger was mixed with the sudden, sobering realization that the country and its people were in mortal danger. As Nazi Germany and fascist Italy moved to support Japan, the political conflict between interventionists and isolationists became irrelevant. It was replaced by argument about whether the Pacific or the Atlantic was to receive priority attention. There was little of the jingo spirit of World War I in evidence, but ideological response to the war was also in short supply. Washed away was the immediate prewar mood of indignation over Nazi cruelty and racism, concern for the invaded nations, and sympathy for persecuted Jews. The mood of introspective self-concern that now gripped the nation brought a rebound and hardening of racist attitudes that was to create new internal conflicts and surprising attitudes toward the enemy.

As the Axis piled up victories in the wake of Pearl Harbor, there was no clear understanding of the national goal except survival; furthermore, the country's morale needed an immediate lift. It came in the usual way in war—a spectacular act of heroism. Even as Pearl Harbor was being mourned and American forces pushed back in the Pacific, an Air Force Flying Fortress attacked and was reported to have sunk a major Japanese warship. The names of Captain Colin Kelly, the pilot, and his bombardier, Sergeant Meyer Levin, flashed across the land as the heroes of the first authentic victory of the war. Kelly died in the attack; Levin lived on to complete 60 missions against the enemy before he, too, lost his life. Far more important than the sinking of a ship was the boost the news gave to the national morale. (The *Haruna*, the battleship in question, in fact survived the attack, was damaged again in the Philippine Sea and was riding at anchor in Tokyo Harbor when American forces took control in Japan at war's end.)

Roosevelt knew that war victories would improve morale, but the Axis powers had to be fought with a sense of democratic purpose if national unity—essential for prosecution of the war—were to be achieved. National unity implied a role and recognition for all the racial and ethnic elements in the land; it implied, too, dealing with the enemy without adopting its racist hatreds. Roosevelt emphasized his purpose in both speech and action. The President's inspiring voice and manner lifted the spirits of the nation. The speeches, the efforts at public education as to war aims, the establishment of symbols (such as the Four Freedoms) came more easily than the actions. Even the considerable power of Rooseveltian exhortation could not dissolve some deep-seated prejudices. And there was a kind of perverse logic as to which prejudices would give way and which were immovable. It is instructive to examine this phenomenon.

The Xenophobic Front

The sense of democratic purpose in the war against the Axis powers failed America in the very first crisis. Within two months of the Pearl Harbor attack, 110,000 American-born Japanese and Japanese resident aliens were taken from their homes on the West Coast and herded into internment camps. The xenophobic cries that went up against the Nisei and the vehemently expressed race hatred of the Japanese enemy were familiar repetitions of corrosive American attitudes in World War I. It was a reflection, too, of the long tradition of fear of "the Yellow Peril." Moreover, most Americans felt humbled and angered by the debacle at Pearl Harbor and the subsequent defeats. They could not readily forgive the perfidious attack; the emotional, even more than the physical damage, was too great. The nation's sense of impregnable strength had been shattered.

The immediate cause of the internment action, which the nation has since come to view as the single greatest wartime violation of its deepest commitments to civil liberty, was a highly vocal, racist minority backed by regional politicians and the military commanders on the West Coast. They carried the day because no public opposition to the plan developed, and without such counteraction, the Administration, uncertain of its own feelings, was only halfhearted in its opposition. Only Attorney General Francis Biddle seemed vitally concerned. The President was not supportive, nor was Secretary of War Stimson. In mid-February, the President signed the order for the Nisei evacuation as a matter of military necessity, and a month later, Congress, many of whose members had been as vocal as the organized groups on the West Coast, endorsed the action. Attempts to release them at various times during the war came to naught. No one would speak up for them. No one would take a chance to challenge the solid xenophobic front, not even the Supreme Court which refused to vacate the order in December 1944. Only Elmer Davis, Chief of the Office of War Information, pointed out that the Japanese had been handed a propaganda bombshell to use against us "that this is a racial war."

Americans of German and Italian extraction did not suffer the cruel fate of the Japanese. In their instance, at least, the nation's democratic vision was not blurred by racist intolerance. Nor were the German and Italian enemy viewed with the emotion-powered hatred visited on the Japanese. (Roosevelt distrusted the German aliens, 600,000 of whom were resident in the country, but would not move against them. However, he favored the vigorous prosecution and the execution of the saboteurs, former American Bund members, who landed on the Long Island shore in 1942.) No doubt the more relaxed attitude toward the Germans and Italians was in part due to the fact that the ideological drive which motivated most Americans at the start of the war soon gave way to less complicated patriotic responses. Fighting Nazism on the battlefield, it also seemed a violation of the American spirit to adopt the hatreds the enemy espoused against Americans of German origin, except clearly disloyal elements such as members of the Bund.

Despite his distrust of Germans, Roosevelt took occasion, at the time of the Nisei internments, to state his awareness of the anxiety that German and Italian aliens living in the United States must feel. He asked Governor Herbert Lehman of New York to assure them "that no collective evacuation of German or Italian aliens is contemplated..."

The sober reaction of the average American made the difference in treatment of the Germans as compared with the Japanese. If there was hatred of Hitler and Nazism, it was not visited on uninvolved Germans in America. Nor did anyone stop playing German music or exchange sauerbraten for Yankee pot roast, as in World War I. But someone did cut down four trees in the Japanese cherry groves of the Tidal Basin in Washington.

For Negroes—Now or Never

Efforts to establish fair employment practices, to desegregate the armed forces, to make the war effort meaningful in democratic purpose to Negroes met with resistance. Black leadership looked upon such resistance as turning the path to unity into a one-way street and the highly touted democratic purpose as a sham. They found that equal opportunity still stopped short of the hiring gate and that Jim Crow held his grip on the armed forces as strongly as ever for most of the war years. The bitterness of Black America broke out in race riots of major proportions—in Los Angeles, in New York and Detroit, and in lesser disturbances in other places. The slogans of democracy, men such as A. Philip Randolph contended, would remain meaningless without the substance they implied.

As a result, the Roosevelt Administration found itself caught between contending forces and trod cautiously. Where reforms could succeed, pressure was applied; where resistance became too great, democratic purpose was thwarted. The strength of the war effort was the first priority, and the risks to that effort were constantly weighed. At best, the general policy of the Administration was "separate but equal" treatment for Negroes in the armed forces and in the government agencies. Integration was approached gingerly. The navy fought for its lily-white status and the Army followed a policy of segregated Negro units usually led by white officers. The Air Force was more tractable and gave blacks greater opportunities to rise in the officer class.

To protesting Negro publishers in February 1944, Roosevelt admitted "discrimination in the actual treatment" of Black troops and expressed his frustration in being unable to meet the "trouble [which] lies fundamentally in the attitude of certain white people—officers down the line...we are up against it, absolutely up against it..." Secretary of War Stimson put it another way: "We are suffering from the persistent legacy of the original crime of slavery." But neither the President nor the Secretary were willing to risk the move to integrated units—either politically or in terms of military efficiency.

Roosevelt's biographer, James MacGregor Burns, found his attitude

toward Negroes "a compound of personal compassion, social pater-
nalism [and] political sensitivity." On the home front, he recognized
their importance to the war effort. But racism was pervasive in Congress, especially among members of the Southern bloc that was a
major element in his wartime coalition; in defense industry, as well as
in some federal departments. He was hesitant to risk any of his
political capital on the issue.

Negro leadership, however, had also found its voice and a new
militancy. For them it seemed a now-or-never opportunity. As early as
the spring of 1941, Negro spokesmen began to press for an executive
order to end discrimination in Federal employment, building up
pressure with the threat of a march on Washington by July 1. Fearing
the policical damage such a protest might bring to his drive for national unity, Roosevelt decided to risk such a regulation. On June 25,
1941, he issued Executive Order 8802, requiring unions and
employers "to provide for the full and equitable participation of all
workers in defense industries, without discrimination because of
race, creed or color or national origin." A Fair Employment Practices
Committee was established, but its enforcement powers were limited.
It was no great victory, but it was a beginning. Ultimately, however,
the war years advanced the Negro cause to the point of setting the
stage for the years of peace when the issue could no longer be brushed
aside or compromised in the name of the national survival. That, too,
was a kind of victory.

Making the Record

The stress of the early war years revealed how deeply certain traditional anti-Semitic attitudes and stereotypic images of the Jew were
rooted in the American mind. Whereas overt anti-Semitic extremism
in the immediate prewar period had been roundly rejected, opinion
polls taken after war began showed a steadily rising level of distrust
and criticism of Jews. To the question whether Jews had too much
influence in business and government, more than half answered yes.
No less than 25 percent saw them as less patriotic than others; a third
or more mistrusted their willingness to serve in the armed forces and
suspected them of malingering. The graph of anti-Semitic attitudes
maintained its upward trend until 1944. With the success of the Normandy invasion and ultimate victory in sight, the tensions in the
nation finally seemed to ease, and the graph took a downturn.

There was a kind of inevitability about all this. The experience of World War I had shown that feelings of distrust, charges of slackerism, suspicion that Jews would seek out the "soft berths" for service were destined to appear. The facts would not matter; the tensions and unhappiness would. Fully aware of this, Jews were nevertheless determined to establish the record of their wartime service. Not that the truth would turn aside the fears and suspicions of the moment, but it would prevent the distortion of history and would meanwhile give Jews themselves a sense of pride in their participation in the defense of the nation and the war on Nazism.

In such a war, logic should have precluded any widespread slander of Jews but prejudice does not respond to logic. So the slanders and numerous individual acts of anti-Semitism cropped up throughout the war years, but never with the intensity or mindlessness of the World War I period. Perhaps logic had penetrated at least to the point where Jewish motivation in a war against Hitler could not be questioned. Perhaps xenophobic impulses were blunted because Jews in the 1940s were recognized as an indigenous group. A considerable proportion of the Jewish servicemen in 1918 were foreign-born and suffered the antagonism vented at the time on all immigrants; in World War II, the Jewish GI was typically native-born and not easily distinguishable from his fellows. Ultimately, the statistical records confirmed the character and extent of their service as Americans. Their numbers exceeded their proportion in the population; the awards they won for valor and merit were equally impressive. More than 550,000 Jewish men and women—nearly 12 percent of the total Jewish population—served in the armed forces. They could have made an army of 37 divisions.

Casualties came to over 40,000, of which 8,000 were combat deaths. Twenty-five hundred others also died in service. Fifty Jewish families lost two sons in the war; one family lost three. Thirty-six thousand received a total of 61,448 medals and awards for bravery. The Congressional Medal of Honor, the nation's highest award for valor, was given to a 23-year-old second lieutenant, Raymond Zussman of Detroit, in the Rhone Valley campaign, a few days before he was killed in action. Seventy-four Distinguished Crosses, 37 Navy Crosses, and 47 Distinguished Service Medals went to others. Distinguished Flying Crosses numbered 2,391 and Air Medals 16,068.

Among general officers, there were six with the rank of major general, including Maurice Rose, a career officer of Jewish parentage who won the Distinguished Service Medal as commanding general of the Third Armored Division in the Normandy campaign. He died in the final drive to victory near Paderborn, Germany. The highest-ranking Jewish officer of the war was a four-star admiral, Ben Moreel, organizer and commander of that remarkable group, the Seabees, and chief of the Bureau of Yards and Docks. Other Jewish officers of general rank included 13 brigadiers, 2 rear admirals, and a commodore. Over 80 percent of Jewish servicemen were in the Army and Air Force; the others in the Navy and seagoing services. Of the Army men, 29 percent served in the Air Force; of these, 20 percent were fliers.

The statistical record could have little impact on public attitudes during the war years. The compilations, though begun as war broke out, necessarily produced no results until the end of the conflict. The War Department might announce—as it did from time to time—that "the current strength of the army is a fair cross-section of American life... including religion" in order to protect troop morale. But neither statistics nor such statements had any immediate effect inhibiting the slanders, the whispered lies, the scurrilous doggerel aimed against Jews and other minority groups.

The problem had been foreseen by those Jewish organizations which during the 1930's had been deeply involved in combating the Nazi propaganda invasion and the home-grown anti-Semitism of the lunatic fringe and nativist groups. In the fall of 1940, the Anti-Defamation League and the American Jewish Committee discussed organization of a current history research and news dissemination program, should war come, of the extent and character of Jewish participation in the fighting. The National Jewish Welfare Board, the official accrediting agency for Jewish chaplains in the armed forces, joined in the discussions. Since World War I the Board had been providing for the recreational needs of Jewish servicemen. To carry on the new project, the three groups formed an Army and Navy Public Relations Committee and were joined by the Jewish War Veterans, the American Jewish Congress, and the Jewish Labor Committee.

The new effort soon demonstrated that where statistics and assuring official statements could not penetrate preconceptions, symbols did. The story of Meyer Levin is a case in point. Hundreds of such accounts were mingled among the thousands of emotion-laden daily reports that reached the public as the mass media sought to bolster the nation's morale. They all had their effect, some of longer duration than others, but all eventually blending into an undifferentiated mass of human travail.

Miraculously, one such story caught the imagination and has become a legend embodying the nation's fondest image of itself. No planning could have produced the great symbol of the self-sacrifice of the Four Chaplains. Yet it was a symbol that might have been lost without the careful researches of the committee that rescued from the depths of the sea one of the most memorable human stories of the war—a portrait of America living its ideal of brotherhood, a drama acted out at the cost of their lives by real flesh-and-blood men— servants of the Lord. It was the obverse side of the hate movements, the bigotry, the divisive forces in the nation. On a most dramatic note, it was evidence of a movement that had been struggling into the sun. Here was evidence that there were men of goodwill in America. There were visionaries who would establish justice and end the evils of ungodly bigotry. There were pragmatists who would turn American ideals into realities. The nation took the Four Chaplains—two Protestant ministers, a Catholic priest, and a rabbi—to its heart. They had touched a chord in the very depths of the American soul.

How their story came to light is a story in itself. In mid-January 1943, the Jewish Welfare Board was informed that Rabbi Alexander D. Goode, who had been accredited as an army chaplain, would shortly be sent overseas. Within the week, the classified casualty list the Board received included the names of Chaplain Goode and three Christian chaplains; Clark V. Poling and George L. Fox, Protestant ministers, and John P. Washington, a Catholic priest. Military restrictions barred any further information. To the knowledgeable, it seemed that whatever had occurred must have happened at sea.

Within a few days, the sharp eyes of the research committee spotted a one-paragraph news item that Daniel O'Keefe, a young sailor who had been an office boy at the *New York Journal-American* was home after being rescued at sea. He told the committee researchers what had occurred. He knew no names and could not mention the ship, but from the lifeboat in which he had escaped, he told of seeing four men, whom he took to be the chaplains, standing together on the deck of the sinking vessel in the dim light of the cold morning. It was not a picture he was ever likely to forget. He said he knew the chaplains had given their life preservers to others; he thought that, standing thus together, they were praying. He had been witness to astonishing acts of bravery. The death of the ship itself was awesome. How much of this was fact and how much the overwrought vision of a distraught young man had to be determined.

The ship had gone down in North Atlantic waters, off Greenland, it was later learned, and 678 persons had been lost. The S.S. *Dorchester* was its name, and it was the only American troop ship to be lost to enemy action during the war. Many of the survivors had been taken to the nearest installation in Canada. Corroboration of young O'Keefe's tale was sought there from chaplains who were assisting the rescued men. Within a short time, others who had been on the *Dorchester* confirmed the events of those critical moments. Bit by bit the story took on its epic shape: the rush for the lifeboats when men, shocked out of sleep, heard the order "Abandon ship!" Some forgot their life preservers; some forgot their parkas or gloves. Even in a lifeboat, in those cold waters, one could not survive for long without these. The Four Chaplains watching and at the same time involved in the scene readily gave up their life belts—and their gloves— to men who had left their own behind and could not go back for them. Always there was the assurance that the chaplain had another handy.

Typical was the report from John J. Mahoney:

When the order to abandon ship came, I grabbed my parka and life

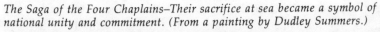

The Saga of the Four Chaplains–Their sacrifice at sea became a symbol of national unity and commitment. (From a painting by Dudley Summers.)

preserver and ran out on the promenade deck, only to find I had forgotten my gloves. Chaplain Goode overheard me swearing at my own stupidity. When I headed back to my cabin, he came after me. "Don't bother," he said, "I have another pair." He pulled off his gloves and gave them to me. I didn't know that he had already given away his life belt to an enlisted man.

I owe my life to those gloves. I landed in a boat that was awash in thirty-degree water. My fingers would have frozen stiff if not for the gloves. I would have never made it without them.

Only 2 men out of 40 in Mahoney's lifeboat survived.

When the War Department released the casualty list for publication some weeks after the catastrophe, the research material on the Four Chaplains so diligently gathered was made available to press and radio. It had an electrifying effect, and the nation seems never to have forgotten these men. Thex have been memorialized in interfaith chapels, in murals and commemorative stamps, in song and story, in sermon and prayer. In all the years since the war, their deed and spirit have stood as a rejection of the bigotry which often plagues the nation.

That the four men represented the finest instincts of America is proven by their personal acts of sacrifice that cold, tragic morning. At least one of them had an opportunity to express his feelings about America and his fellow man before he died. It might well serve as an epitaph for all of them. Rabbi Goode wrote to his wife just before departing for his overseas assignment:

> We are fighting for the new age of brotherhood, the age of brotherhood that will usher in...the world democracy we all want, the age when men will admire the freedom and responsibility of the common man in American democracy...our spirit of tolerance will spread...
>
> Justice and righteousness as dreamed of by the Prophets who gave the world the democratic spirit will cover the earth as a torrent...tyranny will no longer be possible in a united world because...the forces of justice...will have overwhelmed it. Protest against injustice will he heard in every capital of the world....
>
> What has seemed like civilization up to this point is but a crude effort compared to the era that lies just before us....Toward this new world the cavalcade of democracy marches on....

The millennium is yet to arrive, but the vision speaks to us across the years.

The Ultimate Victims

The hardening of anti-Semitic attitudes at the beginning of the war had most serious consequences for efforts to rescue European Jewry from Nazi extermination. As it had all through the 1930's, Congress, responding to public sentiment and its own reluctance, closed its ears to pleas for emergency admission of refugees fleeing for their lives. It blocked every effort at legislative relief. The national origins immigration law now bore its bitterest fruit.

Until war broke out, Roosevelt sought ways to ameliorate the situation by administrative measures. With greater public support, Roosevelt might still have risked pressing for special legislation in the early war years, but public compassion was lacking. The President's own concern for the trapped Jews was evident, but, as always, prosecution of the war was first on his agenda; nothing could interfere with that.

The story of the long, painful decade of the refugees can be told here only briefly. As Hitler assumed power, the outpouring of refugees began with a rush—50,000, principally Jews, in 1933, a steady flow of 25,000 annually through 1938. Most sought asylum in the United States despite the high wall raised by immigration laws. Beyond the approved quota, the wall was unbreachable—the principle of asylum for the persecuted was an ideal, but not even a remote reality. Nothing in the law enabled the nation to respond to the Nazi contingency. Refugees could not be given special treatment. The quota was the last—and only—word.

Not all Americans willingly accepted that word. Liberal forces, Christian church leaders, and Jewish groups pressed for special legislation. Success was out of their reach; they found few allies in Congress for such action, and considerable opposition. The old alliance of patriotic societies, organized labor, and isolationist-minded elements which had pushed through the immigration restrictions in the 1920's held fast. For them, the asylum principle was dead, not to be resurrected under any circumstances. They proved too strong for the proponents of relief measures.

There is little question that they carried the country with them. A national poll in the summer of 1938 found 67 percent opposed to admission of refugees. Nine months later, the figure rose to 83 percent. The closer the world came to war, the more rigid opposition became, the more obvious that the anti-Semitic quotient had become a dominant factor. With action in the Congress stymied, President Roosevelt sought to ease the situation by ordering American consuls in Europe to give special consideration to refugees. A directive went forth from the State Department for "the most humane and favorable treatment possible under the law." What was "possible" turned on a matter of judgment. It quickly became obvious that, not the law, but the predilections of the consular officers determined the treatment. Jewish immigration and relief agencies found many of the consuls less than cooperative. New York Governor Herbert H. Lehman in 1935 and again in 1936 brought their protest to the President. Once more, the President repeated his directive.

In March 1938 Roosevelt called for an international conference of 29

Herbert H. Lehman—The New York governor protested failure of American consuls to help refugees in 1935-1936.

European and South American nations to consider assistance for the refugees, but protected his flank from attack by the restrictionists. The State Department announced that the proposed program would seek no changes in basic immigration policy of the participating nations. "It should be understood," the call declared, "that no country would be expected or asked to receive a greater number of immigrants than is permitted by its existing legislation," and the President emphasized that he did not expect any revision in U.S. quota policy, even as he invoked the American ideal of asylum. However, the restrictionists—in Congress and out—were not mollified. The ineffable John Rankin of Mississippi, already well established as an anti-Semitic voice in Congress, responded that "almost every disgruntled element that ever got into trouble in its own country had pleaded for admission into the United States."

But Roosevelt was not to be deflected. The conference was held in Evian, France, in June with all of the nations that had been invited in attendance. Its one accomplishment was the establishment of the Intergovernmental Committee on Refugees; but even as the conference itself, the committee it gave birth to achieved little. No practical rescue or settlement plans ever were developed as each nation salved its conscience with pious statements while its gates remained closed to the displaced and endangered. Some years later, Roosevelt commented that "unfortunately, most of the governments seemed overly cautious...about receiving these refugees" and "no constructive plans were submitted." He left unremarked the fact that the United States had set the tone that led to that eventuality both in the call to the conference and the opening address by Myron Taylor, the American representative. The expressed American view was that existing immigration laws need not be changed. Indeed, they weren't. The President no doubt calculating the political realities, could not bring himself to buck the quota system, despite the vigorous campaigning for relaxation of the law by liberal and Jewish groups. He recognized that help would never come from Congress.

Old Stock warriors of the restrictionist battles of the 1920's, such as social scientist Henry Pratt Fairchild, now warned anew that anti-Semitism would "burst out into violent eruption" if any considerable number of Jewish refugees were to be admitted. One Southern congressman who also read the polls and watched the unemployment figures wondered about all the government concern for European refugees in face of "the ten million American refugees who have been walking the streets of our cities in vain."

Even a measure to rescue children failed. Congressman Samuel Dickstein in the House and the prestigious Senator Robert F. Wagner in the Senate mounted an effort in the spring of 1939 to liberalize policy to the extent of admitting 20,000 refugee children on a nonsectarian and nonquota basis. Church leaders and others formed a Non-Sectarian Committee for German Refugee Children to back the measure. The committee received wide support from distinguished educators, prestigious public figures and even spokesmen for or-

The Evian Conference–It set up a refugee rescue committee, but the reluctant nations took to heart American Ambassador Myron Taylor's statement that existing immigration laws need not be changed. (Seated, James G. McDonald, former League of Nations high commissioner for refugees from Germany).

ganized labor. For once, on an immigration issue—since no jobs were at stake—the AFL and CIO testified in favor of the measures—no doubt responding to pressure from their idol Senator Wagner. Jewish leadership was content to maintain a low profile and let the Non-Sectarian Committee take the lead, but the anti-Semitic note entered the hearings on the bill almost at once.

Religious spokesmen pleaded that the measure be addressed as a "matter of relief for children and children alone," but the Allied Patriotic Societies stressed that the beneficiaries "would be for the most part of the Jewish race." Senator Wagner agreed that perhaps 60 percent of the children to be admitted were Jewish and then declared "the admission of a handful of European children means a great deal for us and the whole world as a symbol of the strength of our democratic convictions and our common faith."

With the restrictionists expressing the view that the Wagner bill would serve only to breach the immigration laws, the Senate Immigration Committee changed the measure to admit the children only within the quota. Wagner refused to accept the amendment asserting that the "...change would in effect convert...a humane proposal to help children...to a...needlessly cruel consequence for adults in Germany...in need of succor...and fortunate enough to obtain visas...." The amended bill died in committee, and with it another opportunity—in the words of Reid Lewis, an immigration authority, for America to discharge "certain obligations which run with the whole of humanity."

The significance of the congressional hearings was not lost on the Administration. In January 1940, three months after the outbreak of war in Europe, Roosevelt had his Commissioner of Immigration, James Houghteling, once more test the mood of Congress. The report was discouraging. Houghteling found little sympathy for refugees and "hostility to the admission of any considerable number of aliens to compete" for jobs with unemployed citizens. The legislative road seemed definitely closed. Roosevelt once more turned to administrative procedures to provide at least some aid to refugees.

After the fall of France in June, the State Department began to issue visitors visas to "those of superior intellectual attainment...in danger of persecution." In all, 3,268 visas were issued, but only 1,236 were used. The other recipients could not reach neutral ports to escape. The State Department also unblocked quotas so that German refugees could receive visas from consuls outside of Germany to replace prior visas granted in Germany to those who could not get out. Administrative means were also found to convert some temporary visas of refugees already in the United States into permanent quota visas. Small as the numbers were, more refugees thus found a haven in America than in any other single country. Blocked by Congress, unsuccessful in his international initiatives, Roosevelt nevertheless kept alive the ideal of asylum for the persecuted and to a degree broke the congressional monopoly on immigration policy.

American Jews viewed these actions as mere tokenism. The intelligence that came to them through their relief organizations and coreligionists abroad painted an unbelievable picture of death and destruction. By mid-1942 they knew that for every Jew that escaped the Nazis, a thousand were being annihilated. In sheer desperation, they brushed aside the anti-Semitic impulses that were thwarting massive efforts to save the refugees and appealed to the President "as the symbol of humanity's will to fight for freedom." Shortly thereafter the State Department was able to confirm what American Jews knew: that nearly 2,000,000 Jews had already died and that Hitler's "final solution" was in full swing.

On December 8, five men, representing an anguished but activist Jewish community, met with the President and delivered to him a memorandum that detailed in all of its cold horror all they had learned of the "Nazi Blueprint for Extermination." The group included Henry Monsky, Dr. Stephen S. Wise, Maurice Wertheim, Adolph Held, and Rabbi Israel Rosenberg, leaders respectively of B'nai B'rith and the Anti-Defamation League, the American Jewish Congress, the American Jewish Committee, the Jewish Labor Committee, and the Synagogue Council of America. Their urgent plea: Save the surviving Jews of Europe. American and Allied rescue operations were the immediate need. To achieve this, they offered a full catalog of proposals and ideas for action.

The President met the issue with expressions of moral indignation and a pledge that the Nazis would have to pay for their crimes against humanity after the war was won. But there was a wariness in the consideration of specifics that might have helped a rescue operation. At each step there were political and tactical war problems that inhibited action. There was always some other priority. "The mills of the Gods grind slowly," Roosevelt quoted. But human devils were operating the extermination camps of the Nazis.

In April 1943, the United States and Britain held a conference on

refugee problems in Bermuda, but it was hardly more productive than
the Evian conference had been five years earlier. The immigration
laws were held inviolate. While some minor measures were agreed
upon, any large-scale efforts were discounted. Neither government
nor the countries of the embryonic United Nations were willing to face
up to the massive task of rescue or to the awful truth of mass murder.
In August *The New York Times* jolted the country with an "extermination list" that showed 1,700,000 people killed in an organized murder
program and another 746,000 dead of starvation.

Americans could not long withstand such assaults upon their conscience. A prestigious Emergency Committee to Save the Jews of
Europe now joined the Jewish groups in pressing for legislation. On
November 9, 1943, Will Rogers, Jr., in the House and Guy M. Gillette
in the Senate offered a resolution for the establishment of a commission to undertake "the rescue of the Jewish people of Europe." For
once, massive support built up for Congressional action. Unexpectedly further support came as a reaction to testimony of Assistant
Secretary of State Breckinridge Long, who told the hearings on
November 26 that the United States had admitted 580,000 refugees
from Europe since 1933. Two weeks later, it was revealed that he had
fudged the figures and failed to differentiate between ordinary immigrants and refugees from the Nazis. This gave an exaggerated
picture of achievement. Official data showed the refugees admitted to
have numbered only 160,000 in the 1933–1943 decade.

In the meantime, the President was responding to pressure from
another direction. Secretary of the Treasury Henry Morgenthau, Jr.,
deeply disturbed by the State Department's failure to address itself to
the refugee problem wholeheartedly, ordered his own investigation
and faced Secretary of State Cordell Hull with the evidence on January
11. Bluntly titled "Acquiescence of this Government in the Murder of
Jews," the report, written by Randolph Paul, General Counsel of the
Treasury Department, charged State Department officials not only
with failing to rescue Jews from Hitler, but indeed acting to prevent
such rescue and hindering the efforts of others to do so. About Breckinridge Long, Morgenthau was scathing. (He had once told Long that
many considered him an anti-Semite.)

Accompanied by Paul and John W. Pehle, another Treasury official,
Morgenthau now went to the President. Morgenthau's passion, the
impressive indictment and data, and his associates' earnestness
moved Roosevelt immensely. They urged the State Department be

relieved of responsibility for refugee matters and that these be placed in a new War Refugee Board. Morgenthau left with the President the draft of an executive order that would create the new body. On January 22, without waiting for Congress to act on its resolution, the President signed the order with the approval of Undersecretary of State Edward R. Stettinius. The new board was empowered to inaugurate "effective measures for the rescue, transportation and maintenance and relief of the victims of enemy oppression" and to establish "havens of temporary refuge for such victims." John Pehle was named its director. Pehle tackled his job with a verve and skill that might have saved millions if the program had been set up five years earlier. But it was now past the eleventh hour; most of the 6,000,000 victims of the Holocaust had already been incinerated.

Immigration—The Road Back

In the immediate postwar period, President Harry S. Truman, hampered by the continued reluctance of Congress to address itself to the problem of concentration camp survivors, displaced persons, and refugees, followed the procedure of his predecessor and sought by executive order and administrative measures to permit the entry of some of the displaced. However, he could not overcome the basic

Roosevelt and Morgenthau.

obstacles inherent in the national origins quota system. For three years Congress held that a victorious America had no room within its borders for these victims of war and that admission of a proportion of the displaced was not a legitimate claim upon its generosity if the quota system would have to be set aside even for a brief time. However, in 1948, Congress did pass the Displaced Persons Act, providing for the admission of 400,000 DPs without regard to quota limitations for the moment, but with the proviso that those admitted would be charged against the quotas of their country of origin in future years. Thus, one half of a nation's quota could be "mortgaged." The absurdity of this provision became apparent during the three-year term of the Displaced Persons Act. Poland, for instance, because of the large number of refugees from that country, had half its annual quota of 6,488 "mortgaged" until 1993.

When the Displaced Persons Act expired in 1951, the refugee problem still pressed upon the Western World, and the need for continued efforts by the United States was apparent. Congress debated the issue for two years, but in 1953 passed the Refugee Relief Act under which 200,000 persons, mostly from behind the Iron Curtain, were admitted as nonquota immigrants in the ensuing three years. This time the "mortgaging" clause was not included, and indeed the provision in the 1948 Act was subsequently repealed, relieving the heavy burden that had been placed upon the quotas of some European nations. Before the 1953 refugee law ran out, the uprising in Hungary against the Communist regime poured a new flood of 175,000 refugees into the Free World. Despite the fact that the annual Hungarian quota was only 865, the Refugee Relief Act made it possible to admit 6,000 Hungarians before it expired at the end of 1956. But for both political and humanitarian reasons, America had to make a greater effort, though the national origins quota system once more seemed an insuperable obstacle. The sympathetic response of the American people to the anti-Communist Hungarian Freedom Fighters, encouraged the administration to seek a solution. It was found in a provision in the law which authorized the Attorney General to parole individuals into the country on a temporary basis, and 31,000 Hungarians were admitted in this manner.

The lot of the "parolees" was not a happy one. At their discretion, immigration authorities could revoke "parole," nor was there any way for the parolee to change status to that of regular immigrant. For two years they lived in a twilight zone, until special legislation made it possible for them to regularize their stay and eventually to qualify for citizenship. In such piecemeal fashion did the United States keep alive its tradition as a land of refuge for the dispossessed and the persecuted. A 1958 law gave asylum to the homeless victims of earthquakes in the Portuguese Azores Islands and to displaced Dutch from In-

The debate on the Displaced Persons Act in 1946 brought forth this comment from political cartoonist Herbert Block.

donesia. In 1962 a special law provided for several thousand refugees from Communist China in the same manner as the Hungarians had been admitted. Beyond these measures, Americans kept the faith by means of thousands of private immigration bills on behalf of individual immigrants and immigrant families. In the Eighty-seventh Congress alone, 3,500 such bills were introduced, representing about half the total legislative load. But the element in the basic immigration law—the national origins quota system that made all this legislative activity necessary—remained intact.

In these years of desperate effort to help with recurring refugee problems, there was only grudging acquiescence by Congress which in 1952 replaced the basic immigration law of 1924 with the McCarran—Walter Act. It was a long-needed recodification, but it did nothing to reform the racist and restrictionist policies. President Truman vetoed the measure with the comment that "the idea behind [the] discriminatory policy was, to put it baldly, that Americans with English or Irish names were better people and better citizens than Americans with Italian or Greek or Polish names. . . . Such a concept is utterly unworthy of our tradition and our ideals." Truman's veto was overriden, but the long trek back to a democratic, if not unrestricted immigration policy, was on its way. In fact, the McCarran—Walter Act had taken one small step toward the President's position and reversal of the basic racist policy. It established token quotas for all the countries of the Orient which had been subject to complete exclusion. The total quota for all of the nations in the so-called Asia—Pacific Triangle was 2,000. At the same time, however, it introduced a new provision, racist in effect, that placed all persons with even one Asian parent, no matter where actually born, under the quota of that parent's native land.

By the mid-1950s, the mantle of leadership for liberalizing the immigration law, worn so long by Senator Herbert H. Lehman, had fallen to Senator John F. Kennedy. In A Nation of Immigrants, a monograph written for the Anti-Defamation League in 1958, Senator Kennedy pointed out that "despite the heated arguments" the issue between the most liberal and the most conservative positions on immigration policy was not whether there should be restricted or unrestricted immigration, but whether the nation could in all good conscience continue to pursue the discriminatory, racist policy inherent in the national origins quota system.

On July 23, 1963, Kennedy, now President of the United States, repeated the views he expressed in *A Nation of Immigrants* in a special message to Congress. He called for elimination of the national origins quota system in stages over a five-year period, because it would serve "the national interest and reflect...the principles of equality and human dignity to which our nation subscribes." He did not live to see the McCarran–Walter Act replaced, but President Lyndon Johnson picked up where Kennedy had left off and endorsed his proposal in a State of the Union message to the Eighty-eighth Congress in 1964. It now became formalized in a bill in the House sponsored by Con-

Senator Pat McCarran–The McCarran-Walter Act of 1952 brought about a much needed recodification of immigration laws, but preserved the national origins quota system.

A NATION OF IMMIGRANTS

ILLUSTRATED

JOHN F. KENNEDY

INTRODUCTION BY ROBERT F. KENNEDY

HARPER TORCHBOOKS

TB 1118

gressman Emanuel Celler of New York and in the Senate by Senator Philip A. Hart of Michigan. Action on the Johnson proposals was frustrated by the opposition of Congressman Michael A. Feighan of Ohio, chairman of the House Subcommittee on Immigration, who would agree to only minor changes. The bill died with the adjournment of the Eighty-eighth Congress. In the Senate, Senator James Eastland of Mississippi, who also opposed any significant changes, ceded the chairmanship of the Immigration and Naturalization Subcommittee to Senator Edward Kennedy. Hearings were begun, but lapsed as the Senate addressed itself to debate and passage of the Civil Rights Act of 1964, which preceded it on the legislative calendar.

Nevertheless, the battle had been joined, and the nation was soon treated to what amounted to a replay of the debates and the lobbying that led to the adoption of the restrictive Immigration Acts of 1921 and 1924. Many of the old arguments, most of the old fears, nearly all of the old hopes were again heard in Congress, in the press, and in public meetings. Only the cast of characters had changed, not the points of view. Old vinegar was poured from new bottles. But the weight of public opinion had shifted, and so had the comparative strength of the contending forces. Indicative of the change was the editorial position taken by the *Saturday Evening Post*. In 1920 the *Post* had been in the forefront of those who feared the country would be swamped with undesirables unless the law raised restrictions against non-Nordics. In its issue of February 15, 1964, it called for a new immigration "formula...based on need rather than on prejudices in favor of Northern European nations....Our immigration laws are riddled with hypocrisy."

When Congress reconvened on January 13, 1965, President Johnson once more urged immigration reform: "Four Presidents have called attention to serious defects in this legislation. Action is long overdue..." Congressman Celler and Senator Hart reintroduced the administration bill promptly and hearings began within weeks. The President sent his principal cabinet secretaries to the Hill to testify.

Secretary of State Dean Rusk stressed the burden that the racist factors in the law placed on the conduct of foreign relations. "It is the national origins principle rather than the actual immigration which is

(Left) *"A Nation of Immigrants"—President Kennedy set forth his argument against the quota system in this monograph written while in the Senate.*

singled out by our critics," he told the Senate Subcommittee on Immigration. "It makes it more difficult... to establish the good relations which our national interest requires." He cited the record of immigration from the so-called Asia–Pacific Triangle as "far better than a reading of the law would lead one to expect" but it was the racism of the law with which the nation was tarred. A similar situation obtained for the "Good Neighbor" policy in Latin America.

"As a leader in the struggle for freedom we are expected to exemplify all that freedom means... our blemishes delight our enemies and dismay our friends," he said. "What we are asking in effect is that we bring the theory of our law in line with our practice in the postwar period."

A similar message came from Attorney General Nicholas deB. Katzenbach. He told the Senate subcommittee: "There is urgency in terms of our self-interest abroad... the national origins quota system harms the United States... it creates an image of hypocrisy which can be exploited by those who seek to discredit our professions of democracy." And then, turning inward, he commented: "I do not know how any American can fail to be offended by a system which presumes that some people are inferior to others solely because of their birthplace."

The major groups concerned with immigration pressed their view on Congress. This time, however, the opponents of the national origins quota system proved better organized than its defenders. It soon became evident how the wind was blowing. On February 4, Congressman Feighan, who had blocked action the prior year, spoke before the American Coalition of Patriotic Societies, arch-defenders of Nordic primacy, and called for repeal of the national origins quota system. Though hearings in neither chamber had as yet begun, the speech signaled that there was going to be no bitter-end fight. Feighan had "counted the votes" and come up with the answer. His strength as chairman of the Immigration Subcommittee had been undermined when the House leadership enlarged the committee's membership to ensure a majority for reform. He had experienced some gentle Presidential arm-twisting, and he had heard from his home district. It did not favor his stand. Celler, as sponsor of the bill and chairman of the Judiciary Committee, had been the victor in the infighting.

When the hearings opened, however, the opponents of reform pressed their case—often in terms and phrases that had become classic. Senator A. Willis Robertson of Virginia told his colleagues that he could not agree that the immigration law was "incompatible with our

American tradition." Our basic tradition, he said, was Nordic and restrictive, and that tradition had been broken "by some ruthless industrial magnates who brought in thousands of workers from southern Europe...to break the back of a young organized labor movement." Labor leaders who had long ago shifted sides must have listened embarrassedly as Robertson declared that the McCarran—Walter Act was passed to protect organized labor and to preserve "the basic characteristics of our nation." The Senate's self-proclaimed old country lawyer, Sam Ervin of North Carolina, found that the national origins quota system "is like a mirror reflecting the United States" and he liked what he saw. The McCarran—Walter Act, he believed, kept "immigration problems beyond the reach of politicians and pressure groups" and "maintains the historic population pattern of the United States."

The fear of "politicians" was expressed over and over again during the debates by the congressional politicians who opposed reform and distrusted the executive branch which would have greater control under the terms of the Administration's bill. The fears were echoed by spokesmen of the American Coalition of Patriotic Societies, the Daughters of the American Revolution, the major veterans organizations, the extremist Liberty Lobby, and the traditional anti-immigration groups. The coalition's spokesman warned against "precipitate action to rush through...ill-considered...legislation" and expressed touching concern for those "nations whose skilled elite would be decimated" because the proposed law would favor the entry of trained workers. But throughout the hearings the principal concern expressed by opponents of reform—as stated succinctly by the president of the DAR—was to preserve this country's "culture...racial complex, and likely even language." The argument always came back to the racial issue.

For once the proponents of immigration reform were better organized than the opposition. They had worked persistently and effectively since the passage of the McCarran—Walter Act in 1952. Their goals were precise and tenable: an end to the racist national origins principle, more humane procedural practices, and re-establishment of the nation's ability to act in emergency situations and in its tradition of asylum for the oppressed. Beyond this, there was the recognition that the era of unrestrained immigration was long past. In 1960 some 100 organizations came together in a coordinating body; the American Immigration and Citizenship Conference. The membership ran the gamut from the major religious and nationality groups to welfare, civic, and public affairs agencies. Prominently represented were the labor unions, once among the most hostile to immigration. Together these groups mounted a massive educational and political action campaign for the Kennedy and Johnson initiatives.

On another level, some of the nation's best-known public figures in 1965 formed the National Committee for Immigration Reform to back the Administration bill. The bipartisan support of reform was thus reinforced by such members of the committee as Presidents Truman and Eisenhower. A pale imitation of the old Immigration Restriction League called the American Committee on Immigration Policies entered the lists in opposition, but could not match the effectiveness of the National Committee.

The floor fight for reform in the House was led by Congressman Celler, a veteran of the immigration legislative wars since 1924. Seventy-five congressmen participated in the debates. The issue was never in doubt; the opposition had bargained and won amelioration of what they felt to be excessive power placed in the executive branch. This had enabled Chairman Feighan with the support of the Republican floor manager, Congressman Arch A. Moore, Jr., of West Virginia, to present his report as a bipartisan agreement. The floor discussions centered on an effort to place a limit on Western Hemisphere immigration, opposed by the Administration as damaging to the Latin American "Good Neighbor" policy. The argument held and on August 25, 1965, the House passed the total measure, 318 to 95 with 19 abstentions, eliminating the national origins quota system.

The Senate subcommittee adopted the House measure and reported it to the full Senate with some amendments, principally a ceiling of 120,000 for Western Hemisphere immigrants pressed by Senator Sam J. Ervin. The Senate debate, opened by Chairman Edward M. Kennedy, turned into a determined effort by Southern senators to prevent change, maintain and even strengthen restrictions and preserve the racist policies of the past. The names so prominent in the civil rights debates of the time led the opposition: Senators James O. Eastland, John L. McClellan and Ervin, Allen J. Ellender, John G. Tower and Strom Thurmond. Senator Kennedy argued the deficiencies of existing law, the need to adopt emergency legislation ten times in a fourteen-year period and the burdening of Congress with thousands of private bills. Two thirds of all immigrants had entered the country under these measures between 1952 and 1965 while half the authorized quotas went unused. What better evidence that reform was needed? Support came not only from Northern Democrats but Republican conservatives such as Senator Everett Dirksen of Illinois who saw in such patchwork legislation the failure of the existing policy. On September 17 the Senate voted 76 to 18—all the nays were from the South—to adopt the House bill as amended. In the subsequent House–Senate conference the amendments were retained. The House adopted the conference report 320 to 69, and the Senate by voice vote.

"After forty years, we have returned to first principles," Senator Kennedy exulted. "Immigration, more than anything else, has supplied America with the human strength that is the core of its greatness." And one had only to look around the Senate chamber itself to see the great variety of ethnic and racial strains that contributed to that greatness. The new measure struck down the national origins quota and the Asia–Pacific Triangle provision, raised annual immigration to 350,000, and favored those with relatives in the country, the skilled and the educated. At the same time, it preserved the tradition of asylum by providing a capability for emergency action in aid of the oppressed and the persecuted.

No group in the land greeted the enactment of the Immigration and Naturalization Act of 1965 with a greater sense of elation than American Jews. In the final drive to reform the immigration procedures and policies, their self-interest was minimal, but their efforts were undiminished. There were no longer great numbers of their European coreligionists clamoring at the gates which had remained so tightly shut in the critical 1930's and 1940's. Jewish immigrants in the years that were to follow could only be limited in number.

The determination with which Jews had continued to work for reform was grounded in principle. If there was self-interest, it lay in the belief that any national policy which enshrined racism in law undermined their status—as well as the status of other Americans. They fought the national origins quota system because they believed it did just that and because they saw in it a denial of the humane and democratic ideals that showed America at its best. In Congress, through all the years when the immigration battles were being fought, the names of Jewish legislators were in the forefront of the liberal forces: from Adolph Sabath to Samuel Dickstein and Emanuel Celler in the House and from Herbert H. Lehman to Jacob Javits in the Senate. Each in his time was a leader of the Anti-Defamation League and of major organizations concerned with democratic development.

In the final effort, these Jewish agencies and those concerned with service to immigrants, which had long worked cooperatively, joined in the American Immigration and Citizenship Conference. They included the League, the American Jewish Committee, the American Jewish Congress, and that guardian angel of Jewish immigrants, the United Hias Service (known through most of its long history as the Hebrew Immigrant Aid and Sheltering Society).

President Johnson's signing of the Immigration Act of 1965 became a very special occasion. The usual ceremonies were moved from the White House to Liberty Island in New York harbor. There, on October 3, with Miss Liberty looming over him, President Johnson spoke to the nation and to an assembly of those who had fought so long and so hard for the measure—leaders of the immigrant groups and the major public affairs organizations, the men who had steered it through Congress, Senator Kennedy, Congressman Celler and their colleagues, members of his cabinet who were to administer it, and very special guests, such as Mrs. Herbert H. Lehman.

This law, he said, "repairs a deep and painful flaw in the fabric of American justice. It corrects a cruel and enduring wrong in the conduct of the American nation. It will make us truer to ourselves as a country and a people..."

He then affixed his signature to the document which returned the nation to its first principles.

(Left) *President Lyndon B. Johnson, leaving Liberty Island in New York harbor after signing Immigration Act of 1965. A "deep and painful flaw" had been repaired.*

SEVEN

A Time to Begin

As we have seen, the process of social reconciliation which Franklin D. Roosevelt set in motion at the beginning of his Administration slowly ground to a halt in the war years. The xenophobic impulses, ever-present in the nation, expended themselves on the Nisei and the Negroes, Catholics, and Jews, labor leaders and radicals; almost everyone who could be considered different or nonconformist.

In the aftermath of victory over Axis powers, the siege spirit that had enveloped the nation dropped away. In its place came a renewed dedication to equality. The high levels of anti-Semitic feeling had receded. Concern with racial justice stirred men and women who for half a decade had been preoccupied with the deadly conflict for survival. All of their pent-up desires for social improvement, suppressed by the war, now began to find expression. The Great Leader was gone but not his dream or the political coalition he had forged. His heirs—President Truman and such men as Senator Hubert H. Humphrey and Senator Herbert H. Lehman—came to seats of power with a depth of commitment that exceeded even that of the Old Master.

The war had raised national consciousness of race problems to a global level. The impact of genocide, the sudden realization that race was a basic element of colonialism, the salience of racial antagonisms on the home front stimulated thought and action as never before—at the grass roots as well as among committed leadership. The euphemism "human relations," first used by activists and sociologists to describe ethnic and race problems, now tripped knowingly from the tongues of writers and politicians, movie-makers, reformers and churchmen. The late 1940's saw the formation of governmental, state and city human relations councils and citizens "unity" committees throughout the country. Human relations education projects burgeoned in colleges and lower schools everywhere. Efforts to pass improved civil rights legislation by state governments began to achieve successes.

The nation's mass media also began to focus on human relations problems as they sensed the public interest. Catching the spirit of the hour, Hollywood turned out a whole cycle of films attacking prejudice—films such as *Gentleman's Agreement, Crossfire, Intruder in the Dust,* and others with at least a "human relations" incident or two as a subplot to the main story. In one five-month period in 1947, nationally circulated magazines injected their readership of 16,000,000 with a massive dose of "human relations." *Collier's* published "The Outcasts" by B. J. Chute, an indictment of restrictive convenants in real estate, telling what happened when a Jewish family attempted to move into an "exclusive community." The *Saturday Evening Post* told of "The Color Line in Medicine" in an article by Henry and Katherine Pringle. *Harper's Magazine* discussed the progress made against employment discrimination in New York, New Jersey, Connecticut, and Massachusetts where Fair Employment Practices Commissions had been established. Author Irwin Ross found them effective. In *Better Homes and Gardens,* Hodding Carter, the liberal voice of Southern journalism, told "How to Stop Hatemongers in Your Town." And in a seven-part series in the *New Republic,* Bruce Bliven, its editor, discussed the causes, manifestations, and possible remedies of anti-Semitism.

Simultaneously, *Fortune Magazine* published the results of Elmo Roper's current survey of racial and religious intolerance. It took a discerning optimist to find encouragement in Roper's statistics, for they showed the spirit of prejudice in the land to be pervasive. In no category did the unprejudiced make up a majority—whether that category related to Jews or Catholics. Yet, men such as Benjamin R. Epstein, who had succeeded Richard E. Gutstadt as national director of the Anti-Defamation League, looking toward the new day to come, could take heart that only 21 percent now felt that Jews had too much political power and 36 percent that they had too much economic power. In the early war years, as has been noted, the figures in both

categories had been more than 50 percent. But the instincts of knowledgeable men are at times sounder than statistics. In the years that
followed, the prejudicial attitudes continued to drop.

The seeds of that progress were discernible in one fact brought out
by the Roper figures: 28 percent of the population seemed to take the
view that racial and religious minorities were badly treated, and
22,000,000 adults thus formed the base upon which a strong national
leadership might build the effort to end discrimination in practice and
in law. It was not the work of a day, but the time to begin seemed to
have arrived.

Indeed, the process had begun and was gathering momentum with
every passing day and month. A new chemistry had developed. Even
in retrospect, it is difficult to sort out the catalytic elements; nor is it
important to determine who was stimulating the forward movement.
It is enough to recognize that the need to improve the quality of
human relations in the nation was an idea whose time had come. Men
and women and organized groups seeking to end discrimination and
to dispel prejudice were working on government, and in turn government leadership was actively pushing for reform and to give substance to the ideal of equality of opportunity.

*President Harry S. Truman receives from Chairman C. E. Wilson a report
of the President's Committee on Civil Rights as several members of the Committee
attend a presentation ceremony at the White House on October 29, 1947.*

Little more than a year after victory over Japan, President Truman made an all-important move. He established the President's Committee on Civil Rights and a Commission on Higher Education. They issued their reports as 1947 came to a close. In February, President Truman, acting on the Civil Rights Committee's recommendations, asked Congress to establish a U.S. Commission on Civil Rights, a joint congressional committee on civil rights, and a Civil Rights Division in the Justice Department. These were the structural elements of a ten-point program urged upon Congress by the President to eliminate discrimination in employment and education, end the use of poll taxes to limit voting, and suppress lynching. By executive order, Truman made discrimination in employment by government agencies unlawful and moved to end segregation in the armed forces.

The legislative process, especially on matters where a national concensus is yet to be clearly defined, moves slowly. That is equally true of judicial procedures. But in the spring of 1948, the United States Supreme Court gave civil rights advocates and the Administration a major victory in an area of special concern to Jews.

On May 3, the Court ruled 6-0 that the powers of neither state nor Federal Courts may be invoked to enforce restrictive real estate covenants limiting the sale or occupancy of houses on the basis of race or religion. The decision came on review of four cases brought on behalf of Negro complainants that had been moving slowly through the judicial process for many months. It was a major victory for civil rights forces, which together with government had been supportive of the plaintiffs. As so often, the Supreme Court was faced with both constitutional issues and issues of public policy. On the constitutional level, Chief Justice Vinson wrote that the Fourteenth Amendment "erects no shield against merely private conduct, however discriminatory or wrongful" but neither could the purposes of such conduct be "secured... by judicial enforcement by State courts" which the states had been doing. The same reasoning was applied to Federal court enforcement of restrictive covenants.

The Justice Department brief not only came to the same conclusion on the constitutional issues but argued that public policy which forbade discriminatory legislation should apply equally to the courts in the enforcement of discriminatory "private contracts." Though the cases before the Supreme Court were argued on racial grounds, the Justice Department ruled at the conclusion that the Court's decisions were "applicable with equal force to similar agreements based on creed."

The Anti-Defamation League, which, as a number of other Jewish, civil rights and civil liberties organizations, had filed "friend of the court" briefs in the cases, realistically saw the decision as merely the removal of a legal prop for discrimination and not as the elimination of such bias. The victory was one of principle—the principle that the power of government could not be invoked to protect bigotry. It was the obverse side of the defeat suffered when national origins quotas had been legislatively installed to discriminate on a racist basis in the admission of new immigrants. In a sense it was a first tentative step in a judicial revolution that reached a peak with the *Brown* and other school cases in 1954.

Weakened in their legal enforcement status, restrictive covenants, since they had not been outlawed, yet remained as instruments for inhibiting upward mobility and maintaining a pattern of social discrimination against Jews. For the racial minorities the issue was decent housing; for Jews the issue was the right of place in the mainstream of American life. Greeted with enthusiasm by the now-considerable segment of American life concerned with bettering human relations, there was at the same time a panicked reaction to the court ruling among real estate interests and in many cities, towns, and communities throughout the country. On the hysterical fringes, acts of violence were threatened and indeed took place chiefly against Negroes or those selling homes to Negroes. In many an "exclusive" community "gentlemen's agreements" and other collusive devices were proposed, experimented with, and installed to prevent the sale of property to Jews and "non-Caucasians." Real estate brokers reinforced the code of ethics of the National Association of Real Estate Boards:

"Realtors should never be instrumental in introducing into a neighborhood...members of any race or nationality...whose presence will be clearly detrimental to property values."

New organizations sprang up in many parts of the country to thwart the Supreme Court decision. Signs such as "this is a Gentile community" began to pop up here and there and the offices of the League as widely spaced as New England, Chicago and Los Angeles, were deluged during the second half of 1948 with complaints of housing and real estate discrimination. The boldest step was taken by the Los Angeles Real Estate Board which proposed a policy of apartheid by sponsoring an amendment to the Constitution that would "retroactively validate and confer upon the courts...power to enforce...instruments restricting the ownership or occupancy of real property to Caucasians or Negroes, respectively." In Denver, realtors attempted to promote such separation by persuasion, but the Denver Unity Council had a different idea and persuaded the City Council to demand a clear statement of policy on restrictive covenants before granting the privilege of establishing new residential subdivisions.

There was a new ferment in the nation. While the movement was not always forward, the logjam of discriminatory patterns was breaking up, and there was promise in the air. For men who had pioneered the field of human relations in hope that it would also help in ameliorating some of the historic problems of anti-Semitism, it was a time for optimism. The leaders of the Anti-Defamation League met in Los Angeles that May of 1948 to mark the organization's thirty-fifth anniversary. They planned to take note of the work of the President's Committee on Civil Rights and to listen to Charles E. Wilson, its chairman; to review all of the new and encouraging developments already referred to; to honor Mrs. Eleanor Roosevelt and her work with the United Nations Commission for Human Rights. And as the celebration began, word came of the Supreme Court's decision in the restrictive covenant cases. It was a heady moment; and contemplating all of the developments and all of the sudden victories, large and small, the assembled group came to the full realization that they were part of a great American movement, that indeed they were not alone, that they could join with friends and allies in the battle against bigotry.

In this atmosphere, the welcoming words of Governor Earl Warren of California, soon to become the Chief Justice of the United States presiding over the judicial revolution in civil rights, took on a depth of meaning beyond the formal:

> Because intolerance has been directed against Jews does not make it merely the problem of Jews. Whenever and wherever intolerance rears its ugly head, it is the job of all Americans—not of some Americans, but of all Americans—to suppress it.
>
> Anything which limits the opportunity for full American citizenship, because of racial origin, religious or economic status in life, is the direct denial of the principles under which this government was founded. Whenever intolerance has been manifested, it has retarded the progress of this country and diminished our standing before the people of the world.

These men had heard such words before, spoken honestly and feelingly. What was different now was the temper of the movement.

As never before, there seemed a chance of their realization.

The note sounded by Governor Warren—"you are not alone"—had special meaning to Benjamin R. Epstein, now the national director of the League. He had spent two years as an American honor student at the University of Berlin in the 1930's and watched the Nazis achieve power. He had learned what it meant "to be alone."

"The fight against anti-Semitism," he said in his annual report, "is happily past the stage of special pleading, and is recognized as part of the whole problem of prejudice and discrimination affecting not only Jews but the entire American fabric." In the vastness of America, there were allies to be found; there was a great and growing coalition of common concern for fulfillment of the American promise. "The soundest method for combating anti-Semitism," Epstein urged, "is to fight for a healthy society, for those specific issues that others as well as we need to achieve equality of opportunity."

Governor Earl Warren in 1948–"You are not alone."

There was ample evidence out of the American past that Jews had the support of friends and allies in the fight on anti-Semitism. But the ambiance now seemed changed; the realization of mutuality of interest was changing; the intensity of concern and hope of success was growing. Ever-larger numbers of Jews found they were swimming in the mainstream. Yet, there was also continuing evidence of anti-Jewish prejudice and discrimination, banal and unyielding in character, nauseating in the constant, unimaginative repetition of small, hurtful incidents, unsettling in their threatening hostility.

Justice Meier Steinbrink, the national chairman of the League, took cognizance of all this on that spring day in Los Angeles:

> We must not despair when our designs for democratic living are not affected at the snap of a finger or in the course of a week or the course of a year. We may lose many battles but, on examination of history, Americans find they have won the wars for freedom.... We must put teeth into the whole program...that we still have a great distance to travel should discourage none of us for we have already come a long way—perhaps a longer way—than we have still to go.

Ever-larger numbers were caught up in the new concerns for past failures in making the American promise of equal opportunity an American reality. The reports on civil rights and higher education to the President caught the imagination. They pricked the consciences of those in the seats of power and gave encouragement to those long aware of the problems of bigotry. Perhaps the time had come when the nation was at last prepared to meet those problems head on. The "best people" were beginning to talk about the evils of prejudice, in an abstract way, perhaps never applying the transgressions to themselves. But the very talk was having the effect of making bigotry unfashionable.

Everyone was now reading thoughtful little articles in the popular magazines. The editor of *Parents' Magazine* advised her million readers to look upon the Civil Rights Committee report "as a refresher course in the ideals, principles and goals of this democracy of ours." *Seventeen* magazine, addressing itself directly to the young, urged them "to get together and talk over day-to-day things you teenage Americans can do to fight prejudice and strengthen the rights of all people in your communities."

The major mass-circulation magazines, which had begun to focus on the subject in 1947, now found they had touched a responsive chord and pressed on. *Collier's* published the views of Charles

Luckman, president of Lever Brothers Co., that it was to the interest of business to be "a fighting leader in the most liberal of democratic causes—the preservation of our Bill of Rights." In the same magazine, writer Lester Velie warned of the resurgence of the Ku Klux Klan in the South. The ladies' magazines had already staked out the field. *Woman's Home Companion* told what was being accomplished by housewives determined "to rub out the patterns of hate in American life" in an article by Helen Huntington Smith, and *Ladies' Home Journal* introduced America to the home life of a noted rabbi, Dr. Joshua Loth Liebman of Boston, in an article by David Davidson and Hilde Abel. The *Saturday Evening Post* told the story of American war hero Colonel David (Mickey) Marcus, who had died in Israel's War for Independence. And *Reader's Digest* reproduced some of these pieces in its own pages.

If the average American missed the point because he did not read the popular magazines, he got the message in the daily press and over the radio. During 1948, the National Broadcasting Company aired eleven civil rights programs on the "Chicago Round Table." The American Broadcasting Company devoted two broadcasts of its prestigious "America's Town Meeting of the Air" to civil rights, and Mutual presented four programs of dramatic readings from the report of the President's Committee. The Columbia Broadcasting System did a special program, "Liberty Road." Syndicated series, such as "Lest We Forget," produced by the Institute for Democratic Education and the Anti-Defamation League, were aired throughout the year over 500 stations.

While some Americans were reading, listening, and discussing, others were acting. The legislature in New York passed the first state fair educational act prohibiting racial and religious discrimination in higher education. It was quickly signed into law by Governor Thomas E. Dewey. Massachusetts made discrimination illegal in publicly supported housing. Philadelphia, impatient with slow state action, passed a fair employment practices ordinance and Phoenix, Arizona, did as much for public jobs and contractors working for the city.

Church groups rose to the new challenges all through the nation. Archbishop Cushing of Boston told his flock that he found the number of prejudiced people "staggering" and admonished Catholics that "no true Christian could support" such bigotry. The Federal Council of the Churches of Christ, Protestantism's central body, adopted the strongest human rights plank in its history, endorsing the President's program and pledging to work for a "non-segregated church ... and society." One after another, church groups, large and small, fell into line in support of civil rights reform and more specifically the President's program. In the South a regional meeting on civil rights was sponsored by the Southern Regional Conference in February, followed during the year by 47 similar local conferences probing and discussing the new drive for change in race relations.

Finally came the great political debate during the Presidential election. Both parties had adopted civil rights planks, but with the Dixiecrat secession, loss of the Solid South to the Democrats and the defeat of President Truman were freely predicted. But it didn't happen that way. Mr. Truman was returned to office, and despite his unequivocal civil rights position, the Dixiecrats drew only 1,000,000 popular votes.

The College Quota—Revisited

In the glow and ferment of 1948, it seemed appropriate once more to address the problem of the college quota system. Since the 1920's, its insidious effects had spread through the far reaches of the nation's institutions of higher education, unacknowledged, and indeed often denied, by the very college administrators who made use of the quota technique.

Now, however, denial had become a little more difficult and a great deal more embarrassing; the President's Commission on Higher Education had reported that discrimination in college admission because of a candidate's race or creed was creating "serious inequalities in the opportunities for higher education." It found that Jewish students "do not have an equal opportunity" in the choice of schools or fields of advanced study. "The obstacles created... are tacit or overt quota systems," it declared and cited the decrease in the number of Jewish students in professional schools. It found indecent the many ways in which the colleges anxiously sought "to ascertain the racial origins, religion and color of the various applicants for a purpose other than judging their qualifications for admission."

For American Jews, no pattern of discrimination was more emotionally charged than the college quota system. They could and did embrace fervently the findings and program of the President's Committee on Civil Rights, but the report of the Commission on Higher Education evoked a response that welled up out of a quarter century of frustration with a problem they believed went to the very core of their existence as Americans.

The origins of the college quota system in the anti-immigrant, anti-Semitic attitudes, class prejudices and elitist notions of the 1920's have already been examined in prior pages. In the ensuing quarter century, as some of these factors receded and changed, the quota system did not. By 1948 it had become standard operating procedure for elitist schools and freshwater colleges alike to invoke the privilege of discrimination. No school would ever willingly admit it was discriminatory, but nonetheless, the quota procedure became the most widely known secret in the educational field. Off the record, a college admissions officer might offer the opinion that another school was indeed discriminating—but then quickly say he could not prove it. The compliment would be returned by the other school. Like country clubs, many a second-rate college would seek to bolster its prestige by becoming exclusionary. Some would stress their regional character, others their social homogeneity. Major universities would cite their national scope and stress their search for students representing a cross-section of the country. But behind the special claims and the asserted goals lurked the demon of prejudice. The Commission's report, "Higher Education for American Democracy," knocked the props from under the deception, recommending that, as a start, colleges remove "from application forms all questions pertaining to religion, color and national or racial origin" as irrelevant factors in judging a candidate for admission.

In the summer of 1948, the Anti-Defamation League conducted its own survey to determine whether the colleges had been responsive to the commission's recommendations made eight months previously. Applications for admission were made to 541 liberal arts colleges by "counterpart" Jewish and non-Jewish students. Application blanks were received from 450 of these schools. Approximately 10 percent responded to applicants with obviously Jewish names quite differently from those with non-Jewish names: sending different application blanks, suggesting that application be made at a later date or discouraging further efforts to apply, often citing "overcrowded conditions," lack of housing and similar problems at the same time that the non-Jewish "counterpart" was welcomed and urged to pursue his efforts to enter.

If the approach of this 10 percent sector left the Jewish student applicant with no illusions, the replies from the colleges which did send application forms revealed that their responses to the recommendations of the Commission on Higher Education had been negligible. Of the 450 schools, 93 percent asked for information that could have no reasonable relationship to the selection of competent students. Their application papers asked 2,573 potentially discriminatory questions, or an average of 5.7 per school.

The effort to determine whether an applicant was Jewish was persistent. The questions for which "Hebrew" was listed as an answer included religion, race, nationality, and "language spoken at home." If somehow these would not ferret out the fact, there was the request for a photograph, religion of parents, inquiries into change of name, name of pastor, church "preference," church membership, and place of birth and citizenship. Colleges in the Midwest were most persistent in seeking such information, asking 43.8 percent of the discriminatory questions in the survey. The Farwest asked the fewest number—13.9 percent, the Northeast 23.8 percent and the South, where the pattern of black segregation in education was almost complete, found it met its needs with fewer inquiries—18.5 percent in this survey.

Because of the almost universal concern shown by colleges with the religious and ethnic origins of their entering students, the League turned to Elmor Roper to poll the reactions of parents. In September the Roper pollsters asked a "stratified" sampling of parents their preferences. Two out of three (62.5 percent) preferred the "college which admits the best students who apply, whether they are Jews or not." A preference was shown by 15.3 percent for schools that barred Jews and 13.4 percent said they would choose a school that admitted a proportionate number of Jews or only outstanding Jewish students. About 9 percent "didn't know" or gave no answer. Thus it seemed that parents, a year after the issuance of the Presidential Commission's report, had advanced further along the parth of fair educational practices than college administrations. A fascinating side note was the fact that in the South, where the fewest discriminatory questions were put by colleges to applicants, 21 percent of the parents said they preferred schools which admitted no Jews, thus skewing the national average. On a sectional basis, 64.2 percent in the Northeast, 66.2 percent in the Midwest and 68.7 percent in the Farwest expressed themselves as unconcerned with the number of Jews as long as a college chose its students from among the best available.

Cracking the Quota

The accumulating evidence of discrimination weighed heavily on the leadership of American higher education. The continued denials of so many schools that they operated under a discriminatory quota system were wearing thin. In the American Council on Education, principal depository of the aspirations and ideals of the nation's educators, a leadership group examined the possibility of an internal movement to eliminate the quota system. The motive power behind such an effort would have to be a self-study which would either corroborate or disprove the evidence brought to bear by government and other researchers.

Recognizing the values that would flow from an effort at house-cleaning by educators themselves, the Anti-Defamation League and the Vocational Guidance Bureau of B'nai B'rith offered a grant to the council to finance its own study of "factors affecting the admission of high school seniors into colleges." To carry out the project, the council retained the Roper organization to find not what would happen, but what actually *did* happen to the entry class of 1947. Neither the opinions of college admisssions officers nor high school principals was sought; nor the views of the students themselves or their parents. The survey was grounded in the facts: who got into college and who did not, and what were the determining factors.

The Roper survey was based on a national sample of 10,000 high school seniors and a second sampling of 5,000 students from large cities. Approximately a third of the national sample applied and expected to enroll in college if admitted. The interest in higher education, the survey showed, was strongest among Jews: 68 percent of them applied for college admission as compared to 35 percent among Protestants and 25 percent among Catholics. Yet only 69 percent of the Jews seeking to enter college rated their chances of admission as good, while 73 percent of the Catholics and 82 percent of the Protestants looked ahead confidently. The pessimists among the applicants bolstered their chances for admission by avoiding application to their real first-choice colleges—if these had a record of discrimination—and by making multiple applications to other schools.

Ultimately, 88 percent of the Protestant, 87 percent of the Jewish, and 81 percent of the Catholic students gained admission to college. But the story was quite different in the matter of choice. Among Protestants, 82 percent were accepted by their preferred schools, Catholics 71 percent, and Jews 63 percent. In the Northeastern sector of the country, where the Jewish population was heavily concentrated, the Jewish student acceptance rate by the schools of first choice dwindled to 50 percent, and they often found their opportunities limited to state universities and city colleges. The fact that Jewish students overcame the obstacles placed in their path, the report noted, was entirely due to their greater motivation for education. If the Jewish applicant could not get the college of his choice, he settled for what he could get. He played "it safe by applying to several colleges ... in the Northeast Jews filed an average of 2.4 application as against 1.7 for Protestants and 1.6 for Catholics."

Roper further reported that the chief sufferers of discrimination were the brightest and the best and was "especially strong against Jewish first and second quintile seniors... the more favorably circumstanced socio-economically [the student] is, the more discrimination there was against him." No doubt this was caused by the fact that the better students reached for the superior schools. When the statistics were read on the basis of number of applications rather than applicants, the ratio of Jewish acceptances plummeted further. Of the applications filed by Protestants, 77 percent were accepted. Among Catholics 67 percent of the applications were acted upon favorably, and among Jews 57 percent. Since each college acted only on the applications before it, these figures were truer indicators of the bias practiced in 1947 than the ultimate admissions figure.

The Roper survey set the stage for the American Council on Education's effort to end the practices of the quota system. The Council now possessed the ammunition—its own irrefutable data—with which to breach the walls of silence and denial that had met critics of quota practices since the 1920's. For six months after publication of the Roper report, the council planned a campaign that might ultimately achieve the end of religious and racial, as well as economic barriers to higher education "without the coercion of legislation." It turned to the Anti-Defamation League for its experience in the development of action programs.

On November 4 and 5, 1949, in Chicago, the first step in that program was taken: a jointly sponsored "national educators conference on discrimination in college admissions." An observer at that unprecedented event had to be struck by the fervent spirit that permeated the proceedings—in the official addresses, in the testimony from participants, in the candor of admission of past sins, in the expressions of relief that, at last, an intolerable wrong was to be righted. Even the presentation of the clinical data assumed the color of moral imperative.

The choice of Chicago as the site for the historic meeting was in a sense a tribute to Dr. Andrew C. Ivy, vice-president of the University of Illinois and dean of its medical school, who had for years been the goad and the conscience of the educational world on the subject of unwarranted discrimination. Despite his distinguished titles and rank in the world of education Dr. Ivy belied his name, at least to the degree that he was no product of an "ivy-clad" college. He got his education the hard way—part-time study, interrupted courses, earning his way as he went.

That kind of experience molds a man either into a "rugged individualist" or a moralist. In appearance and character, Andrew Ivy was more than a little of both. For him, at least, the dream of a university education came true. Now he wanted the dream to come true for every youth capable of sharing it.

He sounded the keynote of the conference, speaking without oratorical flourish to 100-odd colleagues: university presidents, college deans and registrars, heads of educational organizations and government agencies. His iron-gray hair and austere appearance accented the moralistic note of his message.

Discriminating against deserving students who wanted to get into college was evil, he said. It caused great damage to the United States. It violated the democratic credos which educators are presumed to hold sacred... the Declaration of Independence and the Bill of Rights... the

Crack-the-quota—A Chicago educators' conference in 1949 discussed college admissions discrimination. From left, Professor Samuel Nerlove, University of Chicago economist, Dr. Robert Hutchins, Richard Gutstadt, League Director, and Dr. Kenneth D. Benne, University of Illinois educator.

Golden Rule . . . Judeo-Christian tradition . . . Dr. Ivy paused for a moment and his austerity was softened by a characteristic delayed-reaction smile. The practical man had come to the surface:

> It should not be forgotten that a person can run for public office or for a position of leadership in a labor or farm organization regardless of his race, religion or economic status. No quota system applies to candidates for public office. It would seem essential . . . that our potential lawmakers be provided . . . higher education on a non-quota basis. Equality of educational opportunity [is] the only effective answer to totalitarian ideologies.

The special significance of Dr. Ivy's message lay more in his audience than in his words. Others had made similar comments, equally valid, often more eloquent. But no one had ever had the opportunity to tell it to a cooperative assembly of leading college officials who were directly concerned with the admissions practices of their schools. The presence of these men was tacit admission that enough evidence had been brought to bear to show that religious and racial barriers to higher education did exist . . . and that the time had come for those more directly concerned with school administration to deal with the problem.

The accumulated data were presented by Chicago University's Dr. Floyd W. Reeves, chairman of the American Council's Committee on Discrimination. He made the point:

> All available researches, even though they varied in their investigatory methods show a definite pattern of discrimination.
>
> For many youths, restricted curriculum and inadequate educational facilities are serious barriers to education. Large numbers of youth face economic and geographic barriers.
>
> Desire for higher education is greatest among Jewish youth. Many institutions employ techniques in the admission of students that appear to serve no worthwhile purpose but lend themselves to discriminatory practices.
>
> Race, religion, and national origin all constitute serious barriers for thousands of qualified youths. [State-supported institutions tend not to discriminate against youth from within their own states, except in the case of Negroes in the South and Northern Negroes seeking certain kinds of professional education, but they do discriminate against Jewish and Italian youth who reside in other states.]

The assembly listened to Dr. Ivy's cajoling and Dr. Reeves' facts, then divided their number into four committees to dig into the major areas of the problem: discrimination in admissions to undergraduate and professional schools, and economic and regional barriers. After three half-day sessions of probing, discussion, and sifting of the facts, the conference reassembled to consider the findings and adopt a program that amounted to self-policing.

They agreed on the basic point: the quota system cannot be justified on any grounds compatible with democratic principles.

They proposed to act through:

> Development of a program by the colleges themselves that would eliminate such discrimination.
>
> Enactment of legislation, such as fair educational practices laws, wherever necessary.
>
> Government financial aid to improve the quantity and quality of higher educational facilities so as to eliminate economic barriers facing many who seek college and professional school education.

More specifically:

Dr. George N. Rosenlof, registrar of the University of Nebraska, reporting for the Committee on Admissions Procedures in Undergraduate Institutions, called for a long-range educational program "to eliminate the use of discriminatory criteria" in the selection of students. Every college should publish "a clear and concrete statement of the procedures it follows in admitting students."

Dr. Carlyle Jacobsen, dean of the Division of Health Sciences at the University of Iowa, reporting for the Committee on Professional Schools, (1) urged further research into the barriers of a "social, economic, or educational character" which discourages college graduates from seeking professional training; (2) branded the quota system as "undesirable and undemocratic"; (3) denounced "separate but equal schools for Negro and white as uneconomic"; and (4) declared that "these unjustifiable practices be discontinued..."

Dr. Jacobsen's report also urged elimination of discriminatory questions from professional-school application blanks. It expressed disapproval of overemphasizing the future employment possibilities of a student as a criterion for his admission to school.

Dean Maurice F. Seay of the University of Kentucky and Dr. Karl W. Bigelow of Teachers College, Columbia University, reporting on regional patterns, deplored the fact that "certain variables combine in certain regions of the country to affect particular groups of young Americans to special disadvantage." Their committee found a shortage in the Northeast of higher educational facilities "affecting adversely the abilities of Jews and certain ethnic groups to gain admission to colleges of their preference." Negroes in the South "are particularly handicapped by financial disabilities... and factors relating to race and residence... each region has its own special problem such as those involving Latin-Americans in the Southwest and young people of Oriental backgrounds in the Far West."

President Byron S. Hollingshead of Coe College and Harvard's renowned Dr. Seymour Harris, reporting for the Committee on Economic Factors, called for a system of grants-in-aid for tuition and subsistence to students, who had both need and ability, to be financed by the Federal Government. So that higher education should not be priced out of the market, this committee urged that grants should equal the difference between the full cost of higher education and private resources available to meet these costs.

The national conference was the beginning of the long journey, the springboard for regional conferences, the stimulus for reform and adherence to the democratic ideal by the individual schools, the encouragement of governmental aid and support. Region by region, state by state, the council and the League pursued their program. In April 1950 the first regional conference took place in Washington, D.C., with 28 colleges in Virginia, Maryland, Delaware, and the District of Columbia represented. A Midwest regional conference was held in Chicago in November 1950, with 200 presidents, education officers, and faculty members from 75 schools. In February 1951 the Mountain States conference, held in Denver, brought into being a permanent regional committee on "equality of educational opportunity in higher education." Twenty institutions were represented in March 1951 at the Wisconsin State Committee Conference. An Illinois State Conference, held in Chicago in November, 1951, produced a model policy encompassing all phases of college life suggesting procedures for eliminating discrimination. It was distributed to schools of higher learning throughout the country. Regional conferences were held in Pennsylvania, Indiana, Iowa, Michigan, and New York and ultimately a National Students Conference gathered at Earlham College in Richmond, Indiana.

Perhaps the ideal is never fully achieved, but growth, development, and improvement in these years changed basic, seemingly unyielding, practices of discrimination in college admissions. In the two decades that followed, they continued to make notable progress, without, however, totally eliminating the quota system. That seemed to have a life of its own as a device for preserving or establishing inequities favoring special interests, or for thwarting a rational approach of selection. Too often it continued as an instrument preventing universities from becoming the "social institutions that ... guarantee equality of opportunity" called for by the President's Committee on Civil Rights. Too often it was used to deny the ideal put forth by the committee that "the only aristocracy consistent with the free way of life is an aristocracy of talent and achievement."

The quota system became the preferred instrument for subverting the principle of equality of opportunity or the "aristocracy" of merit whenever special interests intruded, whether out of economic concerns, political goals, or social aggrandizement. The quota system dealt with numbers and their manipulation, and as the students at Harvard long ago had learned, it was numbers—their limitation or expansion—that counted. It will be rewarding to examine three situations in which the quota system was invoked in the years that real progress was being made toward its elimination. The reasons differed. In the instance of two major Midwest universities in the late 1960's, it was a throwback, in the face of campus unrest, to the nativism of an earlier day. In the case of medical schools, the motivation was economic protectionism. In the case of government supported "affirmative action" in the 1970's, it has been the use of the wrong instrument for the best of motives.

The Return to Nativism

The 1960's were not happy days on university campuses. These were the years of the war in Vietnam, the years of rebellion, student activism, and violent encounters. At state universities, especially, administration leaders found themselves caught in the cross fire between students and politicians who threatened to reduce financial support unless peace were restored on campus. As always, in a complex situation that did not lend itself readily to solution, there was a search for a scapegoat. Unable to cope with the depth of disillusion on campus, that "ole debbil" xenophobia was invoked. At the University of Wisconsin in 1961, the administration responded to the backlash by inaugurating a policy that would sharply reduce the number of "out-of-state" students. To the knowledgeable, it seemed ironic that Wisconsin would have to seek "outsiders" to account for rebellious student behavior—Wisconsin with its long history of progressive movements and radical behavior of the left and right; Wisconsin, the state of the La Follettes on the one hand and Joe McCarthy on the other, and a tradition of uninhibited student dissidence.

But the pressure came from the state legislature to get rid of the "out-of-states." The simplistic argument was that by doing so the state would be relieved both of a financial drain and the "troublemakers." Neither assumption was true, for the larger fees paid by out-of-state students and Federal subsidies had to be considered in the financial reckoning. Nor could the campus unrest be placed solely on the doorstep of the out-of-states. The term had become a euphemism for New York Jews, a fact made rather explicit by a blast from the State Chamber of Commerce against students from "Brooklyn, the Bronx and Great Neck, Longgisland" (sic).

To meet the pressures, the Admissions Policy Committee proposed to the university regents a program of "geographic diversity," an Orwellian bit of "doublespeak." When you want to restrict, always call it diversification. The committee suggested that the applications from ten states which traditionally provided most of the university's out-of-state students be "held" while the applications from all other states were processed. It just so happened that the ten "held" states included most of the centers of Jewish population and had been providing 90 percent of the Jewish students on campus. The storm of protest that greeted the announcement forced a quick retreat. Professor Edward Fadell, chairman of the policy committee, publicly declared that the "'go-hold' policy was a bad tactical error. We admit to that." The university went back to the simpler numbers game. In a series of steps, out-of-state enrollment was cut to 15 percent by 1971. The goal was achieved without Orwellian "doublespeak." In 1966 freshman students identified as Jewish numbered 900. In September 1969 the figure was 188. The total Jewish enrollment at the university in these years dropped by 67 percent. In representation to the university regents, the Anti-Defamation League rejected the public discussion and press reports that there was intent to eliminate Jewish students from campus, but expressed concern over the actual effect upon the educational opportunities for Jews at Wisconsin as revealed by the emerging statistics. At the same time it pointed to the new admissions policy as a revival of "educational nativism" rather than a movement for diversity that had made Wisconsin a great educational center.

The Wisconsin situation was calming down when an even more blatantly discriminatory policy appeared at another major Midwest university. In June 1969, the office of admissions at Purdue University in Indiana notified prospective students in New York and New Jersey that "we now know we will not be in a position to serve you." The reason given was that a strict out-of-state quota was maintained with preference given to the children of alumni, but it soon became evident that Purdue's policy toward applicants from New York and New Jersey, the source of most of its Jewish students, was more severe than for those from other states.

In response to representations from the League, Purdue President Frederick L. Hovde asked how "the difficult and unhappy process of selecting the few who could be admitted" might be chosen "without the imposition of quotas." In the discussions, it soon became obvious that other major state-supported universities in Indiana carried on without fixed out-of-state quotas. Purdue now proposed to "remove the least shadow of doubt that discrimination might exist." Unhappily, there was a further breakdown in communication. In the next admissions office directive, the quota was defined as being "based upon the approximate percentage of the population of New York and New Jersey to the total population of the nation." New York's quota for the September 1970 term was 120; New Jersey's, 44.

Throughout the semester, the League's Indiana officials continued to confer with the Purdue administration, contending that the special restrictions being invoked for an area where half of all American Jews resided, was bound to work to the detriment of Jewish aspirants for admission. In March 1971 Dr. Hovde announced that fixed state quotas were to be dropped, but preference retained for children of alumni. Dr. Hovde left the university at the end of the year, believing he had arrived at a reasonable solution. Whereupon the Purdue Board of Trustees added a second preference—special consideration for applicants from bordering states. Reluctantly, the League informed Purdue that it had lost confidence in the university's intentions and suggested that the United States Civil Rights Commission be consulted on policy. That could not have been a palatable idea to Purdue officials, for the commission was headed by the Reverend Theodore Hesburgh, president of the University of Notre Dame, another Indiana institution at which no quota existed.

Once again now Purdue's Board of Trustees changed its mind, and on March 3, 1972, issued its definitive policy statement: no more than 25 percent of the student body would be recruited from out-of-state. New York and New Jersey applicants would be given equal treatment with all others, but the children of alumni would be given preference provided they met the prescribed standards.

It was a small victory, but an important one, because it defeated an attempt to invoke an ethnic quota once more. More importantly, it raised a warning signal that state-supported schools, by establishing excessive and selective barriers against out-of-state students, were promoting a provincialism damaging to educational goals. A League survey in 1970 showed that 73 out of 136 degree-granting state universities restricted the admission of nonresidents, largely for economic reasons. Thirty of these schools had invoked their restrictions within the prior four years. Only Wisconsin and Purdue had seemed to play the quota game. As for the others, while the intent may not have been to cut down on Jewish enrollment, the effect was often exactly that.

Medical Economics

As elsewhere in the educational world of the early 1920's, medical schools hit upon an arithmetic formula for controlling who would and who would not become a doctor. Based on the tribal attitudes of the time, candidates were chosen in proportion to the number of their race or sect in the population. The merit of the individual candidate for admission was subordinated to this quota formula. In 1920 Jewish students formed 40 percent of the medical trainees at Columbia University's prestigious College of Physicians and Surgeons. The figures dropped to 25 percent in the entering class of 1924, when the quota system was established at the school, and to a range of 10 to 15 percent by the mid-1930's, or about equal to the Jewish population of New York State.

In this center of Jewish population, the restrictive policies of Cornell Medical School were particularly rigid and its officials unabashedly frank. In 1940 Dean W. S. Ladd explained to City Councilman Walter R. Hart that Cornell picked a class of 80 out of 1,200 applicants. Of these applicants, 700 were Jewish, but only 10 of those admitted were Jews. A Jewish applicant's chance of admission was therefore one in 70. Among non-Jews it was one in 7.

"We limit the number of Jews ... to roughly the proportion of Jews ... in this state," Dean Ladd said, "which is a higher proportion than in any part of the country." Since schools in other states also played the numbers game and coupled it with restrictions on out-of-state applicants, this was of little solace to the rejected New York Jewish students.

Through the 1950's, as the quota system became increasingly unacceptable to educators, the medical schools slowly relaxed their restrictive policies. Cornell persisted, limiting admission of Jewish students to about 15 percent. In a seven-year period from 1956 to 1962, the Anti-Defamation League tabulated the entering classes of the nation's 80 medical schools. The number of Jewish students admitted moved up slowly from an average of 18 percent in 1956 to 20.5 percent in 1962. Cornell dropped from 18 percent in 1956 to 14 percent in 1962, consistent, as always, with its 1940 explanation of policy. The contrast with its near neighbor, the New York University College of Medicine is telling. NYU, having placed objective standards for admission above irrelevant criteria based on numbers and quotas, and drawing its applicants from essentially the same pool as Cornell, found that each class of approximately 130 included 85 to 90 Jews. Other qualifications being equal, Jews were admitted in the same proportions as non-Jewish applicants.

A policy of economic protectionism by the medical profession provided underpinning for the persistent use of quotas by medical schools in the years when artificial restrictions elsewhere in higher education generally were giving way at a faster rate. A 1955 report of the American Medical Association declared the "need for additional facilities for the education of physicians...exceedingly difficult to determine." At a Senate hearing, the AMA spokesman could not tell Senator Lehman how many doctors the country needed. "It is like answering your wife's question of how many dresses she should have: She can always use one more good dress."

Yet there were answers to be had. Dr. Howard A. Rusk of the New York University College of Medicine reported that the average work week of a doctor was 69 hours, producing for the medical practitioner, in addition to high income, the highest coronary heart-disease rate of any professional group. More than one in four hospital internships and residences went unfilled, even though hospitals recruited thousands of foreign physicians. These doctors offered no economic competition since they could not enter private practice. One out of five public health and hospital posts for doctors also went unfilled. The population kept growing at a faster rate than training facilities.

In contradistinction to the AMA, the President's Commission on the Health Needs of the Nation cited the need for 25,000 additional doctors. It called for increasing the annual number of medical graduates from 7,000 to 10,000 to keep pace with the needs and set as a goal the raising of the total number of medical practitioners by two thirds within a decade to meet the requirements of both a growing and an aging population.

The pool of candidates for medical training in the post–World War II years kept rising rapidly; not so the number of additional places for training. Some years there were two, three, and four candidates for each place, creating a pressure cooker in which discriminatory admissions practices bubbled and boiled. A 1952 report of the New York Board of Regents of the state's nine medical shcools cited the effect of a new "personality appraisal" of candidates for admission. It found that "a combination of cultural traits perhaps related to stereotypes in the minds of admissions officers" contributed greatly to discriminatory patterns. The study found that Jewish and Italian Catholic applicants with two foreign-born parents were more discriminated against than applicants with only one parent born abroad. Those with native-born parents did considerably better, but non-Italian Catholics and Protestants with average grades did twice as well as Italians and Jews in the middle register. Not all of the schools were guilty of skewing the patterns in this way, but a new device had been placed in the hands of those who would discriminate. The severe restrictions on numbers to be admitted into the profession produced other conditions leading to discrimination against minorities. State medical schools began to limit admissions to residents in hope that they would retain the services of the graduates for their home communities, but it didn't work out that way. The University of Tennessee, for instance, found that of 2,500 graduates, only 35 percent remained in the state. This was far below state schools that had not narrowed their choice of students to local applicants. Yet many superior students from other states were thus denied opportunity for training.

The Bakke Variation

At this writing, the story of quotas in educational institutions has acquired an ironic twist. Used so long to deny equality of opportunity, the quota was invoked in 1973 by the University of California Medical School at Davis in order to promote the admission of students of racial origins that in the past suffered discrimination. The purpose was certainly benign; the choice of instruments to achieve that purpose naive in view of its history. But it was indeed a device used effectively by admissions officers for half a century to achieve their goals. Perhaps they knew no other as efficient; and while the means may have been suspect, the ends to be served were obviously desirable, supported by a federal adminstration pressing for "affirmative action" and a large segment of the nation seeking to redress old wrongs. But many of those most dedicated to ending discrimination were unwilling to accept means they considered evil.

The system of admissions set up at Davis allowed for an entering class of 100, with 16 of the places set aside in a special program for members of minority groups "economically and/or educationally disadvantaged." Applicants who considered themselves so deprived could apply for one of the 16 places without competing against those in the general admissions group. In four years, beginning with 1973, 44 minority-group students were admitted to Davis under the special program and 63 under the standard procedures. No disadvantaged white applicant received such preferential treatment. In two successive years, 1973 and 1974, a white candidate named Allen P. Bakke was denied admission though his academic scores were substantially higher than those admitted to the 16 places set aside for blacks, Chicanos, Asians, and American Indians. After his second rejection, Bakke sued in state court, charging that he had been discriminated against on racial grounds in violation of state and federal laws. Ultimately, the California Supreme Court struck down the Davis quota system as violative of the Equal Protection Clause of the Fourteenth Amendment. The university regents appealed the ruling to the United States Supreme Court.

By this time the Bakke case had become the center of national controversy because of the feared effect it might have on the broad program of affirmative action which the government was pressing in many fields. An inordinate number of briefs *amici curiae* were filed with the Court by groups of varying views and interests. It will suffice, however, in our historical narrative to consider the effect of the Supreme Court decision on the quota system and other discriminatory practices in university and college admissions. The Court, on June 28, 1978, handed down its ruling, 5 to 4, that the Davis quota system was unlawful because it denied the right of whites—even disadvantaged whites—to compete for the 16 set-aside seats. It then affirmed by the same vote, but in a different combination of justices, that race could be given consideration in admissions programs seeking redress of past discriminations. Finally, the Court ordered the admission of Bakke to the Davis Medical School. "Solomonic" became the catchword of the legal experts and the public figures commenting on the Court's decision. It was apt enough considering that the nine justices had cut in half the troublesome baby variously called "affirmative action," "reverse discrimination" or "preferential treatment," according to one's point of view.

Those who for half a century had been fighting against the use of invidious quotas in university and college admissions could rejoice at the view of the Court. They had long ago succeeded in branding them immoral; the Court majority now clearly declared them unconstitutional. The force of law was now on their side. So much for quotas as a device. But the favorable consideration of racial factors for the benign purpose of rectifying disadvantages created by ancient wrongs were declared permissible practice. Justice Lewis F. Powell, Jr., who spoke for the Court majority, recommended the procedure at Harvard which, in seeking diversity in its student body, considered race, georgraphic origin, and other factors besides scholarly excellence among the criteria for student selection. Fully aware of the history of

Allan P. Bakke.

quotas, Justice Powell acknowledged that such a procedure "which considers race only as one factor" could be operated "as a cover for the functional equivalent of a quota system," but "a Court would not assume that a university" would do so. "Good faith would be presumed." The presumption was not shared even by all Harvard men. Professor Allen Dershowitz of Harvard Law School, was quick to point out that the university's program "from what I know...results in favoring the wealthy, black and white." Adherents of other schools following procedures similar to Harvard's were equally skeptical.

The use of racial criteria, so long an invidious instrument, for benign purposes, raised a philosophic issue. Could the consideration

Supreme Court Justice Lewis F. Powell—"A Solomonic decision."

of race in admissions programs ever be truly benign? Even for the beneficiaries of such treatment? The issue was addressed in the brief *amicus curiae* of the Anti-Defamation League and an associated group of organizations. Here the League sought to express its long-held commitment to equality of opportunity for each person, without regard to creed or race, its opposition to discriminatory practices that are a denial of such opportunity and its support for corrective measures that would repair long-suffered disabilities without infringement of the constitutional rights of others. The brief asserted:

> It is indeed difficult to discover where the benignity of a racial quota is to be found. Not in the deprivations of benefits to the non-preferred race; not in the stigmatization of the preferred race; not in the effects on a riven society. A racial quota cannot be benign. It must always be malignant, malignant because it reduces individuals to a single attribute, skin color, and is the very antithesis of equal opportunity; malignant because it is destructive of the democratic society which requires that in the eyes of the law every person shall count as one, none for more, none for less.

For support of the argument, Professor Philip B. Kurland of the University of Chicago Law School and principal attorney on the *amicus* brief, quoted from the work of his late colleague Alexander M. Bickel of Yale, *The Morality of Consent*:

> The lesson of the great decisions of the Supreme Court and the lesson of contemporary history have been the same for at least a generation: discrimination on the basis of race is illegal, immoral, unconstitutional, inherently wrong, and destructive of democratic society. Now this is to be unlearned and we are told that this is not a matter of fundamental principle but only a matter of whose ox is gored. Those for whom racial equality was demanded are to be more equal than others. Having found support in the Constitution for equality, they now claim support for inequality under the same Constitution.

The power of the argument thus presented was recognized by Justice Powell who quoted it in his decision after commenting that the California regents urged "that discrimination against members of the white 'majority' cannot be suspect if its purpose can be characterized as 'benign.'... It is far too late to argue that the guarantee of equal protection to *all* persons permits the recognition of special wards entitled to a degree of protection greater than that accorded others."

In large measure, Justice Powell , in the majority opinion, expressed the same doubts about the benign effects of the quota or preferential treatment as was expressed in the League's brief, marshaling much the same supporting arguments and precedents. "Preferential programs may only reinforce common stereotypes, he wrote, "holding that certain groups are unable to achieve success without special protection...." Furthermore, he wrote, "There is a measure of inequity in forcing innocent persons...to bear the burdens of redressing grievances not of their making."

In the decision on quotas, the Court had come a long way toward the view of Justice William O. Douglas, the only member of the Court to address the substantive issue in the DeFunis case of 1974. DeFunis had been denied admission to the University of Washington Law School under an affirmative action program, sued for redress, and had then been admitted while the case was making its way through the courts and was about to receive his degree as the Supreme Court concluded its deliberations. The issues were therefore largely moot, but the case was a direct forerunner of the Bakke case. Justice Douglas wrote:

"The Equal Protection Clause commands the elimination of racial barriers, not their creation in order to satisfy our theory as to how society ought to be organized...."

He conceded that certain physical disabilities, if present, "may in extreme situations justify differences in racial treatment that no fair-minded person would call 'invidious' discrimination. Mental ability is not in that category. All races can compete fairly at all professional levels...any state-sponsored preference to one race over another in that competition is in my view 'invidious' and violative of the Equal Protection Clause."

Justice Powell came much to the same conclusion: "The guarantee of equal protection cannot mean one thing when applied to one individual and something else when applied to a person of another color. If both are not accorded the same protection, then it is not equal."

That should have been the last word. But is it? The Court opened a door to violation when it blessed the use of race as one factor in a university's consideration of candidates for admission. Through that wide door a university's bureaucracy can readily drive a discriminatory procedure to replace the quota system. The past record of such bureaucracies is not reassuring.

EIGHT

The Radicals—
Right and Left

A readily identified thread runs through the extremist movements of American history. It ties together nineteenth-century nativism and latter day right-wing radicalism, weaving through all of those extremist groups that organized to protect their positions against the feared threat of one minority or another seeking fulfillment of the American promise. The minority might be a depressed ethnic or racial group or a highly favored elite; the weapons used against them have been prejudice and charges of conspiracy to undermine the nation. That is the thread, and it binds Samuel F. B. Morse to Tom Watson; Watson to Huey Long and Father Coughlin; Coughlin to Joe McCarthy and George Wallace—and all of them to the myriad bigots and opportunists who have practiced what political scientists Seymour M. Lipset and Earl Raab have called the "politics of unreason."

The nation's renewed march toward its democratic goals recorded in the last chapter brought on for some Americans that fear of loss of status which has always fueled extremist movements and at the same time provided the essential weapon for such a movement—the communist conspiracy. Finding its leader in Senator Joseph McCarthy of Wisconsin, the dominant right-wing movement of the postwar era was not racist or anti-Semitic but a reflection of unhappiness with the Truman Administration's foreign policy and what it regarded as elitist efforts to communize America. Every move toward democratization, toward extension of civil rights, social legislation, and economic liberalization was attacked as communist inspired and promoted by communist agents who had infiltrated government and the basic institutions that "controlled" American life. The minority that McCarthy chose to attack was the social and intellectual elite. Harvard became a swear word and the term "liberal" synonymous with communist—in the parlance of the McCarthyites. Everyone not a blind follower was subject to attack with all of the demagogic fury of which the senator was capable. He was able to manipulate a following that came in large measure from the isolationist Midwest, the less privileged minority ethnic and religious groups, and a very considerable lower-class segment of the nation, traditionally distrustful of intellectualism and high-status groups. As Lipset has pointed out, McCarthy was able to "transpose into a new key the conspiracy theme that has characterized so much of American extremist politics." He was equally successful in attracting mass attention through his outrageous public attacks upon major public figures and minor government officials, charges of treason against State Department personnel and disloyalty in the armed forces. At every turn McCarthy violated that basic tenet of a democratic political system: that political opposition was not to be equated with disloyalty to the nation, nor opponents driven to desperate measures by unfounded charges of treason. Such is the practice of authoritarian systems; a democracy cannot live with it. The tactic eventually destroyed McCarthy, though the media poured their attention on him and he received encouragement from some of his Republican colleagues who saw in it party advantage as long as the Democrats remained in office.

Like so many groups, the Anti-Defamation League watched the rising hatreds and tensions created by the McCarthy tactics with trepidation. "Are we becoming a people blindly, doggedly, fiercely against something we cannot define except to say it is wicked," wrote Henry E. Schultz, the League's national chairman in 1953. The League was finding "the pattern of hate," he said, "easily transferable to minority groups and reflected in the anti-Semitism of the time." As a member of the Board of Higher Education in New York, Schultz had been through the "communist wars" on the city college campuses and seen the damage they could do. He put the question on anti-Semitism to McCarthy directly in a personal meeting and came away with the feeling that though the Senator was "not an anti-Semite in the sense of a Gerald Smith . . . [his] methods injured many of our democratic institutions on whose strength the security of minority groups are largely dependent."

Looking at McCarthy's America, the poet Archibald MacLeish cried out that "there is more substance in our enmities than in our loves. . . . A man who lives, not by what he loves, but by what he hates is a sick man. So, too, is a nation." Indeed, Joe McCarthy's America in 1953 was a sick nation—but one about to pass the crisis in its illness. Its obsession with the fear of communism fed the fevers induced by the radicals of the right. MacLeish spoke at the fortieth-anniversary meeting of the Anti-Defamation League at a moment when McCarthy's attacks on the government establishment had become intolerable to his own party and to his Senate colleagues, possibly the only group in the nation that could silence him. A Republic administration had come to power, but the McCarthy fury continued unabated. He took no notice of the Democratic defeat at the polls; as far as McCarthy was concerned, the communists controlled and manipulated the government; nothing had changed. No doubt President Eisenhower writhed under McCarthy's lashing tongue, but for almost the full year he had been in office kept silent.

On November 23, 1953, the day after MacLeish had spoken, the President came to the League's celebration as the guest of honor at dinner. No doubt he looked upon it as a social event, for he came in a

Poet MacLeish—"There is more substance to our enmities than our loves. . . ."
Mrs. Eleanor Roosevelt is seated at left.

jovial mood without a prepared address, and, as he reported, he had been "briefed and briefed" by his staff on civil rights and had turned down the briefings. This was no night for politicking. He was warmed by the friendly reception, amused by some favored entertainers, and moved by a stage presentation of high moments in American history. The closing lines, read by Helen Hayes in the role of Harriet Beecher Stowe, recalled the Civil War:

> A day will come when this our little life, will be ended.... All who raged, all who threatened; the weakling who yielded; the man who, like our President [Lincoln] stood and bore infamy and scorn for truth. Yes, life will be over, but eternity will never efface from our souls whether we did well or ill... whether at the end we could say, with truth, "I have fought the good fight—I have kept the faith."

The words from the stage triggered an emotional chord in the President. The time and the place seemed just right for him to address the subject uppermost in the mind of the nation. He had no carefully prepared phrases or polished ghost-written sentences. The thoughts tumbled out of him as he responded to the encomia of Henry E. Schultz, who presented him with the League's "America's Democratic Legacy" Medal. That phrase, too, seemed to have its effect.

"I want to tell you about an idea that came to me as I was sitting here," the President said.

> I was raised in a little town, a famous place....It is called Abilene, Kansas....Now, that town had a code, and I was raised as a boy to prize that code. It was: Meet anyone face to face with whom you disagree. You could not sneak up on him from behind or do any damage to him without suffering the penalty of an outraged citizenry....You live after all by that code....
>
> In this country, if someone dislikes you or accuses you, he must come up front, he cannot hide behind the shadow; he cannot assassinate you or your character from behind without suffering the penalties an outraged citizenry will impose....
>
> There must be no weakening of the codes by which we have lived...by the right to meet your accuser face to face...by your right to speak your mind and be protected in it.

(Above right) *President Dwight D. Eisenhower delivering the "Code of Abilene" speech before the Anti-Defamation League in 1953, his first clear attack on Senator Joseph McCarthy.*

(Below right) *Eisenhower receiving the America's Democratic Legacy Award from Henry E. Schultz. "The patterns of hate (are) easily transferable."*

In the context, there was no mistaking Eisenhower's meaning. McCarthy's name was not mentioned, but a signal had been given. James Hagerty, the President's press secretary, sitting among the diners, stiffened with surprise as he listened, but then calmly proceeded to punctuate the transcript handed him by the White House stenographer. The press corps buzzed with excitement. The President's message had been carried simultaneously by the four major television networks, running four minutes overtime; 38,000,000 viewers and another 20,000,000 radio listeners had received the signal. Most importantly, the Senate got the message. There had been almost a senatorial quorum in the room.

The pressure of his colleagues on McCarthy now began to mount, but he continued his extremist tactics as if Communists and not his own party controlled the Adminstration. He was confident of his own power and believed himself invulnerable. The Senate's patience came to an end on December 1, 1954, and it took that rare step—censuring one of its own, citing him for "obstructing the constitutional process of the Senate" and tending to bring it "into dishonor and disrepute." The effect on McCarthy was devastating. With his loss of standing in the Senate, his power oozed away; the press lost interest in him and he lost public attention; his following faded, and he, too, almost disappeared from sight. Bereft of power and notoriety, he died suddenly of a heart attack on May 2, 1957. Political extremism moved to regroup under new banners.

The Post-McCarthy Right

The extensions of McCarthyism paraded under a variety of names led by men committed to the conspiracy theory of history, bound together by their pathological fears of communism and their distrust of democratic process, but with none of the animal force or charismatic quality of the Senator. They provided a home for that considerable following the Senator had left behind—perhaps 20 percent of the electorate—even as the lunatic fringe groups had inherited a following from the Nazi and Coughlin movements of an earlier decade. One of the differences lay in the fact that there was no substantial anti-Semitic carryover. Senator McCarthy had never shown any anti-Semitic propensities, and neither did the new Radical Right organizations. Yet they were enormously attractive to the anti-Semites, the racists, bigots and yahoos. Recognizing that its cause was often damaged by their presence, the Radical Right had the constant problem of cleansing its ranks of anti-Semites.

There was obviously also a community of interest between the Radical Right, as typified by the John Birch Society, and right-wing conservatism. Both elements saw the country imperiled by the "dangerous" policies, foreign and domestic, of government and the established powers. The former found the direction set by the "Communist conspiracy"; the latter saw "the mess in Washington" as the inept and misguided functioning of government under all Presidents since Herbert Hoover. The alliance between these two wings of the right came more easily after 1960 when Eisenhower went out of office and a Democratic administration returned to Washington. The liberal policies of a Kennedy, the flowering of the civil rights movement, the advance of social-welfare legislation and the strains of the Cold War all added to the fears of right-wing extremists. Nor was the party of John Kennedy able to exercise the restraints on the right wing that the Eisenhower party ultimately invoked against McCarthy.

A study conducted in 1963 by a group of social scientists from Stanford University, Washington University in St. Louis and the California Department of Public Health lends weight to the thesis:

Senator Joseph McCarthy—The end came quickly after his attack on the Army. Seated to his left is Boston attorney Joseph Welch.

The allegations of Communist influence...are less convincing to the public when a Republican is President. Hope, party loyalty and organizational alliances all restrain right-wing leaders at [such a] time....All these conditions are reversed when the White House changes hands. There is no incumbent President to restrain right-wing dissidents....During a Democratic administration, alarmism about Communism is more plausible...particularly [to] those with very conservative ideas.

Much to the discomfort of Dr. Frederick C. Schwartz, an Australian who organized the Christian Anti-Communist Crusade, a lucrative Radical Right operation, the researchers had based their findings on investigation of a "school of anti-communism," one of many he ran. For its first seven years the "Crusade" had stagnated. Its income jumped 350 percent in the first year of the Kennedy Administration.

In the political spectrum to the right of center, there was a tendency toward blurring of the lines. Right-wing conservatives could, and did, find some common ground with the Radical Right. Similarly, centrists among conservatives shared positions also held by the right wing. Thus William Buckley, Jr., was critical of Robert Welch, leader of the John Birch Society (and called a communist dupe for his pains) but would not reject the organization, many of whose members held views congenial to his own. Buckley cited the dilemma of such conservatives as he. To agree with Welch, he said, was to accept the thesis that the government was "under the operational control of the Communist party"; to remain silent was to "egg him on." But principally he lamented that the Birch Society could not be "an effective instrument when it is led by a man whose views are...so far removed from common sense."

What had set Buckley off—and other conservatives such as Senator Barry Goldwater—was the appearance of a Welch monograph, *The Politician*, elaborating his conspiracy theory. The politician of the title was President Eisenhower, whom he charged with being "a dedicated, conscious agent of the Communist conspiracy." Welch, in fact, went so far as to express "my opinion [that] the chances are very strong that Milton Eisenhower is actually Dwight Eisenhower's superior and boss within the Communist Party," a statement softened in a later version to read, "...boss within the whole Left Wing movement."

Nor could conservatives—appalled as many of them were by Welch's scribblings—be less pained by some of the Neanderthal and disruptive tactics of the Birch Society that paralleled the lunatic fringes. Their embarrassment at the local "book-burnings," attacks on teachers, minor officials, churchmen, and civic institutions was sometimes as acute as that of liberals who had been too uncritical of allies of the left in the years of the Popular Front.

The conservative embarrassment could be particularly painful when the peddlers of bigotry climbed aboard the Radical Right bandwagon, taking the conspiracy charges several steps farther away from common sense. Their contribution was that the Communist conspiracy was really a pro-Soviet Jewish conspiracy. That the Radical Right would be of concern to the Anti-Defamation League was apparent— not so much because of its attraction for anti-Semites as for its antidemocratic thrust and its threat to the political fabric of the nation. In their 1964 study, "Danger on the Right," Benjamin R. Epstein, the League's national director and Arnold Forster, its general counsel, wrote:

> [The Radical Right's] fears and warnings are, to all purposes, baseless. The real danger is that in continuing endlessly to cry wolf, they confuse and divide America, diminishing her ability to recognize a real peril when it appears...they constitute a serious threat to our democratic processes...[it] should be the concern of all Americans.

They found the "fevered phantasies...the counsels of fear and confusion...the unfounded suspicions" broadcast by the Radical Right as subversive as any of the conspiracies it imagined and particularly damaging to legitimate conservative positions.

In essence, the League was arguing that conservatives could not long tolerate the extremist tactics of the Radical Right and at the same time maintain the integrity of their own political programs. This became even more apparent as Birch Society leaders moved into the American Independent Party in support of the backlash politics of George Wallace. It was a marriage of populism and elitism on the extremist right such as the nation had never quite seen before and cut a considerable swath in the Presidential elections of 1964 and 1968.

Wallace, a populist and racist in the Southern political tradition of Tom Watson, appealed to the less educated, lower economic strata among rural and small-town voters. In industrial areas and the cities, he won support among poorly educated low-income groups and blue-collar classes who had followed Joe McCarthy and perhaps Father Coughlin before him. He made a serious dent among trade unionists, normally followers of a liberal line. Wallace offered them an attractive combination. His populism permitted him to back those economic and social programs that had kept these groups loyal to the Democratic party; his racism, his opposition to integration and his calls for "law and order" fed their fear of blacks. His common ground with the Birch Society was his view of the communist conspiracy. He drew into his orbit the whole complex of extremist and Radical Right groups with attacks on intellectuals, the concentration of power in the federal government, its failures in foreign policy and its "no win" Vietnam war policy. The fact that the Birch Society itself was an elitist group whose members were affluent, often the heads of substantial businesses, with better-than-average levels of education did not inhibit Wallace's opportunistic politics. He could endorse the Society and its goals wholeheartedly even while he promised more social welfare legislation to his worker constituency—programs the Society violently opposed.

Wallace's campaign in 1968 was enormously successful in terms of a third-party effort. He got on the ballot in every state in the Union, received 13 percent of the votes, and for a time seemed to shake the electoral process. Pre-election polls showed he had the approval of as much as 40 percent of the electorate. Ultimately, he received an unprecedented 9,000,000 votes. Birch leaders had helped provide competence and organization to the campaign, but not conservative votes. The votes for Wallace came from those who responded to the race issue in the small towns and rural areas of the South, and from the blue-collar workers of the cities who voted their prejudices rather than their social objectives. Trade unionist support for him slackened as union leaders, alarmed by working-class defections, worked vigorously to hold the line for the two major parties. The middle class, too, largely held to its old allegiances and stayed in the political mainstream. Significantly, the type of voters to whom the Birch Society appealed did not vote their bigotry, but their conservatism, and remained in the Republican party. They could not enter into the alienated politics of the Wallace coalition.

Those torn by doubt had the consolation of having Spiro Agnew as the Republican vice-presidential candidate, traveling the low road in the Wallace footsteps. His campaign speeches inveighed against "phony" intellectuals and found the Democrats "soft on communism." He spoke deprecatingly of the problems of blacks and feelingly of the threats to "law and order." He thus beckoned to extremists that they could find a home in the Republican party and perhaps enticed enough of them to give the Nixon-Agnew ticket its narrow margin of victory over the Democrats. Several years later— after Agnew resigned as Vice-President under the shadow of criminal conviction—it was not strange to find him heading up an anti-Semitic organization, Education for Democracy, Inc.

The Radical Right has been longer-lived than extremist movements of past eras, many of which had far greater political successes. The John Birch Society in 1978 continued to claim a membership of 60,000. To maintain this figure, which is probably exaggerated, it from time to time moved over into the shadier areas of racism and anti-Semitism. From the very beginning of his public activity, Welch had been obsessed with the notion of conspiracy. For Welch, the Illuminati—that fiction of an eighteenth-century Masonic conspiracy of intellectuals—still lives and continues to be responsible for all of the social and political progress he despises and considers evil. Latter-day exemplars of the Illuminati, Welch reported in his pamphlet, *The Truth in Time,* destroyed Senator McCarthy and powered the communist conspiracy. His faith in the myth caused the Birch Society to reprint John Robison's 1798 book *Proofs of a Conspiracy.* The Society's stamp of belief in the conspiracy and its anti-intellectualism is contained in an introduction:

> One tends to think of professors, philosophers and writers as ... perfectly harmless to the world. Robison and history prove otherwise.... From Woodrow Wilson—himself a professor—to Lyndon Johnson, we have had nothing but Presidents surrounded by professors and scholars ...which brings to mind Weishaupt's [Illuminati] plan to surround the ruling authorities with members of his Order.

Thus, Welch, like McCarthy, made an intellectual elite and agencies of the government the target of his attacks, eschewing anti-Semitism. But in 1972, in preparation for the Presidential elections, he directed the Birch Society in a massive effort to distribute a paperback book, *None Dare Call It Conspiracy,* by Gary Allen. Forster and Epstein, in their book *The New Anti-Semitism,* point out that Allen did not show the care that Welch might have. His book was "steeped in the blatant lies and half truths that have characterized the recognized standards" set by *The Protocols of the Learned Elders of Zion.* Conservative comment was equally critical. William Loeb's conservative Manchester (N. H.) *Union Leader* called the book "anti-Semitic nonsense." The right-wing periodical *Human Events* refused to accept advertising for it, and other newspapers and magazines of similar viewpoint joined in the criticism.

None Dare Call It Conspiracy became a prime campaign document for the American party in 1972. With George Wallace out of the running, the Birch Society took virtual control of the party. Representative John Schmitz of California, who had written the introduction to Allen's book, became the party's Presidential candidate. Both Schmitz and his running mate, Thomas J. Anderson, were members of the Society's National Council. The heaviest contributors were Birch members, and the Society's conspiracy theory was the basic thesis of the campaign. Schmitz branded the two major parties part of the "conspiracy" and offered the Allen book, which he inserted into the *Congressional Record*, as evidence. Without the Wallace charisma and force, however, the American party attracted small attention and little criticism. With a massive 78,000,000 votes cast, the Party polled 1,080,541 in the 32 states in which it was on the ballot. That provided a more accurate reading of the strength of the Radical Right and the lunatic fringe than the 9,000,000 votes Wallace had polled in 1968. It is doubtful that the injection into the campaign of the anti-Semitism of the Allen book had been helpful to the candidates.

Moving to the right of the Birch Society, one encounters Liberty Lobby, Willis Carto, its founder and manipulator, and finally that fringe of society where the unabashed hatemongers, anti-Semites, and racists live and thrive. Carto has been a connecting link between the Radical Right and the salesmen of bigotry. He founded Liberty Lobby in the 1950's as a respectable conservative front while, out of personal predilections, he carried on as an anti-Semitic propagandist for profit through a chain of publications and organizations. Though he kept a low profile within Liberty Lobby, he remained its real power. He brought into the group such known professional bigots as Joseph P. Kamp, Ned Touchstone, W. Henry McFarland, Richard Cotten, and Kenneth Goff. In Curtis B. Dall, a retired army colonel and one time son-in-law of President Roosevelt, he found a prestigious spokesman and chairman for the organization. Ultimately, Dall had no difficulty in adjusting his Radical Right propensities to Carto's anti-Semitism. By the 1970's, Liberty Lobby was moving rapidly from its basic conservative stance toward the anti-Jewish line of the rest of the Carto operations. They came together on the gound of American foreign policy in the Middle East. For both the Radical Right and anti-Semitic elements that policy fitted into their concept of conspiracy; for the former, it was treason in high places; for the latter, evidence of the "world Zionist conspiracy" manipulated by Israel.

Dall and Liberty Lobby began by spouting the standard anti-Semitic line in a pamphlet titled *America First*. It pounded away at the old canards: "The Jews rejected their Messiah, even had him crucified." "Almost all of the early Bolsheviks were Jewish." "...Hitler's hostility toward Jews originated in the Zionest leaders having pushed the United States into World War I on the side of the allies" "...those who singled out the Jews for their part in getting us into war [World War II] were scorned and ridiculed."

Soon Dall was warning Americans that "your sons could be drafted to fight for Israel...and probably will be, unless some changes are made immediately." He foresaw no such changes. In the 1972 Presidential campaign, he was outraged that both major-party candidates, Richard Nixon and George McGovern, supported the integrity of the State of Israel. "Just what does 'integrity' mean," he asked. "Does this mean the two candidates favor ordering Christian soldiers to fight, perhaps die, in furthering the political objectives of the Zionists?"

How effective Dall was, to what degree his message came through to the American public is questionable. No doubt he reached his own following, and that was substantial; but such Radical Rightists as the Reverend Billy James Hargis and the Reverend Carl McIntire, religious fundamentalists, stayed clear of both Dall and Schmitz on the issue of American sympathy for Israel. Echoes of support came only from the hatemongers on the Right fringe.

Politics of the Left

The politics of the Radical Left is sometimes frighteningly similar to that of the Right. In tactics, insistence on orthodoxy, as they see it, and perception of their own high-mindedness, they are alike. They may regard each other as evil incarnate, but their primary attention is given to undermining the center holding the existing order together. In that sense, they are both revolutionary and both attract violent elements from the fringes of society. The Radical Left grew in strength during the 1960's as the nation was beset by domestic turmoil. Flocking to its ranks was an alienated younger generation critical of things as they were. The focus of unhappiness was the Vietnam war, the slowness of civil rights progress, the evident poverty amid plenty, the seeming failure of democracy as a system. As blacks rioted in the ghettos in the "long, hot summer" of 1967, college students, caught up in the idea of confrontation politics, rioted against continuation of the Vietnam war. Everyone seemed to have suddenly acquired a set of "nonnegotiable demands" that had to be satisfied immediately. Frustration and alienation became truly threatening forces, fertilizing the ground for radical politics of the left.

Until the Vietnam war wound down, both Radical Right and Left— and indeed the lunatic fringe—had a common foreign-policy target. If the Radical Right could charge three succeeding administrations with following a "no win" policy that constituted a "communist conspiracy," the Radical Left was just as ready to see the war as an opportunity for "anti-imperialist struggle." As the war ended, both Right and Left shifted their attacks to American foreign policy in the Middle East. The shift brought the Radical Left into an arena which suited its style and gained for it allies it could not reach otherwise.

In politics on the left, everyone has to take in everyone else's washing—or there is no alliance. The propaganda lines emanating from Marxist revolutionaries of every stripe, alienated black power groups, and Arab sources merged into a single pattern. Once again the United States was cast in the role of "imperialist," Israel was its cat's-paw, and an "occupying power" against which Arabs were bravely fighting a war of national liberation. Zionism was racism and the "fight against" it "a vital part of the world revolutionary struggle." Arab guerrilla warfare and terrorism were justified in the name of that struggle and criticized only when they were counter-productive, because the world recoiled from such wanton acts as the murder of Israeli Olympic athletes in Munich. Nor was the Radical Left hesitant in using the Shylock canard and other old anti-Semitic myths against American Jews, or to impugn the integrity of such eminent public officials as U.S. Ambassador Arthur Goldberg and Secretary of State Henry Kissinger. After years of repetition in publications of the left and at their myriad meetings and public demonstrations, the world should not have been totally shocked to hear the same theses expounded in debate at the United Nations or coming from the mouth even of so eminent an Arab statesman as Anwar Sadat.

Once the Vietnam war ended, the Radical Left, seeking new ways to attack "American imperialism," began the deliberate transfer of its propaganda mechanism to the problems of the Middle East. In 1971 the Trotskyist Socialist Workers' party, which had long regarded Israel as American "imperialism's beachhead" in the Mideast cited "... the necessity for closer collaboration and solidarity between American revolutionaries, Arab organizations in the U.S. and the revolutionary movement in Arab countries." The Trotskyists proposed to support the Palestinians in their "struggle to destroy the State of Israel." The

transfer of their activities from the Vietnam issue to Israel would be
made easy, they reasoned, because "the mass anti-war movement has
sensitized large numbers of people to the role of U.S. imperialism."
Even the slogans could be "analogous to the slogans around the issue
of Vietnam." Realistically, however, a spokesman for the Socialist
Workers' party found that the "leadership of the anti-war coalition...don't yet understand that Zionism serves the same U.S. imperialist aggressors who are destroying Vietnam." This was quite a
switch in approach because two or three years earlier the party had
opposed injection of other issues into the programs of their satellites,
the National Peace Action Coalition and the Student Mobilization
Committee to end the War in Vietnam, because it might lose them
allies.

With its national convention of 1971, however, the Socialist Workers party, making common cause with pro-Arab propagandists,
sought to harness the "anti-war coalition" to its program for the
Middle East. The concentration was on the youth and student organizations, their own and those of their allies, and, of course, of Arab
groups such as the Organization of Arab Students. The efforts included the usual array of "teach-ins," rallies, demonstrations and
literature distributions on and off the university campuses—
adaptations of the devices that had been developed by Vietnam war
protesters. The propaganda lines dwelled obsessively on the iniquity
of Israel and the evil of American imperialism, but as always, among
extremists, the venom spilled over into all-purpose anti-Semitic
tirades. American Jews, supporters of Israel, had to be "discredited"
among the true believers. Usually the line followed was the one
expressed in an article in *The Militant*, a party publication:

> ...there is a deadly symmetry between the attitudes of the Israelis toward
> the Arabs and that of American Jews toward the Afro-Americans and
> their liberation struggle...the upper and middle ranges of American
> Jewry...some of them bankers, landlords, big and little businessmen,
> participate in the system of oppressing and exploiting the black masses,
> just as the Zionists have become oppressors of the Palestinian Arabs...

The Socialist Workers' party pursued that line in all of the ramifica-
tions of its political activities and turgid discussions. The lunatic
fringe of rightists could do no better. Among those repelled by it were
the best of black civil rights leadership. "I can not believe," wrote
Whitney Young, Jr., executive director of the Urban League in 1970,
"that the criterion for relevance in the black struggle for liberation here

in the United States is dependent upon adopting slogans and ill-informed opinions about issues of foreign policy. Black people have a duty to free themselves from other people's propaganda..."

The Communist Party–USA was not be be outdone by its competitors. As the senior theoreticians of the left, they not only had targets to attack, but ramparts to defend. Through the years it predictably followed the Soviet line, harshly critical of Israel yet conceding its right to exist, calling the faithful to "the battle [that] must be waged against the machinations of U.S. imperialism in the Middle East and for the liberation of the Arab peoples." The point man in Communist Party–USA attacks was Harry Lumer and his vehicle, the party ideological journal *Political Affairs*.

It is "in this country, the heartland of U.S. imperialism and the home of the largest Jewish community in the world [that] the fight against Zionism takes on exceptional importance," he wrote in 1971. Then, going on the defensive, he charged that "an alarming growth of racism and chauvinism within the Jewish community" had produced "a campaign of vilification and slander" against the Soviet Union "based on the Big Lie of official 'Soviet anti-Semitism' and persecution of Soviet Jews, which has been built since 1967 to frenetic proportions." Lumer, of course, had taken his line on the Middle East from the policy set forth at the Soviet Twenty-fourth Party Congress earlier in the year.

Once established, the propaganda line was repeated with the regularity and persistence of a detergent commercial. The party convention in New York in 1972 called for an "end" to the "alliance of U.S. imperialism and Israeli expansionism." The *Daily World* charged "Zionist supporters in the U.S. have sold themselves to the U.S. State Department. They support the Vietnam war and spread State Department slanders about 'Soviet Anti-Semitism.'" Over and over came the denials that there was even a trace of anti-Semitism in Russsia, that it was all a figment of "Zionist agents of U.S. imperialism." Again the ultimate defense came from Lumer.

"Today Soviet Jews live on a plane of full quality with all other Soviet citizens," he told a fiftieth anniversary party gathering in New York, "an equality which is not enjoyed by Jews in any capitalist country.... Anti-Semitism in word and deed are outlawed... the Jewish question has been fully solved..."

Having established his defense by assertion, Lumer went back to the attack. "Zionism is not only anti-Soviet," he told the faithful, "it is in its very essence a racist ideology."

The "Zionism is racism" line and "U.S. imperialism" charges were played repetitively like a reprise by the splinter groups of the Old and New Left through the years. Typical of these was the Progessive Labor party, a faction of the Communist Party—USA which had broken away in 1965, to side with Communist China, then broke with the Maoists when China moved toward the United States. But it remained loyal to the universal Radical Left policy on the Middle East. Its great achievement was to capture control of the remnant of the Students for a Democratic Society in 1967 after its Weatherman leaders went underground. The SDS collapsed in 1969. New groups of varying stripes kept forming and disappearing through the 1970's, as Radical Leftists cut loose by this process sought new associations. There always seems to be a cadre in the wings whenever new resources and new opportunities become available.

The Black Extremists

That alienation was never an important force among Negroes is one of the miracles of American politics. Perhaps their deep religious faith—so long the only source of hope for a better world to come—made them conservative. Blacks never rejected the system; they strove to be included in its beneficence. For a hundred years, except for an isolated incident here and there, they abjured the call of the revolutionary and fought for integration, equality of opportunity, and the civil rights accorded to others under the Constitution. From the founding of the National Association for the Advancement of Colored People to Dr. Martin Luther King's Southern Christian Leadership Conference, the central Negro goal was reform, not revolution; inclusion in—not separation from—the rest of America.

The cause of separatism had a moment in the sun in the 1920's when Jamaican-born Marcus Garvey preached black nationalism and promoted a "back to Africa" movement. He was a rejected messiah who ended up in jail for using the mails to defraud. Not until after 1964, when passage of the Civil Rights Act did not bring an immediate utopia, did restive young blacks turn to left-wing revolutionary and separatist ideas. They found their theorist in Frantz Fanon, the Martinique-born revolutionary who preached violence as the means whereby "colonized" peoples could free themselves. They found their white allies among the Radical Left, financial support and sometimes asylum from Arab sources. Their radicalization was thus nurtured by the turmoil of the times, both at home and abroad. Their view of themselves as an exploited "colony class" made for easy acceptance of the Radical Left charge that America was an imperialist oppressor and the full propaganda line stemming from it. And even as Garvey had been infected by the anti-Semitism of his day, so the black rebels of the 1960's absorbed into their programs the anti-Semitism of the Radical Left: Jews as oppressors of the black ghettos, Israel as the instrument of American imperialism, Zionism as racism.

The growth of anti-Semitism among blacks after 1966 was an expression of the black power movement which was as much a rejection of the established Negro leadership as a revolt against the white-dominated society. Black power was grounded in the idea of separatism; it rejected white support for the Negro cause and Jews most of all because they had been so prominent in civil rights activity; it turned away from the Christian ethic so central in American Negro life and countered Martin Luther King's nonviolence strategy with calls for the use of force, fire, and riot. Malcolm X, the stormy petrel of the Black Muslim movement, was a prophet more to its liking than King; for he, too, had turned to the tactic of force, and long ago, under the guise of a distorted Muslim philosophy, adopted, as did Elijah Muhammad, leader of the Nation of Islam, an anti-Semitic stance. Malcolm X sounded the note that was to be heard again and again from black power advocates: "In America," he charged, "the Jews sap the very life blood of the so-called Negro to maintain the State of Israel, its armies and its continued aggression against our brothers in the East." Malcolm X had the charisma and the intellectual baggage to rise in the black power movement, but he fell victim to the very violence he preached. In 1965 he was murdered, under dramatic circumstances, by some of his "brothers" as a consequence of an internal power struggle in the Nation of Islam.

After 1966, the black extremist groups maintained a steady drumbeat of anti-Semitic propaganda. Much of it came from sources with intellectual pretensions. The magazine *The Liberator*, founded by Daniel H. Watts in 1960, turned from critical attacks on whites generally, to baiting moderate Negro leadership, and ultimately to anti-Semitism. It was a classic journey for those who ended up in the radical camp. Particularly pernicious was a series of articles in early 1966 that purported to tell the story of Jewish exploitation of the Harlem ghetto: "... the first line of resentment against slum housing, inferior grades of meat, spoiled food ... is directed against the living person who perpetuates these conditions. In general it is ... the Jewish population which has grown rich exploiting Black Americans for decades." This was pretty primitive stuff for a magazine with intellectual claims, and not supported by the facts, but Watts argued that they were "valid" and were his way of starting a "dialogue" between Jewish leaders and the black community. But *The Liberator* indicted Jews not only for their alleged exploitations, but for their very support of the Negro cause. Jews, it was alleged, had dominated the civil rights movement, the black colleges, the black organizations. The most selfless, generous acts were described as a sort of Jewish imperialism.

"More than any other, the Rosenwald Foundation, established by Julius Rosenwald, contributed in great measure to the almost absolute dominance of Negro colleges and organizations by Zionists," wrote Eddie Ellis, author of the series. Rosenwald was indeed the philanthropist who first recognized that education was the road that would lead Negroes to equality as it had other groups. To see "exploitation" in such matters was clearly provocative and perverse. The series provoked two of the best-known of *The Liberator*'s contributors. Author James Baldwin, who had done some serious soul-searching of his own, found *The Liberator* taking "refuge in the most ancient and barbaric of the European myths."

"I think," he wrote, "it is most distinctly unhelpful, and I think it is immoral, to blame Harlem on the Jew." Actor Ossie Davis, certainly an activist, found the charges "wild and unsupported contentions" and clearly racist. "In a war against all exploiters whomsoever," he wrote, "I am an ally. But Mr. Ellis seems to be calling for a war against Jews. If that is the case, I am an enemy." Both resigned from *The Liberator*'s advisory board.

The unhappy fact was that the "line" projected in *The Liberator* was being peddled by numerous black extremists during this period, determinedly and consistently. Every tense situation provided its opportunities; the debate of every community issue had its infusion of bigotry. Perhaps most critical was the long confrontation that resulted from the decentralization of the New York City school system. It was tailor-made for a black-Jewish confrontation because of the historic large Jewish representation in the teaching staff and the black community's frustration with the school system. The extremists had a propaganda field day and the debate often descended into antiSemitism, racism, and anti-Negro prejudice. The use of "fighting words" developed in the New York situation became a pattern for black power advocates in other cities.

By mid-1967, the principal black groups had begun to augment their own anti-Semitic effusions with the propaganda of their newfound friends of the Arab world. From then on and far into the 1970's, as long as they remained viable, they maintained a drumbeat of anti-Jewish and anti-Israel propaganda, drawing on Arab sources and support. To pick one's way through extremist movements is at best a tricky business. The black revolutionary organizations have been characteristically volatile—splintering often, changing leaders frequently, internal power struggles and internecine warfare a common condition. Adding to the instability were police pressures and the resistance of the general community. Nevertheless, there was little deviation from the anti-Semitic program the movement pursued.

The Student Non-violent Coordinating Committee (SNCC), which after 1966 belied its very name, is a case in point. Dr. Martin Luther King was its sponsor when it was organized in 1960 to channel the efforts of idealistic youth, black and white, into his nonviolent civil right demonstrations in the South. And so it did. Its members dreamed his dream; they were dedicated to integration and they sometimes risked their lives in nonviolent protest. But in 1966, Stokely Carmichael became its chairman and King saw the group slip into a policy of violence that was anathema to him. Carmichael preached black power, guerrilla warfare, and getting "whitey... off the backs [of blacks]." He sounded the end of the black-white coalition in the organization. The restless Carmichael moved on after a year to greener fields, visiting several Arab countries to express his allegiance to the Palestinian cause, and finally settling in Guinea, West Africa, where he became a naturalized citizen and a university lecturer. He became a propagandist for Arabs, returning to the United States frequently to express his hatreds. He missed no opportunities in college lectures and public meetings to label Israel an "immoral, illegal, and unjust state" and American Jews "an enemy ethnic group" of the black community.

Carmichael was succeeded at SNCC by H. Rap Brown. Talk of violence increased and his involvement with guns and exhortations to riot and looting eventually resulted in his becoming a fugitive from justice. SNCC's orientation toward the left grew as it began to see itself part of the "international liberation movement." As its financial troubles also grew, SNCC gave itself over ever more readily to Arab propaganda. The June–July 1967 issue of its *Newsletter* was devoted to reprinting verbatim material from a Palestine Liberation Organization (PLO) pamphlet so hateful and anti-Jewish in content as to also attract the white racist, neo-Nazi National States Rights party. SNCC readily admitted the source of its diatribes, adding a few of its own anti-Semitic items and some lurid cartoons for local color.

At about the time SNCC was turning away from Dr. King's tutelage, a far more dangerously effective armed black revolutionary group was being organized on the West Coast. The Black Panther party was better led, more tightly organized, clearer in its revolutionary ideology, and firmer in its alliances with the white organizations of the Radical Left. Its membership was never very great—perhaps 3,000 at its peak—but its supporters may have numbered as many as 60,000. The circulation of its weekly publication passed 100,000 and it seemed to attain a vogue in some fashionable and intellectual circles. But the Panthers were committed to the overthrow of American society, considering themselves a "vanguard" party in the Marxist struggle against capitalism and blacks the instrument for revolution. It saw no hope for black liberation in a democratic and capitalist state.

No group suffered more from splintering, internal conflicts, and power struggles so characteristic of leftist movements than the Black Panther party; nor were other groups exposed to more police power and community pressure. Their threats of guerrilla warfare and armed revolution were taken seriously. Shooting confrontations with police occurred from time to time, and there were casualties as a result of internal quarrels. A police raid on Panther lodgings in Chicago on December 4, 1969, during which two of its members were killed led to a Federal grand jury investigation. The report was critical of the extent of police force used. In New Haven, Connecticut, Bobby Seale, the party chairman, and 13 other Black Panthers were tried for the murder of a dissident member.

The reporting on Panther activity and clashes with the law has been extensive. Less thoroughly explored have been the party's forays into anti-Semitism. From its very founding in the San Francisco Bay Area in 1966 by Huey P. Newton and Bobby Seale, the Black Panthers allied themselves with Al Fatah, the Palestinian terrorist organization, and became the principal supporter of the Arab cause in the black community. It fitted the party's image of itself as a guerrilla group. The standard leftist line developed from this starting point—Arabs, as part of the Third World, fighting for national liberation; the United States as imperialist oppressor, both at home and abroad; Israel its Mideast "lackey" and American Jewish intellectuals the inventors of domestic policies oppressing blacks. These banalities were repeated in infinite variations and tailored to suit every occasion. When Bobby Seale and Huey Newton were imprisoned in 1969, Eldridge Cleaver, who himself had fled the country in 1968 to avoid imprisonment after a gun battle between Black Panthers and Oakland police, announced from Algiers that they were jailed by "Zionist magistrates." When a public-spirited group headed by former U.S. Supreme Court Justice Arthur Goldberg formed a "Commission of Inquiry" into the clashes between police and Panthers, Cleaver charged that "the power structure is trying to take control of the situation by using a well-known Zionist."

A split developed in the party in mid-1971 between Cleaver and the Huey Newton–Bobby Seale group. Newton and Seale in Oakland turned to seeking control of community institutions; Cleaver established a base in Harlem for a new publication, *Right On*, to continue the original revolutionary policy. But both continued their anti-Jewish stance. They saw no evil in the massacre of Israeli athletes at the Munich Olympics, played infinite changes on their accusations of Israel's perfidy, railed against American Jews for oppressing Blacks and supporting "Israeli terrorism."

The passage of time brought its fascinating changes. After years in Algeria and elsewhere in the Middle East, Cleaver returned home a born-again Christian and a considerably changed man. Huey Newton had fled to Cuba in 1974, as Cleaver before him, to avoid a murder charge in the death of a seventeen-year-old girl. He returned in 1977 with a quite different view of America than when he had left. In the meantime, Bobby Seale had run for mayor of Oakland, made a very respectable showing, but then left the party. Until Newton returned, its leadership fell to Elaine Brown, who pursued the direction he had set, before he fled, toward community and service programs and increasing acceptance within Oakland political circles.

Newton's change of heart about America—that violent revolution was no longer necessary to bring about "full employment first and socialism based on the American experience at some distant time"— did not carry over to his feelings about his revolutionary colleagues. He blamed Cleaver for the Black Panthers' violent image that in the early 1970's sent "a lot of our most courageous younger brothers" to prison and some to their death. Panther violence he found "antagonized the black community."

"I never understood him," he said of Cleaver. "If he's a born-again

Christian, that's between him and his God. But he seemed to always be in whatever is in vogue in the country, and that's the revivals now as it was the black revolution in the 1960's."

After his Middle East experience, Cleaver's turnabout on the American political system was even more complete:

"With all of its faults," he wrote in *The New York Times* explaining why he was returning, "the American political system is the freest and most democratic in the world. The system needs to be improved, with democracy spread to all areas of life, particularly the economic. All of these changes must be conducted through our established institutions, and people with grievances must find political methods for obtaining redress."

Gone the fiery rhetoric of the revolutionary; gone the threat of guns and violence; gone, too, the cheap anti-Semitic propaganda he had spouted for so many years. Out of his Middle East experience, he wrote in 1975 in criticism of the Arab-sponsored United Nations resolution which equated Zionism with racism.

"To condemn the Jewish survival doctrine of Zionism as racism is a travesty upon the truth.... I am surprised that the Arabs would choose to establish a precedent condemning racism because it can so easily and righteously be turned against them. Having lived for several years amongst the Arabs, I know them to be amongst the most racist people on earth."

Describing black slaveholding among Arabs, he wrote: "I have seen such slaves with my own eyes. Once I pressed an Algerian official for an explanation... and he ended up describing a complicated form of indentured servitude...it was nothing but a hypocritical form of slavery."

His disillusionment brought him back home to a prison cell in California where "I write these words." Of the United Nations, he said, "The General Assembly is no longer filled with Mahatma Gandhis...it is now a forum for crude hired killers like Idi Amin....Concrete steps must be taken to render the U.N. structurally incapable of cynical manipulation by hypocritical power blocs that devour freedom...with a reckless distortion of the right to vote."

The recantation seemed complete. The man who for years had "cynically" allied himself with the "hypocritical power bloc" and repeated its vilification of Jews now "speaking out from a prison cell" recited his *mea culpa*; "...of all the people in the world, the Jews have not only suffered particularly from racist persecution, they have done more than any other people in history to expose and condemn racism."

The Nation of Islam

Not quite in the tradition of Radical Left politics but radical nevertheless is the sectarian and separatist movement popularly called the Black Muslims and formally designated by its founder as the Nation of Islam. It is the creation of one Elijah Poole, who styled himself Elijah Muhammad, Messenger of Allah. Whatever pretensions it has as a Moslem sect, is rejected by orthodox Moslems. It is messianic in the manner of a Father Divine, seeking religious conversion and the self-improvement of the converts. It is rigid, disciplined, and self-righteous as might be expected of an orthodoxy. All this might have its social value if the Black Muslims were not also hate-filled, violent, and prone to criminality.

The movement was founded by Poole in the early 1930's. Its dissidence and separatism came to public attention during World War II, when many of its members refused to register for the draft and the organization expressed its hatred of whites by sympathizing with the Japanese. Elijah Muhammad was put in jail for a number of years. Yet the organization grew in stability, testimony to the zeal of its adherents and the organizational abilities of its leadership.

Despite its successes, the Black Muslims remained a fringe group within the Negro community, eaten away by internal feuds, never entering the mainstream because of its separatism and its rejection of the basic religious traditions of the community. Nevertheless, it was a force to be reckoned with. This was dramatized by the turmoil created in the New York community in the 1960's when Malcolm X, Elijah Muhammad's second-in-command, broke away to form the Organization for Afro-American Unity. Malcolm X's stepped-up efforts to gain support among Arabs abroad called attention to the anti-Semitism in the Black Muslim credo. There now developed a competition as to which group could be more vitriolic.

Muhammad Speaks, the Black Muslim weekly periodical, maintained a steady tigade of anti-Jewish charges. Understanding the uses of violence, these usually stressed fictitious violence allegedly practiced by Israel against Arabs, quite the reverse of the reportage from the Mideast that appeared in the general press: "Is Life of an Arab in Israel like a Black Man's in Alabama?" "Arabs Describe Israeli Torture,"

"Israel Building New Concentration Camps," "Israelis Imitate Their Former Oppressors," "Israel Torture, Theft Cause Hijackings." Eventually, the tactic paid off for Elijah Muhammad. In 1972 *Muhammad Speaks* was able to report a $3,000,000 interest-free loan from Libya and gifts totaling nearly $300,000 from Abu Dhabi, Qatar, Syria, and Bahrain.

In its attacks on Jews, the Black Muslims leaned heavily on *The Protocols of the Elders of Zion* thesis. Not American "imperialism" but the Jewish "conspiracy" to manipulate the world was their target. American Jewish "Zionist millionaires" are brought "together by the common exploitative essence of capital, by their common hatred of progress and freedom of the peoples." They manipulate the big monopolies and banks of America, the politicians and the press. And all the evidence could be found at the bookshops of the Nation of Islam such as the one in the principal mosque in New York where at least two editions of *The Protocols* were available, one published by Gerald L. K. Smith and the other by the Reform Society of Kuwait. There was also a collection of Smith's anti-Semitic pamphlets and such delectable items as *A History of Jewish Crime* published in Karachi, Pakistan, by the Asia Book Center. The burden of that work of scholarship: "the Jews always commit crimes because they are incapable of everything else . . ."

Elijah Muhammad died in February 1975 and was succeeded as leader by his son, Wallace D. Muhammad. A man not burdened with his father's pretensions to be the messenger of God, Wallace Muhammad almost immediately began to open the windows of his separatist society to the outside world. He expressed an interest in entering the mainstream of the black community, conforming to more orthodox Mohammedanism and even to end the isolation of the Black Muslims from the white world around them. From the beginning, he exhibited the qualities of the practical politician. He dropped the title "Messenger of Allah," changed the name of the Nation of Islam to the World Community of Islam in the West, freed his followers to pursue non-Moslem activities, to serve in the armed forces, and to vote in elections. The latter fact was not lost on political and civic figures in Chicago, the home base of the organization, who in 1977 joined in a public dinner in his honor—an event designed to exhibit the new face and interest of the changed World Community of Islam.

The changes in policy and tactics were most evident in the group's newspaper. The title *Muhammad Speaks* was dropped in favor of the name *Bilalian News* (bilalian means black). The column of the Arab propagandist Ali Baghdadi disappeared from its pages, and so did attacks on Israel. News from Arab lands reflected their support of the organization, usually of a financial nature. In place of the continuing attacks on both Christianity and Judaism which had characterized *Muhammad Speaks*, the renamed publication on June 4, 1976, recorded that Wallace Muhammad "demonstrated the unity of all believers and the oneness of all the great heroes of Judaism, Christianity and Islam" and admonished all to do more about combating social injustice. Editorially, in June 1977, *Bilalian News* played on the same theme:

> ...we hold on to our truth and we do not allow a Judaic interpretation of that truth or a Christian interpretation... to influence us or to distract us [but] we have to recognize that we are all people in one group... we are all in one boat together. We have only one enemy... that enemy is ignorance, arrogance, greed and moral corruption. These are the enemies of all of us, so we all have to band together to overcome the common enemy.

Difficult Allies

The black power groups made prickly allies. Intoxicated with the notion of power, they flexed their muscles in public and took arbitrary stances within the conclaves of both the Radical Left and the black community. The Radical Left showed little ability to cope with their difficult allies and often gave way to their more untenable demands. On the other hand, responsible black leaders, surer of their ground, could not readily be budged from principled positions. They better understood the weakness and the dangers of black power pretensions.

How well the black power groups succeeded in imposing their programs depended upon the composition of the meetings. At the National Conference on Black Power held in Newark in July 1967, shortly after the devastating riots in that city, the delegates went far afield from their most urgent concerns to condemn "Israeli oppression against Arabs." No one objected effectively, because in the aftermath of the riots, anti-Jewish feelings were widely expressed. A follow-up meeting of the same groups in Philadelphia in 1968, seeking ways to express their animus found the Nigerian-Biafran civil war part of an Israeli "plot" to take over Africa.

More significant was the ability of the black radicals to impose their will on the National Conference for New Politics, a convention of Old and New Left groups which drew in many civil rights, antipoverty and peace activists and organizations. The convention was held in Chicago in September 1967, and its goal was to explore the possibility of a third-party ticket in the Presidential elections of 1968. The explorations quickly descended into factionalism and to a split along racial lines. Forming a caucus, the black delegates promptly faced the convention with a set of "nonnegotiable demands." Though they constituted only 30 percent of the delegates, they demanded 50 percent of the votes. Presenting a set of thirteen resolutions, they insisted these be adopted without change or deletion. If not, they would all walk out. The Radical Left majority at the conference were not unfamiliar with such tactics; they engaged in such practices themselves, but they could not afford to have the blacks bolt. The convention adopted the Black Caucus demands by a two-to-one vote including a resolution condemning "the imperialistic Zionist war."

The Radical Left could not have found that resolution unpalatable, for they added the other side of the trite equation calling on "United States imperialism" to cease "interfering in the Middle East." But black leaders like Dr. King did. The Southern Christian Leadership Conference people who attended the conference he said, "were the most vigorous and articulate opponents of the simplistic resolution on the Middle East question," and denounced the convention's anti-Semitism as "immoral." Israel's right to exist, he said, was "uncontestable." The New York Times editorially expressed the general public view of the convention travesty, finding "appeasing Negro extremists" morally inexcusable. "Negro extremists are using old Stalinist tactics and their victims will find—as did the Stalinists victims earlier—that they have paid a high price for very little or nothing."

Responsible black leadership was sensitive to the tactics but constantly exposed to a tug-of-war with extremist groups. Typical of the problems they faced was an anti-Israel resolution introduced in the closing minutes of a National Black Political Convention held in Gary, Indiana, in March 1972. The convention was a gathering of the full range of Negro interest groups to plan an agenda for effective political action. It was chaired jointly by Mayor Richard Hatcher of Gary, Congressman Charles C. Diggs of Michigan, and Le Roi Jones, the poet whose anti-Semitic verse and extremist politics had made him an influential figure among black power groups. With 3,300 delegates and 5,000 other attendees, the convention at best faced a difficult task to achieve a consensus. The last-minute Mideast resolution practically destroyed the effort. After the convention's "Continuations Committee" made its report, Congressman Diggs and Mayor Hatcher dissociated themselves from the anti-Israel resolution. Congressman Louis Stokes, chairman of the Congressional Black Caucus, speaking for his 13 fellow congressmen, reaffirmed their support of Israel and detailed its "cordial relations" with the developing nations in Africa. Roy Wilkins, executive director of the NAACP, announced the organization's withdrawal from the convention "because of a difference in ideology as to how to win equality for the Negro minority," at the same time condemning the anti-Israel resolution. And finally, Samuel Jackson, the highest-ranking black official in the Administration, in a letter to the Anti-Defamation League, wrote that "the views expressed in that resolution are not those held by the great majority of blacks in this country. We are both aware and appreciative of the role which Israel has played in the economic development of many of the African nations."

The National Black Political Convention offered merely another example of the disruptive power of black extremist groups. But even in the years that they flourished, the leaders and organizations that espoused separatism in the black community had an evanescent quality. One after another, they rocketed to prominence and then faded from view to be replaced by others. Excessive violence, troubles with the law, failure to hold constituencies together, loss of financial support, but mostly a failure to penetrate to the solid center of the black community which clung to the hope of the ultimate success of integration led to increasing isolation of black extremists.

NINE

"...Hatred...Is Sacred."

In 1968, shortly after the Israel victory in the Six Day War, the director general of UNESCO received a letter from the Syrian Minister of Education, rejecting the findings of a UNESCO Commission that had examined textbooks used to teach Arab children in refugee camps financed by the United Nations Relief and Works Agency (UNRWA). The report had noted that a majority of the 127 textbooks reviewed by the Commission employed the "deplorable language of anti-Semitism," distorted history, incited to violence, and were educationally destructive because "...student exercises...[were] often inspired by a preoccupation with indoctrination against Jews rather than by educational aims."

Wrote the Syrian minister: "The hatred which we indoctrinate into the minds of our children from their birth is sacred."

The Western mind is startled by such unabashed bluntness, perhaps because it is centuries removed from its own history of religious wars. In an Arab world where everyone is either a "believer" or an "infidel," and everything is either "holy" or "profane," even hatred can be called "sacred." Even the minds of children—perhaps especially the minds of children—are weapons of warfare.

The educational system to which the international commission had taken exception was all part of the total war against Jews and it washed against American shores as elsewhere. It had its small victories here as Nazism did in the pre–World War II period. Arab propaganda efforts won acceptance, at first, on the rightist lunatic fringe. But as we have seen, it had greater success—because of the different political climate—on the Radical Left and with alienated groups of the 1960's. Though victory over Israel was its ultimate purpose, the Arab propaganda attack was aimed not against Israel alone—it was aimed against Jews everywhere: Jews as supporters of Israel, Jews as possible settlers in Israel, Jews as infidels whose fate, according to the Koran, was "humiliation and wretchedness" and who had been "visited with the wrath of Allah."

Arab propaganda left little to the imagination. *The Protocols of the Learned Elders of Zion* became a staple as early as 1920 and has in the sixty years since then appeared in a number of Arabic translations and editions. It has been quoted and serialized and peddled all over the world by Arabs. As conflict in the Middle East grew, even before the establishment of Israel, leading Arab politicians turned to it as a text with increasing frequency. Gamal Abdel Nasser found it "very important" as a key to Zionism. He told an Indian editor in the 1950's that it "proves beyond a shadow of a doubt that 300 Zionists, each of whom knows all the others, govern the fate of the European continent"—this after the destruction of European Jewry. Wasfi Tal, the Prime Minister of Jordan, later assassinated by Palestinian terrorists, lectured in 1970 at the Jordanian University on "the world Jewish conspiracy" and documented his thesis with *The Protocols*. In Libya, Colonel Muammar el Qaddafi keeps a copy on his desk and recommends it to visitors as "a most important document."

Hitler's *Mein Kampf* also found favor in the Arab world. Considering that Arab leaders, such as Haj Amin al-Husseini, the Grand Mufti of Jerusalem, backed the Nazis in World War II, and in the postwar period provided havens for fleeing war criminals, this is not strange. Interest in Hitler and the possibility that he might yet return was a recurring subject of discussion in the Arab press of the 1950's. Arab leaders followed Nazi propaganda methods diligently and came to rely on the Goebbels technique of the Big Lie and the repetition of the most outrageous libels. It is difficult to determine whether Arab propagandists were apt pupils or inept practitioners who actually believed their own fabrications. David Hiost of the *Manchester Guardian*, reporting on a 1972 interview with King Faisal of Saudi Arabia, found him "apparently carried away" with the "blood libel" myth that Jews killed Gentile children for ritual purposes in the preparation of Passover matzoth. It was "an extraordinary outpouring of anti-Semitic prejudices,'' Hiost wrote. Extraordinary or not, Faisal repeated the story to the Cairo weekly, *Al Mussarrat*:

"Two years ago when I was in Paris, police discovered the bodies of five children.... Afterwards it turned out that Jews killed the children to mix their blood into their bread."

Arab propagandists, Faisal among them, also learned to make their fabrications "newsworthy." In the spring of 1973, American government officials and other public figures received a letter from the chairman of the Palestine Arab Delegation, a lobbying group, warning that "Zionist-Jew leaders in the U.S. have converted the Watergate incident...into a great 'scandal' to blackmail the President...[in order] to dictate to the President the Middle East policy of the United States." He then asked: "Are you willing to sit back and helplessly watch Israel and the Zionist-Jew leaders in the U.S. complete their domination of the U.S. government?" King Faisal repeated the theme a couple of months later with an added fillip. He was reported by United Press International as seeing both Watergate and the Lambton parliamentary sex scandal in London as "Zionist plots" to undermine the two governments because they were beginning to favor Arabs.

Such forays into the thickets of anti-Semitic diatribe did not prove very helpful in winning friends for the Arab states among troubled Americans seeking a solution for the problems of the Middle East. The responses came primarily from the political fringes and from such front groups as Arab money could buy or organize, even as the Nazis had done in the 1930's.

Boycott as Warfare

In their efforts to wage total war against Jews, however, the Arab states hit on a device considerably more disturbing than the primitive anti-Semitism of *The Protocols* and the blood libels. The instrument chosen was an economic boycott of the Jews of Palestine (and later the State of Israel) by all of the states in the Arab League. The League's formation was sponsored in 1944 by Britain to foster some semblance of unity among Arabs that might lead to peaceful development in the Middle East. The Arab interpretation of unity was to unite against the Jews of Palestine. At the close of 1945, a boycott declaration placed a ban on "Jewish products and manufactured goods"; it urged all Arabs "to refuse to deal in...or consume Zionist products," and called for the opening of boycott offices in each of the Arab capitals—all this at least three years before Arab rejection of the United Nations Palestine partition plan and the establishment of the State of Israel. Having lost the military battle in 1948, the Arabs turned to intensified economic warfare against the new state. The boycott was followed by closing of the Suez Canal to Israeli shipping or neutral vessels headed for Israeli ports. This led to the second Israeli-Arab war in 1956 and Egyptian blocking of the canal with sunken ships.

The economic boycott had by this time entered a second phase. It was extended to include companies in the United States and Europe that traded with Israel. Ultimately it was extended further to all American and foreign companies doing business with companies already blacklisted for trading with Israel. The ability of Arab nations to enforce such triple-tiered economic sanctions—first Israel, then companies doing business with Israel, then companies doing business with companies doing business with Israel—was questionable and led to Arab inconsistencies and absurdities that diminished their effectiveness. But it also had its successes.

American Jews, vitally concerned with the fate of Israel, soon found that they, too, were in the line of Arab fire. Once more from a foreign source came, not only anti-Semitic propaganda, but efforts to tilt American business and even American government agencies against Jews, their employment, their economic opportunities and their civil rights. As early as 1950, the Anti-Defamation League protested State Department acquiescence to a clause in an agreement with Saudi Arabia that barred American Jewish servicemen "as members of the U.S. armed forces at Dharan Air Base." For the next quarter century, the League was to conduct a vigorous countercampaign against Arab boycott pressures in the United States.

The story of the boycott in all its myriad detail of Arab-Israeli conflict and Western business manners and political morals—both good and bad—has been well told in two books: Dan S. Chill's *The Arab-Boycott of Israel* (1976) and Walter H. Nelson and Terence Prittie's *The Economic War Against the Jews* (1977). The effort here will be to relate the story to the American scene, the impact upon anti-Semitism in the United States and the key role of the Anti-Defamation League.

Despite Arab protestations that the boycott was conceived as a defensive measure, in practice and performance it has always exhibited the characteristics of guerrilla warfare—the economic equivalent of the terrorist tactics favored by Al Fatah, the Palestine Liberation Organization (PLO) and their associates. As with the international acts of violence and plane hijackings, bystanders often suffered more than Israel, the principal target. Indeed, Israel found the boycott a not very effective economic weapon for the Arabs up to 1973, when the Arabs were able to bring to bear their newfound strength as a vital source of oil for Western industry. In particular instances, the Arab boycott served to stimulate the growth of some Israeli industries and development of new ones, such as shipping and the El Al airline. In the score of years from 1950 to 1970, Israel's economy flourished, some years rising at a rate of 10 percent. Yet, the boycott was costly, too; it impeded foreign investment and trade with major international companies fearful of losing Arab markets. The Israeli economics ministry played the issue in low key, seeking to avoid public conflict with companies whose products were needed and which were submitting to Arab pressure. The Israeli foreign ministry pursued the problem more aggressively. It took the view that boycott was not solely an economic, but also a political and propaganda matter and saw in it a denigration of Israeli sovereignty.

For years the Arab boycott remained a quixotic affair. Each Arab nation made its own rules—or changed them, if it served its own purposes—even to the detriment of the common goal. The inconsistencies which the world saw were dictated by the weakness of the Arab attempt to make the boycott serve three functions—as economic, propaganda, and political weapons. This often led to ludicrous situations. The humor was not lost on Americans when it was learned that the film *Funny Girl* was banned as offensive because actor Omar Sharif, an Arab, playing opposite singer Barbra Streisand, who is Jewish, kissed her in a romantic moment of this sentimental movie. Often names were placed on boycott lists simply because they were well known and would attract attention to the boycott. Elizabeth Taylor had her movies banned because she was a "Zionist" and had bought Israeli bonds; Sophia Loren, the Italian actress, because she had played in *Judith*, a film about the 1948 war. The film *Exodus* brought down the Arab wrath on all its participants—Paul Newman and Sal Mineo, the stars, and even actress Joanne Woodward, Newman's wife in real life. Otto Preminger and United Artists were placed on the blacklist because they had produced *Exodus*. That was not a new idea. According to *Variety*, the theatrical newspaper, the major American movie producers were asked in 1954 to report whether their principals were Christians or Jews and how many Jews were employed. It was fairly obvious the answers for the four major companies—MGM, Columbia, Universal, and Paramount—would not win friends for them in the Central Arab Boycott Office, but it really did not matter much because there were no movie audiences to speak of in Arab countries except Lebanon and Egypt. Yet, for the propaganda value—at least so the Arabs believed—dozens of stars, from Harry Belafonte to Marilyn Monroe and Esther Williams, then the darlings of Hollywood, were blacklisted.

Some blacklistings brought forth sardonic responses and nowhere more than in the field of art and music. Verdi's opera *Nabucco*, which tells the biblical story of the Babylonian captivity, was blacklisted because it presented "an historic event in a way to create sympathy for Jews and serve Israel propaganda." Walt Disney's film *Snow White and the Seven Dwarfs* could not be shown in Syria because the Prince's horse was named Samson. The Syrians suggested a name change to "Simpson." Folk-singer Joan Baez came under a ban because she sang of "the children Moses led through the desert" and again of holding a "ticket to the Promised Land."

In 1975 Arab sensibilities were outraged in the very halls of the United Nations when they learned that a cantata based on the Twelfth Psalm, composed for the occasion by Austrian composer Gottfried Von Einem contained the words "Behold, He that keepeth Israel shall neither slumber nor sleep." Shocking Zionist propaganda, the Arabs charged. The phrase was dropped. The Temple University Choir which was to sing the cantata protested the omission. Chaim Herzog, the Israeli ambassador, commented that, in view of its recent record, he "was not surprised" to find the U.N. "trying to rewrite the Bible." Von Einem insisted that he, at least, was not politically motivated and offered to write a chorale to be called "The Keeper of Israel."

Pressure on U.S. Business

But the Arab boycott was not to remain the stumbling, bumbling effort reflected in these incidents. The lack of discipline and the ineptitude among Arab officials concerned with the boycott was in time offset by businessmen eager for Arab trade and willing to compromise in order to get it. The major change in the boycott's effectiveness came with the development of oil as a weapon of economic warfare and the growth of business opportunities to billion-dollar levels for American and other foreign companies in the Arab Middle East. As long as the stakes were small, major industries—the great

multinational companies and banks—were able and generally inclined to fend off Arab attempts at boycott blackmail. It was more
difficult for smaller firms. The boycott battles in the 1960's swirled
about four American corporate giants: Coca-Cola, Ford Motor Company, Radio Corporation of America (RCA) and American Express.
Each in its way fended off the Arabs, valuing its image in America
more than the Arab connection.

Coca-Cola became a public issue in March 1965 when an Israeli
bottler charged that his company had been denied a franchise because
of the Arab boycott. When the story appeared in *The Wall Street
Journal*, Coca-Cola issued a prompt denial and cited a series of reasons
why there was no Israeli franchise—reasons it had presented earlier to
the Anti-Defamation League. Briefly, Coca-Cola declared that it was
disposed to grant franchises only in instances where the arrangement
could be mutually profitable, where the franchise applicant had a
$1,000,000 investment and was willing to give primary attention to
Coca-Cola as against its other soft drink interests. The League's own
investigation of these criteria, however, had shown that they seemed
to be tailored to keep a franchise out of Israel. Ten bottlers in eight
different countries approximately the size of Israel, including Kuwait,
Iraq, and Lebanon, had franchises. Their capital investments aver-
aged $245,000, and one bottler in Ireland was capitalized only at
$14,000. The Israeli firm, Tempo Soft Drink Company, which had
applied for a franchise as early as 1960, owned a new $3,000,000
bottling plant and had a net worth, as rated by Dun and Bradstreet, of
$500,000 above that figure. Furthermore, Tempo had offered to change
its name to Coca-Cola of Israel.

The League felt that Coca-Cola had really bowed to Arab boycott
pressure, but James A. Farley, then board chairman of Coca-Cola
Export Corporation, insisted that as early as 1950 Coca-Cola had
offered a franchise to Israel only to have the Government refuse the
proposed franchiser a permit to operate. Coca-Cola would not deal
with Tempo, Farley said, because "in 1963 the Israeli courts found [it]
guilty of infringement of the Coca-Cola trademark and bottle design."
Actually, the case had been settled out of court, and the bottle design
had not been at issue. As for the 1950 franchise, it had been offered to
an American businessman, Abraham Feinberg, who decided that
only two years after the establishment of the State, that Israel could ill
afford to commit any of its limited foreign exchange for the luxury of
having a popular soft drink. In 1966 this was no longer true. Israel was

economically stable and the Arab states were threatening every major company that might consider dealing with it. Coca-Cola felt public pressure all over America at the point of sale in restaurants, grocery stores, and soda fountains. Coca-Cola quickly moved to end the matter. Two days after the League made public its findings and negotiations with Coca-Cola at a press conference, the company announced its own reassessment and the granting of a franchise to Feinberg and his group. In talks with the company, Arnold Forster, who was the League's spokeman, expressed the view that Coca-Cola officials were moved by "the fact that they could not stand the heat of a public argument about whether or not they had submitted to Arab blackmail."

Ma'ariv, the Israeli newspaper that had first made the issue, commented editorially that "... while in any other country Coca-Cola is just a soft drink... we [saw] in Coca-Cola... a political device. The struggle to obtain... production of Coca-Cola in Israel... was a political struggle against the Arab boycott...."

The Coca-Cola decision was clearly a propaganda defeat for the Arab boycott forces. A wide public had become aware of Arab blackmail of American business and reacted with anger. Now a major American company had publicly decided that the price of dealing with the Arabs was too great in terms of its own interests and image. Within the highest circles of American industry, the action of the Ford Motor Company, in the same period, was an even greater blow to the boycott. In 1966, Ford simply decided that it would submit to no outside dictation as to where and when it might do business. It announced that it was completing a deal in Israel whereby the Palestine Automobile Corporation, Ltd., which had been a distributor of Ford products for thirty years, would build Ford trucks and tractors from "knockdown" kits supplied by Ford. The assembly plant would be in operation within the year, and Ford would thus become the first major American automaker with such a facility in the Israeli market.

The Arab response was immediate. Saudi Arabia ordered Ford agents to leave the country within three months. The Arab League Boycott Committee voted unanimously to ban dealings with Ford. Plants in Egypt and Morocco were closed down. But the Ford company held to its principled position. "We are definitely going forward with our plans for Israel," Henry Ford II wrote the Anti-Defamation League in 1967. "We feel we have the unchallenged right to compete in any market of the world willing to accept us as an industrial citizen." And in 1973 he told a meeting of Israeli industrialists: "We are more than willing to do business with any country, but we are unwilling to refrain from doing business with one country as a prerequisite to doing business with others."

But for all the threats and blacklistings, Ford's market in Arab countries did not dry up; it continued to sell trucks to Jordan, and Ford vehicles captured by Israel from Arab forces in the 1973 War numbered in the thousands. By 1975 Egypt was again asking Ford either to reopen its old plant or build a new one for the manufacture of diesel engines, cars and trucks.

The position taken by Ford was followed by other major corporations with muscles to flex and reputations to protect. The Radio Corporation of America was blacklisted by the Arabs in 1966. It had licensed an Israeli company to issue records under the RCA label. Since records represented but a tiny fraction of its several million dollars in sales in the Arab states, RCA was offered the opportunity to "buy" its way off the blacklist. Recognizing that it was opening the door to outright blackmail, RCA refused the deal. To RCA, the boycott was both "capricious and insidious." Said Eugene P. Seculow, RCA's international vice-president, with much the same reasoning as Ford: "Our position has been very simple. We believe in free trade and we are attempting to do business everywhere in the world where it is not against U.S. laws. But we won't comply in any way with the boycott or try to negotiate our way off the list."

American Express, perhaps a more vulnerable company because, as a travel service, it is subject to all of the vagaries of international politics, represents the giant that panicked and then regained its composure. In 1956 American Express closed its Israeli offices, claiming that the operation had become unprofitable. The figures did not bear this out. Tourist traffic had in fact increased, and the Israeli tourist office found itself "convinced beyond a doubt" that the company had responded to "threats of the Arab boycott"—a fact confirmed by American Express asking for State Department aid in its dealing with the Arabs. But it also had the problem of dealing with pressure from home. "We pointed out to them", Forster reported on a meeting with company officials, "that there was another factor at play...important in the American scheme of things: one's reputation in business." Before it became a public issue, American Express reopened an office in Israel; its Arab offices continued to operate, for once more the Arab nations showed they would blink at violations of their boycott when it suited their purposes. They needed American Express.

But for every company that stood its ground, there were scores of weaker or hungrier ones that bowed to the boycott whether they needed to or not in order to benefit from what they thought to be the rich Arab market; they got encouragement in this from the actions and policies of some key American government departments.

The Oil Weapon

With the oil embargo of 1973, Americans suddenly became aware that economic pressure was capable of unsettling their lives. In the long lines at gasoline service stations during this period, the word "boycott" took on menacing meaning. By 1975 congressional leaders were looking with troubled eyes on the seduction of American business, the collusive actions of Government bureaucracy, and the intrusion of foreign influences into certain hallowed American precincts.

At the same time, American Jews began to see themselves, as well as Israel, as prime Arab targets. The boycott pressures and the flexing of Arab muscle at the United Nations brought American Jewish organizations to a decision to pursue an aggressive and coordinated program to counter the boycott. They were led in this effort by the Anti-Defamation League, the American Jewish Committee, and the American Jewish Congress, and were to have a telling effect.

In the years from 1975 through 1978, moves to counter the boycott revolved around the strengthening of the antiboycott provisions of the Export Administration Act of 1969, which stated American policy as opposed to "restrictive trade or boycott" and to compliance by American companies with such practices "imposed by any foreign country against another . . . friendly to the U.S." It required business to report all boycott demands to the Commerce Department, but did not call for compliance with such illegal demands or require reports on the actions taken. Even failure to report boycott demands, however, went largely unchallenged by the Commerce Department, and other departments were found to encourage business to comply with Arab demands. Congressional hearings in 1975 focused on these problems.

Ever so slowly, but increasingly with the passing years, the American public—and certainly American leadership—became aware that the boycott weapon in the hands of the Arab states was being used to subvert American civil rights laws and practices. The economic strength derived from oil emboldened the Central Arab Boycott Committee beyond the point of discretion. If the world could be blackmailed into refusing to do business with Israel, why not use the boycott for other Arab purposes? Why not tell the media that it had to see things the Arab way? It seemed worth a try. On March 1, 1975, United Press International reported that the Columbia Broadcasting Company and the National Broadcasting Company were threatened with expulsion from Arab countries unless tmeir news coverage was "beneficial to the Arab cause and under the supervision of the Arabs."

The immediate response of Richard Salant, president of CBS News was: "CBS News has covered news in all major Arab cities but never 'under supervision,' nor would CBS permit any government, including the U.S. Government, to dictate the contents of our news coverage." NBC spoke in a similar vein. That ended the matter; the Arabs backed off, and a year later, to save face, announced that the two networks had been dropped from the blacklists but would be kept "under supervision."

Not all American business was inclined to act so forthrightly. On February 25, 1975, almost simultaneously with the Arab attack on American freedom of the press as revealed in the CBS and NBC incidents, Seymour Graubard, national chairman of the Anti-Defamation League, made public a report which charged a long list of American companies with violation of the nation's antiboycott regulations and antidiscrimination laws—some responding to Arab pressure, others acting voluntarily "as they scrambled for a piece of the Arabs' new wealth." Most unseemly was the dropping of Jewish staff members by some companies seeking Arab business. "Anyone with a sense of history," Graubard commented, "can see that Jews are once more being singled out" for discrimination.

The activities of the offending companies were sometimes startling in their crudity. Such blunt strictures against employment of Jews had not been heard in decades and had long been outlawed. But here was a teacher recruitment agency issuing job orders for Middle East schools, announcing that teachers who are Jewish, have Jewish surnames, or Jewish ancestors need not apply.

— A mortgage company offering investments to a Midwest bank provided "no board member or director shall be Jewish."

— An engineering firm, recruiting for projects under the supervision of the U.S. Army Corps of Engineers, asking applicants to state their religion.

— A chemical company setting forth a policy of not dealing with Israel "either directly or indirectly" because it "represents too serious a risk to even consider."

— A Midwest American medical supplies company which agreed to prohibit Jews from handling any aspect of the shipment of goods under a $20,000,000 contract with Saudi Arabia.

— An East Coast architectural-planning company which told a qualified Jewish applicant he couldn't be hired because it was actively seeking contracts with three Arab countries and had received a letter stipulating that no Jews be employed on the project; another which asked the sales representative of a nationally known building supply firm whether he or his company was Jewish "because we have a contract with Saudi Arabia and it's been implied that we're not to do business with Jews"; a third which eliminated all identifiably Jewish names from its company brochures as part of a sales campaign to solicit Arab business; and yet a fourth working on Saudi Arabian projects under the supervision of the U.S. Army Corps of Engineers, which told Jewish applicants it could not hire them because the contracts prohibited Jewish employees and even the products of certain manufacturers.

In response, President Gerald Ford, at a press conference in Florida the next day, ordered investigation of the League's charges by the State, Justice and Commerce departments, warning that his Administration would not tolerate discrimination "repugnant to American principles." They have "no place in the free practice of commerce as it has flourished in this country...." He warned foreign investors to take note that they were "welcome in the U.S." so long as "they were willing to conform to the principles of our society."

Government and public thus became newly aware of the issue and the degree to which the law and deeply held American beliefs had been flouted. The involvement of the Army Corps of Engineers was particularly troubling. Corps officials had admitted carrying out Saudi Arabian exclusionary policies in testimony before a Senate subcommittee investigating its work. A Corps spokesman said merely it was "acquiescing on instructions of the Department of State," and a State Department official had testified that it took a "low-key approach" and preferred to make no issue, even though Saudi Arabian anti-Jewish policies were being abetted within the United States itself by the American Government—the very thing the President was to warn against.

On March 6, in testimony before the House Subcommittee on International Trade and Commerce, Graubard stressed the admitted complicity of the Army Corps of Engineers and urged legislation "to prevent the intrusion of offensive foreign discriminatory practices" in American affairs. "Relations with foreign countries" he testified, "must be premised on the inviolability of our own constitutional principles and declared policies."

On June 10 and thereafter, the League filed legal complaints under the Civil Rights Act against several American corporations, a first test of the Act's extraterritorial jurisdiction. It was an effort to compel companies to cease their collusion in discrimination and to obtain a ruling nullifying the clause in the 1974 U.S.–Saudi Arabian trade agreement, whereby the U.S. agreed to be "sensitive" to the Saudis' "religious contexts"—the euphemism for barring Jews. Some companies quickly entered into negotiations with the League and settlements were reached, for the U.S. Equal Employment Opportunity Commission early took the position that the Civil Rights Act of 1964, as the law of the land, took precedence over any executive agreements entered into with other nations.

The League thus filed charges against a personnel procurement firm, the American Bureau of Shipping Worldwide Technical Services, for denying jobs to American Jewish engineers on projects in Iraq and Bahrain. The complaints came before the EEOC and the New York State Division on Human Rights. The EEOC started an investigation. The New York State organization found "probable cause" and set a hearing. Not to prolong the proceedings, ABS came to a settlement with the League. It agreed that it would no longer accede to the discriminatory policies of foreign governments and would correct past discrimination by active recruitment of Jews for overseas posts.

A similar conciliation agreement was reached with International School Services, Inc., the teacher recruiting agency, after the League had filed complaints with EEOC and the New Jersey Division on Civil Rights, charging that the Princeton-based firm had specified that it would not hire Jews. Against formidable odds of official apathy, the League thus proved that the law could be applied successfully.

Within a week of its boycott report, the League issued a second survey. It charged that America's banking and shipping industries were major boycott participants, disclosing that commercial banks, at the behest of the Arabs, required American exporters to submit certificates of anti-Israel boycott compliance before letters of credit would be validated and paid, thereby setting up a secondary boycott in violation of declared U.S. policy in the Export Administration Act. It also charged that steamship lines signed certificates of boycott compliance in possible violation of U.S. shipping laws, naming 14 lines, including federally subsidized American flagships. Graubard urged President Ford to order corrective action and then placed the data before the House International Trade and Commerce Subcommittee. Over the next several weeks, League representatives discussed the boycott practices with officials of a number of major banks, many of whom indicated that while they did not wish to take the initiative, they did hope that the practice of including the restrictive certificates with letters of credit could be halted.

On May 31 a meeting was held with Arthur F. Burns, Chairman of the Federal Reserve Board. After thorough study, on December 16 the Federal Reserve Board issued a warning to the approximately 5,800 commercial banks within its membership, that their honoring of boycott-tainted letters of credit "constitute a direct violation to Federal antitrust laws or of applicable state anti-boycott laws." The board's warning added that "participation of a U.S. bank, even passively, in efforts by foreign nationals to effect boycotts against other foreign countries friendly to the United States, particularly where such boycott efforts may cause discrimination against United States citizens and businesses, is a misuse of the privileges and benefits conferred upon banking institutions." Cited as a "specific abuse" was the processing by banks of letters of credit requiring boycott compliance in order to receive payment.

"Contradictory Policies"

Press and public reaction to the revelations of the extent of American compliance with the boycott spurred on the congressional probers and those who favored corrective legislation. Administration leaders, however, began taking clear stands in open opposition to the proposed laws. Despite oft-repeated general statements of American principles, Administration officials appeared before Congress in opposition to the antiboycott legislation. Charles W. Hostler, Deputy Assistant Secretary for International Commerce, testified that the Commerce Department believed legislation prohibiting American

firms from complying with the Arab boycott "would be ill-advised."
A high Treasury Department official, while expressing hope that
Saudi Arabia would end its anti-Jewish discrimination and boycot-
ting, said that his department was opposed to strengthening the U.S.
Export Administration Act because it might stifle Arab investments
here.

The Defense Department passed the buck on the League's charges
that the U.S. Army Corps of Engineers was violating the Civil Rights
Act of 1964; Defense announced it would refer the matter to the State
Department. The State Department, for its part, sent spokesmen to
testify before Congress that a lifting of the Arab boycott would come
with a final settlement of the Arab-Israeli conflict—thus, in effect,
denying that the violation of American policy by American firms and
the boycotting of American firms by other American firms constituted
an American problem.

Yet the threat of legislation brought some administrative action.
The Commerce Department reminded exporters of the existing regulation requiring them to report all boycott requests received, and then
on May 21 initiated proceedings against five exporters that failed to do
so. However, the department continued its adamant opposition to any
new law forbidding compliance with such requests.

The League now charged that key executive department agencies
were handling the boycott questions with "contradictory policies,
buck-passing and confusion." Their reactions were characterized as
"rationalization" and marked by "protestations that the documented
wrongs are unavoidable or do not exist at all." Quoting a White House
letter that officials of various departments had testified before a House
Committee "addressing many of the issues," the League pointed out
"that most of the officials had testified *against* the proposed legislation" and followed a "soft policy" with respect to the boycott operation's abuse of American principles.

Six months later, at the League's 1975 annual meeting on November
8, Deputy U.S. Attorney General Harold R. Tyler delivered a message
from President Ford, advising that he had directed that steps be taken
to see that laws prohibiting discrimination against Americans "are
rigorously observed" and that he had requested and received "recommendations for further action" that might be necessary. On
November 20, as promised, the White House announced a series of
measures dealing with Arab-instigated discrimination against
American Jews. But while the announcement dealt with acts of religi-

ous discrimination already illegal, it did not address the restrictive aspects of the boycott which so many Washington officials had indicated they were willing to see continue unchallenged and unchanged.

Throughout the second half of 1975, the League pressed the Department of Commerce to cease circulation of Arab trade tenders with boycott specifications. In August it wrote Secretary Rogers Morton urging that the Department "comply with public policy" by ending this "routine practice." The department replied that refusal to disseminate Arab tenders because of the boycott clauses would deny U.S. firms "access to business opportunities" but agreed to stamp such tenders with a warning that it was against American policy to boycott a friendly nation. The League refused to accept this device, and on September 10 filed suit against the Secretary of Commerce in Federal District Court in New York to stop the practice of "promoting, aiding and abetting Arab boycott operations, thereby restricting free trade and discriminating against American Jews" since many firms had been blacklisted because they were Jewish-owned. The matter never came to court as League leaders and Secretary Morton met on November 3 to talk out the issues. Toward the end of the month, Morton issued orders barring the department from further dissemination of "foreign trade opportunities containing boycott provisions . . . or based on documents containing such provisions." Furthermore, Foreign Service officers were instructed to no longer forward documents with boycott provisions. In April 1976, after a meeting with League representatives, Elliot Richardson, who succeeded Morton, took the department a step further. "Public disclosure is appropriate" he agreed with the League, in the case of firms that violated the reporting requirements of the Export Administration Act.

Nothing changed much, however, as industry went its way in pursuit of Arab business deals. No one took to heart the belated Government warnings, as they were obviously countered by Government actions that encouraged flouting of the Export Administration Act. The Federal Reserve Bank's admonition was ignored; the Commerce Department's statements not taken seriously. Business worried only about public exposure, and the possibility of legislation with enforcement provisions. Recognizing this, opponents of the boycott began to build a public case of the violations of law by industry. On March 11 the Anti-Defamation League released a survey that charged 200 American companies and 25 major banks, including the 6 biggest, with waging "economic war" as collaborators of the

Arabs. To rely on voluntary compliance with antiboycott policy, the League showed, was a mistake and a delusion. Both businessmen and bankers ignored the policy and went about the process of validating boycott documents. The League followed up its report with testimony before the House Judiciary Committee's Subcommittee on Monopolies, urging remedial legislation that would enforce the antiboycott policy.

The disclosures had some salutary results. A number of companies announced changes of policy, others offered support for new legislation. Two Philadelphia banks and a number of banks in other cities announced they would cease to accept letters of credit with boycott stipulations. Two giant food processors, General Mills and Pillsbury, agreed to support legal enforcement, and General Mills urged the House International Relations Committee to adopt amendments to the Export Administration Act that would prohibit, rather than merely warn against boycott compliance. General Mills' testimony termed the Arab restrictions "contrary to the long-term policies and interests inherent in the American tradition.... Free trade is inexorably linked with human freedom...."

By the summer of 1976 two antiboycott bills—out of two dozen that had been thrown into the hopper—started to move through the legislative process. In the Senate, the Stevenson-Williams Bill called for a ban on "tertiary boycotts"—that is, the boycotting of blacklisted American firms by firms doing business in Arab states. It also mandated public disclosure of the names of firms reporting requests or compliance with the boycott to the Commerce Department. In the House, the Bingham–Rosenthal Bill went further, seeking to prohibit secondary boycotts—that is, refusal of companies to do business with Israel at the behest of the Arabs.

Administration officials spoke out in opposition. For the Commerce Department, Deputy Assistant Secretary Hostler took the position that "American firms should not be restricted in their freedom to make economic decisions based on their own business interests" except in cases of illegal religious discrimination. For the Treasury Department, Assistant Secretary Gerald L. Parsky offered the view that "a peace settlement is the best way to bring a definite end to the Arab boycott" and that passage of the Bingham–Rosenthal Bill would "cripple the United States effort" for peace. Testifying for the League before the House International Relations Committee on June 10, Seymour Graubard replied to Hostler that "Commerce seems to feel that American firms may properly have business restrictions forced on them by foreign powers" but not U.S. law forbidding "compliance with the boycott." Addressing Parsky's argument, Graubard pointed to the long years of war and asserted: "We cannot wait passively any longer ... before seeking to halt Arab coercion of American business firms ... it is necessary for firms wishing to stand up to the Arab boycott to be protected."

The Senate passed the Stevenson–Williams Bill, weakened by the Tower Amendment, which exempted bank letters of credit from the export law's reach. The House adopted the Bingham–Rosenthal Bill. Congress was now ready for a Senate–House conference committee to adjust differences, but unanimous consent to appointment of the committee was blocked by Senator John Tower of Texas. A rare parliamentary maneuver, it worked because time was running out on the ninety-fourth Congress. An informal committee was named and the Administration proposed a watered-down version of the bills before it. The conferees opposed it and it came to naught. When the Export Administration Act expired on September 30, President Ford continued the Commerce Department's powers by executive order. He also instructed the department to make public the names of business firms reporting Arab boycott requests and any actions by such firms either rejecting or complying with the requests. The order satisfied the remaining complaint in the Anti-Defamation League suit against the Commerce Department in September 1975. As for Congress, it closed out its legislative year with passage of the Tax Reform Act, which included an amendment introduced by Senator Abraham Ribicoff, cancelling the benefits—originally provided to encourage overseas operations—of companies with foreign subsidiaries that complied with the Arab boycott. All sides had now built their defenses for the 1976 national election campaign debate.

While President Ford took the necessary steps to preserve the existing regulations affecting the boycott and to make some minimal improvements, he failed to shift the onus for failure of the legislative effort onto Congress. His Democratic opponent in the campaign was generally stronger in support of reform. Jimmy Carter denounced the boycott in clear terms "... in my judgment legislation should be passed to make compliance with the secondary boycott of Israel illegal. I regret that the Ford Administration continues to oppose such legislation which seeks only to bring America's commercial practices into harmony with America's humane principles." If that sounded like campaign oratory, he was at least reading the public mind correctly. Shortly after the election a Louis Harris public opinion poll revealed that a 71 percent majority disapproved of the refusal of Arab countries to do business with U.S. companies that also deal with Israel. Only six percent took the opposite viewpoint.

In February 1977 Congress picked up the legislative burden once more. The Senate began consideration of a measure, now known as the Williams—Proxmire Bill, and the House took up the Bingham—Rosenthal Bill again. They called for outlawing both secondary and tertiary boycotts and heavy penalties for violations. Commerce Secretary Juanita Kreps and Treasury Secretary Michael Blumenthal supported the legislation, and President Carter said he saw the boycott as a moral issue. Among Administration spokesmen, only Secretary of State Cyrus Vance voiced unhappiness. He said the proposed measure would make his task in the Middle East more difficult.

No longer able to find substantial support in the Administration on the issue, Arab propagandists and their allies in American industry stepped up their tactic of preaching doom and predicting destruction for America if Congress should enact the tough measures before it. Two broad coalitions appeared on the scene to oppose antiboycott legislation. The first drew together a number of major firms that included important banks, oil and construction companies with large Arab interests, and trade organizations such as the National Association of Manufacturers, the U.S. Chamber of Commerce, and the Emergency Committee for American Trade. The second was sponsored by the National Association of Arab—Americans under the pretentious title, "Full Employment in America Through Trade" (FEATT) and for a time drew the participation of oil firms and other industrial giants. These left quickly when the organization was exposed as harboring extremist and anti-Semitic elements. The propaganda line fostered by FEATT and its allies included dire predictions that the antiboycott laws would lead to American economic collapse, rampant unemployment, and even the disappearance of the United States as a major power.

The Petroleum Equipment Suppliers Association predicted that a billion dollars in wages would be sacrificed by the antiboycott bills in its industry. The Association of General Contractors foresaw all Arab trade going to Europe and Japan if the new bills were enacted, and FEATT itself prophesied loss of a million jobs in five years. The American decline to "a second-rate power," recession, and massive unemployment had even earlier been predicted by Mobil Oil in newspaper advertisements, and the doomsday line was repeated over and over again by pro-Arab lobbyists and flacks. A newcomer to this group was onetime Vice-President of this "doomed" land, Spiro Agnew. Now acting as a business consultant, Agnew warned that an "insurmountable wall" was being raised between "staunch friends" that would cost "millions of American jobs" as Arabs withdrew their trade. The antiboycott bill, he said, was the way to "commit hara-kiri to satisfy the small but powerful Zionist lobby." Agnew was only repeating—to borrow his own phrase—the charges of the "nattering nabobs" and lobbyists of the pro-Arab camp.

The Senate Subcommittee on International Finance at its hearings on the Williams–Proxmire Bill which began on February 21, heard these arguments repeated interminably. An answer for the record came from Maxwell Greenberg of Los Angeles, chairman of the Anti-Defamation League's national executive committees. He spoke for the Jewish groups most vitally concerned with the issue: the League, the American Jewish Committee, the American Jewish Congress, and the National Jewish Community Relations Advisory Council. Arguing for adoption of the Williams–Proxmire proposal, he dismissed opposition to it as "specious in content, fear-mongering in intent, and, in some instances, simply designed to curry favor with Arab business clients." He asserted it would cause American businessess no measurable loss of international trade and would strengthen the nation's moral position:

> Experience bears out that Arab boycotting countries will buy the best available product for the cheapest possible price in the shortest delivery time offered. They are first and foremost, businessmen. . . . American know-how, technical genius and product superiority . . . have been the major factors in Arab trade with the United States. If and when the American business establishment loses these special characteristics and qualities, the Arabs will go elsewhere—whether or not our businessmen have knuckled under to the boycott . . . the Arabs will not turn their backs on American enterprise . . . even in the face of an effective antiboycott law . . . if we remain competitive in terms of quality, service and price.

The time had long passed, he told the committee, for endless rejoinders to opponents of antiboycott legislation: "The question, simply stated, is whether this great nation will acquiesce to improper foreign demands which generate practices clearly in conflict with American principles and interests."

A Joint Approach

Greenberg spoke thus in full knowledge that not only the committee members, but some of the nation's most powerful business leaders were listening sympathetically. Three weeks earlier he had participated in a remarkable closed-door meeting between contending parties looking for a solution to the emotionally charged boycott issue that would be in the nation's best interest. Within another month, that and subsequent sessions were to produce a formula that resulted in legislation acceptable to Congress and the President and to the parties in conflict—the leaders of big industry and those of the Jewish community.

It began with a casual meeting on November 30, 1976, between Irving Shapiro, Chairman of the Board of duPont, and Benjamin R. Epstein, the national director of the Anti-Defamation League. They were attending a League dinner. As recalled by both men later, Shapiro said in passing: "You know, you're going about this boycott thing in the wrong way if you are taking on a major fight with the American business community." Epstein recognized it as no idle comment. He knew Shapiro to be one of the most respected voices of American industry. As chairman of the prestigious Business Roundtable whose 170 members included the chief executives and board chairmen of the nation's major corporations, Shapiro had a reputation for statesmanship. They were joined by Burton M. Joseph, the new national chairman of the League and himself president of a major Minneapolis grain concern, the I. S. Joseph Company; Frank Carey, Chairman of the Board of IBM, and Nathan Perlmutter, who was to succeed Epstein as the League's national director. Their talk took on substance. Shapiro thought a bitter struggle could be headed off if men from the Business Roundtable and the League sat down and talked things out. It seemed to him that a meeting of the minds was possible. Joseph was delighted with the idea. "Let's see if we can make it work," he said.

It took a month to clear the decks. Then a meeting was set for January 28, 1977. Twelve men from the Business Roundtable and an equal number from the League met in the boardroom of the Seagram Company, together with legal counsel and consultants. The group included Clifford C. Garvin, Jr., of Exxon, Thomas A. Murphy of General Motors, Reginald H. Jones of General Electric, George P. Schultz of Bechtel, Robert H. Mallot of FMC Corp., Walter Wriston of Citicorp, and Ralph Lazarus of Federated Department Stores, all chairmen of their companies. Chase Manhattan and Mobil Corp. were represented by high-placed executives. The League had its principal officers and executives present, many of them also heads of major companies. Three or four men in the room were leaders in both organizations. If the men did not all agree and the bargaining was hard, at least they spoke the same language and the commitment from the beginning was to find an acceptable accommodation. The drafting of the joint statement of principles which was to serve as the basis for legislation was placed in the hands of a committee of lawyers that

Saudi Black List—As Congressional interest in the Arab boycott grew, Senator Frank Church briefed the Senate Subcommittee on Multinational Corporations, exhibiting the 1975 roster of 1,500 blacklisted American companies.

included Greenberg, Forster, and Max Kampelman of Washington representing the League and Hans Angermueller of Citicorp, Gerry Kandler of duPont, and Vincent Johnson of General Electric, representing the Business Roundtable.

The finished draft was circulated to the Business Roundtable executive committee and received the approval of 38 members. Two expressed reservations and one, Rawleigh Warner of Mobil, dissented. The League throughout had been in consultation with its associates in the antiboycott battle, the American Jewish Committee and the American Jewish Congress. On March 3 it was forwarded to President Carter who had signaled his interest in the procedure and now adopted the draft as the Administration position. Soon, however, public conflict broke out over interpretation of a clause permitting an Arab country to select a product by brand name. Under questioning by Senator Adlai Stevenson III in hearings of the Senate Finance Subcommittee, Shapiro declared the understanding of his group to be that there was no limitation to such selection. To the same question, Joseph replied that the statement clearly rejected selection if it was designed to comply with the boycott. The firebrands were ready to start fighting again. As Epstein described this moment, "Everything seemed to break down in misunderstanding, confusion and anger. But with White House urging, the two chairmen brought the teams together again." The legal team, with Alfred Moses of the American Jewish Committee and Paul Berger of the American Jewish Congress included, met and reworked the disputed clause. It left the conflict to be reconciled by the regulations to be issued by the Commerce Department implementing the law. Shapiro still had the problem of bringing the diehards in the Business Roundtable along with him. He turned to Clifford Garvin of Exxon to quiet the rebellion, especially among the oilmen. Secretary of State Vance added his voice and Garvin responded favorably. The Business Roundtable executive committee as a result acted unanimously in support of the reworked clause.

Congress finished voting on the bill—actually a set of amendments to the Export Administration Act of 1969 which outlawed both secondary and tertiary boycott—on May 16, and President Carter signed it into law on June 22 at an elaborate ceremony in the Rose Garden of the White House. He took particular note of the unusual role taken by the Roundtable and the League as citizen groups helping Congress and Executive branch solve a critical legislative problem. No doubt with

(Above) *Consultation–League officials Benjamin R. Epstein and Burton M. Joseph with Vice President Mondale.*

(Below) *The statement of principles which led to the adoption was drafted by a joint law committee gathered here for the signing ceremony. From the left, Maxwell E. Greenberg, then chairman of the League's national executive committee; Hans H. Angermueller, Citicorp; Vincent Johnson, General Electric; John Hoffman, Citicorp; Arnold Forster, ADL general counsel; Gerry Kandler, DuPont; Max Kampelman, member of ADL's national executive committee.*

the disputed clause in mind, the President commented that ''the new law does not threaten or question the sovereign right of any nation to regulate its own commerce with other countries... the bill seeks to end the devisive effects on American life of foreign boycott aimed at Jewish members of our society. If we allow such a precedent to become established, we open the door to similar action against any ethnic, religious, or racial group in America.''

The principal provisions of the law declared that:

> An American firm may not refuse to do business with Israel as a condition of doing business with Arab states.

> An American firm may not refuse to do business with another American firm because the latter is owned by Jews or has Jews among its board members or executives, or because it is on a blacklist.

> American firms and individuals are forbidden to practice any form of religious or ethnic discrimination to meet boycott requirements.

> American firms are prohibited from acting in any way as enforcers of the boycott, and they may not respond to any request for boycott-related information—such as information about a person's religion, a company's present or contemplated dealings with Israel, or the presence or nonpresence of a company or individual on an Arab blacklist.

> American firms may make no agreements, secret or otherwise, with Arab states concerning participation in the boycott.

> Boycott-tainted letters of credit were outlawed and negative certificates of origin were to be banned within one year.

Beyond the legal prohibitions against the principal features of the secondary and tertiary boycotts, the law also provided additional important safeguards. For example, although an American firm resident in an Arab country may be required to comply with that country's laws, including its regulations as to what may be imported, it was forbidden to use that situation intentionally to evade American law on the boycott.

The Arab boycott was a testing of American business ethics in a political context. It came down to the question: What price democratic commitment? There were some heroes, some villains, and many who were easily seduced. Government itself waffled badly on political principles, and there were some in high positions who shortchanged the nation's democratic commitments for what they thought was its diplomatic advantage or economic need. Public concern swung the tide. It was expressed in the halls of Congress, in public discussion, and ultimately in meetings of some of the contending parties seeking solutions and compromise that would best serve the ideals and needs of the nation. Other nations, too, had been subjected to heavy Arab boycott pressures, and few did as well in resisting. Some of the leading democracies failed the test. As for American Jews: They fought the issues from positions of strength, and came away reasssured that the American system worked.

Anti-boycott measures—President Carter signed the amendments in the White House Rose Garden with Congressional leaders, the Business Roundtable and League officials looking on. "The bill seeks to end divisive effects on American life."

TEN

The Prevalence of Prejudice

America has always had an ear cocked to the sound of that different drum pouring forth its messianic message of a kindlier society in the making. Too often the promise has been drowned out by the clashing noises of conflict, for America has never fully escaped its European heritage of religious tensions, ethnic rivalries, and their political consequences. From the very beginning, the prevalence of prejudice stood as a stumbling block on the road to that better social order.

Let us look once more, briefly, at American beginnings. There is for instance the remarkable achievement of religious liberty—a truly revolutionary achievement. Few who came in search of freedom were prepared to share it. Most settlers brought with them a full bag of hatreds, religious animosities, experience in the persecution of dissenters, though themselves often the victims of attack. European immigrants in every era arrived with their bundles of prejudices intact, prepared to carry on Old World wars. This they proceeded to do, only now they were acting as Americans. The belief systems that nurtured these conflicts gave birth to American nativist, extremist, racist, and fundamentalist movements which in turn represented attacks on America's democratic institutions and a weakening of commitment to the democratic system.

How America treated its minorities became through the years a valid test of the health of that system. The current level of anti-Semitism, one of the prize packages in the bag of imported hatred that

259

in time became naturalized into an American phenomenon, would seem to attest to the strength of the nation's democratic institutions. Overt discrimination, unbridled expressions of prejudice against Jews have been at low ebb. But anti-Semitic attitudes have receded slowly indeed. Is that important? Why be concerned with prejudices that are not acted out in antisocial behavior? Is there a tendency, in focusing on anti-Semitic beliefs, to exaggerate the extent of the problem? The answer to the last question, of course, is yes, even as to judge the extent of anti-Semitism by placing stress on discrimination is to minimize it.

In four decades of opinion polling, a curiously consistent finding has been that Jews are inclined to overstate the extent of anti-Semitism and non-Jews to underestimate it. Jews seemingly respond most sensitively to prejudicial attitudes; the non-Jew, whatever his biases, feels he does not act on them and sees improvement in nondiscriminatory practices. These views reflect two warring elements of American life: the durability of historic prejudice and commitment to democratic process.

Furthermore, in the second half of the twentieth century, these trends were complicated by responses to anti-Semitic manifestations elsewhere in the world. America could no more isolate its spiritual problems from the rest of the world than it could isolate itself. It therefore entered into the great reappraisal by Christian conscience of religion's past role and present responsibilities for the anti-Semitism that led to the Nazi persecutions and the Holocaust. In the postwar period, anti-Semitism became an international concern in a way that it had never been in all the centuries of Jewish persecution. It led to Vatican Council II and to similar conclaves by the World Council of Churches and other major Protestant bodies. What were the root causes of such incredible hatreds? How awful must be the prejudice that can lead to the immolation of 6,000,000 human souls.

Even if the practice of anti-Semitic discrimination is under control, can anti-Semitic attitudes be ignored? Sometimes the question was phrased differently. As long as discrimination is at low ebb, is there need—or is it even possible—to change inbred prejudices? There was no agreed-upon answer.

Swastika Epidemic, 1959

Then, on Christmas Eve 1959, a minor act of vandalism—daubing paint on a building—occurred in Cologne, Germany. Normally, that should have been of interest only to the local police. But the time and the place, the character of the vandals and the object of their desecration turned it into a sensational incident that had worldwide repercussions—an incident that once more bore witness to the extreme durability of anti-Semitism. The building selected by the German youths for their vandalism was a synagogue, the symbol smeared on its walls a swastika. A nasty little incident, but seemingly of little significance until—within days—similar daubs appeared on synagogue buildings and in cemeteries and homes throughout Germany, then in hundreds of other European cities, and finally, spanning the ocean, in hundreds of places throughout the United States.

Desecrated synagogue–Within two months 643 such incidents took place in the U.S. in 1960. It led to the League's California studies.

Within two months, 643 incidents were recorded in this country. Then the brief storm subsided, the sense of shock faded, but the old, unanswered questions remained. The epidemic of swastikas had flowed from the paintbrushes of young people, not hardened, hate-filled old Nazis. Fifteen years after World War II, could anti-Semitic hatreds survive the horrors of the Holocaust even in the young? Was the evil hopelessly and forever uneradicable? Could the whim of a few wayward youths set off a worldwide orgy without let or hindrance, and could it be repeated time without end?

When the shock and the sensationalism faded from the public mind, the questions remained, and a search for some answers began. The Anti-Defamation League sent a study team to Germany to go over the ground where the events had originated. There were no definitive answers to be found. Whatever the complications of German life, whatever the failures of its educational efforts and the difficulties of establishing a democratic society, in the matter of anti-Semitism, Germany remained an exceptional case. It was both more vulnerable to anti-Semitic outbursts, and, out of its past guilt, quicker to take uninhibited police action. But it had no answers to the core problem.

In Germany one could rationalize the causes for the swastika epidemic. One could find them in the Hitler period and in its people's long history of anti-Semitism. But what evoked the responses in the United States? To find some answers, the League in 1960 undertook a massive research project—proposed by Oscar Cohen, its program director—into the patterns of prejudice in America with emphasis on the nature and causes of anti-Semitic attitudes. Cohen believed fervently that the social sciences could provide new tools and new approaches to the old problems. At the League's behest, the plan for the study was drawn by the Survey Research Center of the University of California at Berkeley and carried out over a five-year period by a team of social scientists led by Dr. Charles Y. Glock, a specialist in the sociology of religion and director of the center. At this writing, the vast amount of data accumulated is still being mined.

Dr. Glock has described the study as "a group of interrelated projects focusing on those aspects of American society which were crucial in determining the extent and course of anti-Semitism." Answers were sought for penetrating and disturbing questions. Were Christian beliefs, church teaching, and clerical attitudes continuing to nurture anti-Semitic attitudes in America? What were the links between anti-Semitism and political extremism, and what was the potential for political anti-Semitism in contemporary America? What, indeed, were the anti-Semitic beliefs and practices of the day? How did children acquire anti-Semitic beliefs? And young people? How had the civil rights movement affected the relations of Jews and Negroes? Did understanding of the Nazi period influence American public opinion toward Jews?

Historians have long recognized anti-Semitism as Christianity's most disturbing legacy to the Western world. That, too, is the way Jews see the matter. To them, Christian teaching through the ages has been the most effective agent in the promotion of hatred of Jews. Christians generally find such uncompromising charges unacceptable and self-defeating. Why dwell on the past in a time of growing consensus on ethical concepts, increasing religious harmony and common action promoting social justice? Why continue to look to the depressing past in this new day of an exhilarating ecumenism? Christian leaders were not ready to concede that Christian beliefs continued strongly to affect anti-Semitic attitudes. They skeptically viewed historian Raul Hilberg's thesis that pagan Nazism found in religious based anti-Semitism the means for exploiting political anti-Semitism.

On the other hand, social scientists looking at the Nazi phenomenon, paid little heed to the religious factor. They sought more contemporary sources of anti-Semitism: economic, political, social, and psychological. An inventory of thirty years of research into anti-Semitism prepared by Princeton sociologist Melvin M. Tumin for the League in 1961 included 183 studies, of which only 13 touched on religion. Too frequently, the study of anti-Semitism had become subordinate to the study of Nazism, and sometimes the two were equated and seen as one. The possibility, suggested by Hilberg and others, that religious bigotry might have prepared a state of mind that made possible acquiescence by so many in the horrors of the Holocaust was lost on most social scientists.

The Religious Factor

The first of the studies to come out of the League's program at the University of California provided jolting evidence that Hilberg's thesis might have validity. The findings left "no grounds for complacency" and was in time to change the perceptions of the nation's religious leaders.

Advance data from the study, for instance, were presented to Vatican Council II in statements by Cardinal Cushing of Boston speaking for the American prelates and by Cardinal Bea, who headed the committee in charge of the schema on the Jews.

The mass of scientific data gathered revealed the strongly negative affect of Christian teaching and beliefs on attitudes toward Jews: 25 percent of all Americans with anti-Semitic attitudes derived their prejudices from their religious indoctrination; another 20 percent were influenced to some degree by their religious orientation. Only one in 20 prejudiced Americans acquired their anti-Semitic bias through purely secular sources.

What were the religious influences? Dr. Glock and Rodney Stark, who carried out this phase of the research, found the answer in a causal chain that coupled "orthodoxy—commitment to a literal interpretation of Christian dogma—to particularism—a disposition to see Christian truth as the only religious truth." The combination leads to hostility toward the religious dissenter who will not see the "truth" or accept salvation. With such hostile religious ideas about Jews, the move to secular anti-Semitism comes easily.

To the investigating sociologists, the evidence was unsettling. "We were entirely unprepared to find the religious roots of anti-Semitism so potent and so widespread in modern society," they reported. Jewish responsibility for the Crucifixion remained "a common belief" and with it the belief that Jews continued under a divine curse, the Lord punishing them for rejecting Jesus. Thus, particularist Christians often held to the view that they had divine approval for their hostility to Jews since they were doing the Lord's work. Such a contemporary view of the Jew does not differ greatly from the medieval age of faith when Christians considered that their continued rejection of Jesus marked Jews as religious outsiders and Judaism as without legitimacy. Only through conversion could Jews attain salvation and acceptance. With such perspectives, an inordinate number of American Christians cited their belief that such great figures of Hebrew Scriptures as Moses, David, and Solomon were not Jews and denied the Hebraic origins of their own faith, seeing only Judas Iscariot, among the Apostles, as a Jew.

American Christians, however, cannot be regarded as a unitary

(Right) *Contrasts—In the Middle Ages, disputations between Christians and Jews were not colloquies between equals but fierce attacks upon the Jewish position (figures on the right are wearing identifying "Jew hats").*

group. There are considerable theological differences among the denominations. The California study found an average 23 percent of
Protestant church members accepting the notion that Jews are being
punished by God and another 13 percent expressing uncertainty on
that score. Fifteen percent of Roman Catholics stated their belief in the
divine wrath; and 8 percent were not sure. But within Protestantism,
the range was a low of 7 percent among Congregationalists who
accepted the thesis to 35 percent among Southern Baptists. When the
Protestant churches were grouped, the combined figure for moderate
denominations was 16 percent, and for the conservative 31 percent.
Glock and Stark found in these figures "dubious basis for . . . [Chris-
tian] interest in the tribulations of Jewry . . . let alone great sympathy
for Jewish victims of persecution."

On a broad scale of anti-Semitic beliefs, only 20 percent of Protestants and 26 percent of Roman Catholics expressed no anti-Semitic
biases. Within the Protestant denominations, the range was 5 percent
among Southern Baptists, on the conservative end, to 26 percent

*Catholics, Protestants, and Jews participated in a colloquium in New York
after publication of study on "Christian Beliefs and Anti-Semitism."*

among Congregationalists and Episcopalians. Anti-Semitism was shown to be lowest among church members on the West Coast and in the East and highest in the Midwest and South, where the orthodox and particularist sects are predominant.

Where, then, was religion's commitment to those ethical standards of brotherly love and social justice which precludes racial and religious prejudice? As always, democratic America safeguards its most precious ideals in its basic institutions. So, too, with religion in America. The organized churches expressed their ethical commitments through their governing bodies and leadership. Their voices have been loud and clear. All major denominations have expressed their opposition to anti-Semitism; they have developed agencies to promote racial justice and to oppose prejudice and discrimination. They have acted as the voice of Christian conscience, but they have not always been heeded by their own most devoted communicants because, while Christian faith requires all men to be regarded as brothers, there are the specific contradictory beliefs that encourage prejudice. The effect on American Protestantism has been to create an inherent tension. Those who seek in religion the inner peace that comes from unquestioning faith find disturbing the activities of those who respond to Christianity's moral challenges. Thus there is often a built-in resistance among the most committed laity to church efforts fostering social justice and combating prejudice. The ethical message from church leadership does not penetrate. Even when of the same mind, pastoral clergymen are often reluctant to project the changes in official church position so as to avoid confrontations within their congregations.

In a survey of Protestant clergymen much like that which produced the data on anti-Semitic prejudices among the Christian laity, the California researchers found ministers considerably less prejudiced against Jews than their flocks, but their anti-Semitism was more highly correlated with their religious beliefs. Despite church pronouncements exonerating the Jews of Jesus' day of the charge of deicide and substantially qualifying Christian judgment of present-day Jews, the general clergy did not accept these judgments to the degree where they could deal with the now officially false beliefs held by the laity. With the clergy largely unconvinced of the revised official doctrine, the message could hardly get through to the churchgoer, and the causal chain remained uninterrupted. The more conservative the clergyman, the less likely he was to preach on social and political issues; the average minister devoted perhaps three sermons a year to such matters, often without committing himself on the issue. In the survey, over half the Missouri Synod and American Lutherans and 42 percent of the Southern Baptist spoke not even once on a social justice issue. In such instances the breakdown in church communication was absolute: deaf ears and closed minds in the presence of a silent pulpit.

Herein lies a major element that sustains the durable prejudices evoked by Christian beliefs. Glock and Stark summed it up in 1969:

> When national conferences of church leaders meet and issue pronounce-ments, they are made up of men who are not directly vulnerable to member opposition...the majority of laymen never even find out what policies their leaders enunciated. But when the risks are high, as in face-to-face confrontations with the laity, the actions are minimal...the churches do not have sufficient authority over their lay members greatly to alter their prejudiced views or even to speak boldly about them....
>
> If we accept the evidence that religious ideas are important in pre-judice, we must then face the fact that at present they more commonly function to sustain prejudice than to overcome it.

Persistent Fantasies

In 1964, when sociologists Gertrude J. Selznick and Stephen Stein-berg addressed themselves to anti-Semitic attitudes in the nation as a whole, they found them fairly low-key but persistent, pervasive and peculiarly grounded not in direct contact or experience with Jews, but in "fantasy images"—the very stereotypes which had so troubled Sigmund Livingston at the start of the century. An anti-Semitic belief system, created by invidious interpretation of very ordinary facts, continued to hang on, winning adherents who learned their pre-judices from distortions. Having no corrective experience with reality, the prejudiced in the 1960s, as in 1900, regarded their biases as objec-tive fact, and therefore as tenable and true. When some measure of personal acquaintance entered into the experience of even the most prejudiced, startling acceptance of positive stereotypes of Jews also entered the picture. Thus, 75 percent agreed that "Jews were warm and friendly people," 67 percent said that with contact one "gets to like" Jews and 73 percent found "Jews becoming more like other Americans."

One last observation no doubt derives from the fact that the immi-rant Jew of the ghetto as an American social type has been replaced by acculturated native-born later generations that increasingly appear inappropriate targets for prejudice. No negative belief about Jews was as widely accepted in the survey as these favorable views. Xenophobia seems to drop away when the purported "stranger" does not turn out to be strange at all and confounds the stereotype of the anti-Semitic myth. But the myth is not necessarily destroyed. Selznick and Steinberg found that "both pejorative and favorable beliefs about Jews [are] . . . a reflection of the familiar assertion of anti-Semites that some of their best friends are Jews" and implicit recognition that they became anti-Semitic "by [first] becoming acquainted not with individual Jews but with anti-Semitic ideology."

To assess the depth and extent of anti-Semitism in the nation, the Selznick-Steinberg study examined not only the prevalence of anti-Semitic beliefs and stereotypes, but the extent of support for discriminatory practices and tolerance for political anti-Semitism. As a measuring rod to establish the intensity of anti-Semitic belief in the individual and ultimately in the general public, they constructed an index of eleven anti-Semitic beliefs on these factors. As administered to the sample, 37 percent were ranked as highly anti-Semitic on the basis of their acceptance of five of the eleven beliefs. Those ranked low in anti-Semitism—indeed, as unprejudiced—numbered 31 percent and accepted only one of the beliefs on the index. The figures were an encouraging improvement, for the most anti-Semitic third of the population twenty years earlier would have accepted as many as eight of the beliefs and the least anti-Semitic third as many as four or five. Selznick and Steinberg concluded however that in 1964 "if the population as a whole were as anti-Semitic as the most anti-Semitic third, Americans would be very anti-Semitic indeed."

The statistical data lend color to that view: 37 percent retained negative images of Jews based on the old myths and canards, and many among these did not consider themselves prejudiced because they regarded as objective fact their beliefs that Jews were "too powerful," clannish, prideful, overly aggressive, intrusive and unethical. More than 25 percent defended the right of social clubs to exclude Jews, and another 29 percent, while opposed in principle to such discrimination, would do little or nothing to oppose the practice. A minority of 36 percent was firmly opposed.

Only 5 percent said they would vote for an anti-Semitic candidate, but a full third of the sample said a candidate's anti-Semitism would make no difference to them. Such indifference to both political and social discrimination was also common among the least-prejudiced third of the population. Only 16 percent rejected the anti-Semitism inherent in all three of the criteria set up in the survey. This small minority constituted the "principled and consistent opponents of anti-Semitism." They exhibited strong commitment to democratic ideas, rose above the apathy of the majority, and rejected the distortions of anti-Semitic ideology.

These statistics bring into focus the discussion of the comparative importance of attitudes and discrimination as measurements of anti-Semitism in national life. Anti-Semitic attitudes and discrimination are in fact indivisible. In a noncritical period, even the most prejudiced may be unwilling to support discriminatory practices or to act out their beliefs. But it is equally true that even the unprejudiced have their sticking point and will raise discriminatory bars under given circumstances that serve their interests. It is sometimes a matter of fashion. The anti-Semite will be tolerant when intolerance labels him too clearly as the bigot; the unprejudiced will go along with barriers against Jews when these are approved by his social or economic peers.

The critical mass lies in the apathetic majority, the indifferent who lack a principled position on bigotry and whose commitment to democratic ideology wavers. Should the anti-Semitic pendulum swing violently to the right, they will follow, for they possess no countervailing commitments and readily assume extreme positions. This is especially troubling in the area of political anti-Semitism were that to become a critical issue as it was for a time in the 1930's and 1940's. In the 1964 survey the indifferent third, who though "not intolerant of Jews are tolerant of anti-Semitism," expressed the view that they would not be bothered by a candidate's anti-Semitism. They could readily render political anti-Semitism a dangerous possibility in a period of turmoil and domestic conflict. From time to time, men with strongly expressed anti-Semitic views have indeed been elected to Congress and other important public offices. That there can be recurrences is a distinct possibility unless there is widespread principled opposition to political anti-Semitism. It is a matter not to be taken lightly.

Adolescent Attitudes

When the California project turned to study anti-Semitism among adolescents, it was found that teen-age images of Jews were largely governed by the traditional stereotypes so deeply imbedded in American culture. The young were not averse to applying these stereotypic traits to their age-group peers, having been exposed to anti-Semitic ideas from the adult world long before they became aware of Jews or understood the meaning of prejudice. They would rarely admit that their knowledge of Jews was limited or perhaps even nonexistent. The model of the study was built on three communities. In the largest, Jews formed 43 percent of the population, the smallest town's population was 23 percent Jewish, and the middle community, far from a metropolitan center, had a Jewish group of less than 1 percent. Contrary to expectations, the greater the Jewish presence in the community, the more extensive the hostility toward Jews seemed to be. The ratio of teenagers with anti-Semitic attitudes in the town with the largest number of Jews was 66 percent, the second town's figures was 53 percent, and the town with the minimal Jewish group was 41 percent.

Nevertheless, under circumstances where interreligious friend-ships developed, there was a natural drop in the incidence of anti-Semitism. In the town with highest Jewish presence, anti-Semitic teen-agers without Jewish friends reached a level of 76 percent and dropped to 20 percent for those with five Jewish friends. In the com-munity with the median Jewish population, the ratio dropped from 60 percent to 25 percent for those with four Jewish friends, while in the town with a minimal number of Jews the figures moved from 41 percent to 31 percent for those with one Jewish friend, to complete absence of anti-Semitism in those with two Jewish friends.

The adolescent absorbed his anti-Semitic beliefs and feelings from a variety of sources: family, friends, social and economic class influ-ences, and competitive school situations. Their lesser ability to make sophisticated judgments of personal traits, historical influences, group cultural differences, and community attitudes added to the surprisingly large amount of hostility found by the sociologists. Young people with the lowest degree of educational achievement and those of low economic status were found to be most anti-Semitic. Surprisingly, this did not apply to blacks laboring under similar or worse deprivations. Students came out of high school with the same prejudices with which they had entered and often with more rigid social distance attitudes. The schools seemed to have failed to recog-nize the prevalence of prejudice or to have skirted the issue, relying on intergroup contacts to resolve the problem. And the question re-mained whether teachers were equipped with sufficient understand-ing of the nature of prejudice to deal with it in classroom situations. In

fact, teachers interviewed at the schools studied were of the opinion
that prejudice was not a serious problem. The self-delusion was part of
the problem, since it denied the need for a sustained program of
education that would lead the adolescent student away from the paths
of prejudice.

The major findings of the California studies, some of which have
been reviewed so briefly here, were offered by the League and the
California University Survey Research Center group not as an indictment but as a challenge to the basic American institutions that have a
collective role in sustaining or opposing prejudice and dealing with its
social effects. As Dore Schary, then national chairman of the League,
phrased it in 1968 at a university symposium in Berkeley, "we em-
barked on the studies in order to determine how the phenomenon [of
prejudice] is maintained in order to develop more effective remedial
steps." The Reverend Theodore M. Hesburgh, president of the University of Notre Dame and chairman of the U.S. Civil Rights Commission, offered the view that "no force in our culture systematically
opposes" prejudice, and his comment was borne out in three days of
discussion of the successes and failures of the basic social institutions
of the land by men directly concerned with and deeply committed to
them.

Their analyses cited the infectious quality of prejudice from child-
hood onward, the nurturing of bigotry in children by adults through
example, the sometime supportive actions of the very institutions

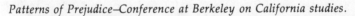

Patterns of Prejudice—Conference at Berkeley on California studies.

which should in fact be principal reforming agents, and the need for that systematic opposition to prejudice cited by Father Hesburgh. They agreed that the learning of prejudice begins within the family setting where concerned social institutions can hardly reach and where the child is exposed by parents to prejudicial acts and attitudes sometimes deliberately, often inadvertently. It is not likely that parental ways can easily be changed and children taught tolerance unless the parent travels that path first. But they also found in their research, evidence that when the child is exposed to school, church and the mass media, he may have his absorbed prejudices confirmed, for these institutions also occasionally and inadvertently teach prejudice. Yet they are the principal hope for corrective learning; their influence, teaching power, and commitment can be the nation's main instrument for the control of prejudice. To these should be added the civic and political organizations which in American life are so basic to the operation of the democratic system.

In commentary on the political institutions, political scientist Seymour M. Lipset pointed out that while in every era in American history politics has been the handmaiden of prejudice, the political arena has been the scene of most victories against prejudice in the past and that it was in this arena that victims of prejudice were most likely to win their struggle. The power of protest by the victims of prejudice remains a potent force. Ultimately, however, success depends on a coordinated effort by the basic institutions, stimulated by greater commitment and greater public awareness of the need. To encourage such commitment and knowledge was a primary objective of the League's research program.

Time and again in the American experience it has been a determined minority that has effected change. The majority may not readily give up its prejudices, but it does give way—often grudgingly—to the justice of a cause. A mix of political action, social action and education in human relations has moved the nation along the democratic path. It has not merely been a matter of ameliorating prejudice in order to eliminate discriminations; as often as not, the elimination of discriminations has led to lowering prejudiced attitudes. The essence of the programs of the human relations agencies lies in a recognition of that fact. The California studies revealed how difficult the process can be, how complex the factors, how slow the progress.

The Critical Sixties—And Beyond

The studies were conducted in years when America was a troubled land. The 1960's were a painful experience remembered for the Vietnam war, and a youthful generation distrustful of an "establishment" that had led the nation into the agonies of that war. It was a generation in revolt because it saw the war as a negation of democratic ideals. America was subjected to that uncomfortable phenomenon: confrontation politics. As already described in previous pages, radical elements of right and left were making political capital, and always at the expense of the existing system.

Memories of conflict fade slowly, but the 1960's and 1970's may yet emerge as a time when idealism triumphed, when the nation won a stunning victory of principle that will color our lives long after the Vietnam defeat becomes dusty history, the wounds of internal conflict healed and the whole misadventure forgiven. For these years saw the victory of the civil rights movement, at least in law. After a century, the nation at last went marching down the road to fulfillment of stifled promises of equality. These years also saw—and this is yet not fully appreciated—the churches and religious leadership addressing the problem of prejudice with a maturity that was the beginning of a quiet revolution in interreligious relationships.

The California survey data that had the most dramatic effect and drew the most concerned responses were those relating to church attitudes and Christian beliefs. Critical as the data were of the church-goer and the lower clergy, church leadership was well aware of the problems of anti-Semitism and concerned with its historic effects. But religious leaders were startled to find that their efforts to deal with Christian-Jewish relations had brought such little success in redirecting the attitudes of their followers.

The history of efforts at interfaith amity goes far to explain the apparently meager results. The men of good will who began organized efforts in the 1930's moved gingerly past theological controversy to hopeful expressions that all who believed in the Fatherhood of God had to accept the idea of the brotherhood of man. Round-table discussions, brotherhood meetings flourished throughout the country as trios of liberal clergymen—Catholic, Portestant and Jewish—led what were essentially informational sessions. The brotherhood movement had its uses. At least some clergymen talked to each other across the barriers of conflicting theology and bitter past history. As superficial as the talk might be, new human contacts were established. Avoidance of the controversial evidently permitted the idea of interfaith colloquy to mature and in time to draw in the conservatives and the institutions of religions. For in the beginning the conservative churches did not participate. It was difficult to find a Catholic priest or fundamentalist minister who would appear with those of other faiths. Sometimes only a representative layman could be found to fill out a trio. The brotherhood movement was the domain of the liberal clergyman; the orthodox, whether Christian or Jewish, were unprepared for the encounter.

The change came sometime in the 1950's, because the world had changed. The Nazi onslaught, the war years, the social upheavals of the 1930's and 1940's moved the great theologians of Europe and America to re-examine the place of religion in modern life, to rethink the traditional postures of their churches and their relationships to each other. Such introspective re-evaluation soon had its effect upon interfaith dialogue. There was a searching for greater depths, for problems of "common concern" as Protestants phrased it; or the "common good" as Catholics viewed it. The social issues raised by events of those years dominated religious thought in America. European theologians sought to redefine their historic and present-day relations to Jews in the baleful light of the Holocaust.

Throughout the 1950's small cooperative ventures, chiefly on social issues, were undertaken by Catholics and Jewish organizations. The contacts were informal, exploratory, and at times very tentative. The Anti-Defamation League strengthened its program directed toward Catholic cooperation by establishing a separate department, building on the growing recognition that there were areas of common concern between the two communities other than the religious. In 1959, the growing Catholic-Jewish colloquy achieved a breakthrough, largely at the initiative of Bishop John L. Wright of Worcester, Massachusetts, a prelate known for his liberal views. It seemed time, Bishop Wright told Dr. Joseph L. Lichten, who headed the League's intercultural affairs department, for a more structured approach to issues bearing on the common good. On May 9, such a planned, jointly sponsored colloquium was held at Assumption College on "the Person and the Common Good." The idea caught on and within a short time similar institutes were held at Catholic colleges throughout the country—

some 150 in the past two decades, supplemented by thousands of less formal discussion sessions. At least on an intellectual level, communication had come into vogue.

Jewish-Protestant dialogue in the same period benefited from an easier relationship that had developed through the era of round-table interfaith symposia and traveling trios of clergy. At least this was true for the more liberal denominations. Here too social issues became paramount and the "common concern" for improvement of civil rights and improvement of race relations led to cooperative action and joint planning. Public affairs kept the lines of communications open on a group to group basis and made approaches on religious issues possible. Always concerned by anti-Semitic fallout from Christian teachings, the Jewish agencies raised questions that brought thoughtful responses from many church educators. What church-school textbooks said, what religious teachers taught about Jews colored all relationships, it was pointed out. To remove distortions, to eliminate offensive judgment of Jews went to the heart of the matter, and change could be achieved without compromise of faith by Christians. There was gratifying cooperation from liberal churchmen; to fundamentalists who saw the words of the gospel as literal truth it was a painful decision. For Jews it was the essence of the matter. Progress was made, but slowly.

The Glock-Stark study held up a mirror for those churchmen most committed to improvement of group relationships in America. What they saw was not a total surprise to them, but it was thought-provoking. For many, complacency went out the window. Some saw they had avoided facing up to the real problems; some became painfully aware that for all their diligence, their work had brought limited results. The inner tensions in the churches and their impact on prejudice startled many of them. The findings moved one Protestant theologian to cry out that he was "left appalled as a human being, embarassed as a Christian and flabbergasted as an educator," as much by the revelation of how many churchmen were "anti-Christian" as by how many Christians were anti-Semitic. He was only one of many such voices. A moment had come in the long history of religious conflict when the facts, spread on the record with all the authority of scientific method, struck a critical chord and gave force to a movement and ideas that had been bubbling up for some time.

In the meantime, the drama played out in Rome by Vatican Council II reached its high point. The Protestant World Council and the Lutheran World Federation were first to adopt manifestos repudiating, as the Lutherans phrased it, the "especially reprehensible...notions that Jews rather than all mankind are responsible for the death of Jesus and that God for this reason has rejected his covenant people." But it was the Vatican Council that focused the eyes of the world on the issue. Unquestionably, it was Pope John XXIII who took the initiative for a new approach to the Church's position on Jews. During the war years he had been witness to the Nazi persecutions. He must have thought deeply about Church attitudes toward Jews before he ascended the Papal throne; he was impressed by the work of the great French-Jewish historian, Jules Isaacs. In 1960, he invited Isaacs to the Vatican to hear directly from the scholar his case for the argument that the Christian "teaching of contempt" was the root cause of anti-Semitism. The audience took place in July; in September, the Pope asked the liberal Cardinal Bea known, as a scholar of the Old Testament, to prepare a declaration on the Jews and in November, Cardinal Bea invited the Anti-Defamation League and the American Jewish Committee to submit memoranda. Within the year a series of papers on various aspects of Catholic-Jewish relations was submitted to Cardinal Bea's Secretariat on the Promotion of Christian Unity by the two organizations and the World Jewish Congress.

The American Catholic hierarchy at the same time evidenced its support for improved relations and became early supporters of a Conciliar statement that would express church rejection of anti-Semitism and revise its historic harsh judgment of Jews. The complex four-year story of the writing and countless revisions of the Council's statement on the Jews need not be fully chronicled here, but it is worthy of note that the American bishops at all of the crucial moments were unwavering supporters of a strong statement. This was especially important during the discussions of 1964 and 1965. When it was revealed in June of 1964 that the statement was being weakened, Cardinal Spellman of New York undertook a private intervention with the Papal Secretary of State. He asserted with some urgency that the declaration must "clearly proclaim that the Jewish people are not to be held guilty of the crucifixion..." The American bishops caucused in September and six of their number prepared to speak on the issue at the third Council session. At the same time the California study's findings on the deicide charge, made available by Dr. Lichten, were distributed to the bishops by the Dutch Documentation Center. As the American prelates fought for an improved statement, opponents in the curia sought to have it re-submitted to the conservative theological commission. Cardinal Spellman and Cardinal Cushing of Boston intervened directly with the Pope in protest.

The issues were hard fought. Fundamentalists held to their literal interpretations of the harsh judgments in certain New Testament passages. The liberal majority among the prelates acknowledged that Christians had harmed Jews and were still supportive of anti-Semitism. Political factors came into play. Arab governments brought pressures to bear. They construed the proposed statement as an act of political friendship for the State of Israel.

The statement on Jews became a contest of maneuver. Between sessions of the Council, the conservatives of the Curia would weaken the text and seek delay. At the sessions the liberal majority pressed its views. Ultimately, the statement was moved out of the schema on ecumenism or "Christian Unity" to the schema on Catholic attitudes toward non-Christian religions. The key word "deicide" was dropped in the final version, but it repudiated Jewish guilt, past or present, in the death of Jesus and deplored "hatred, persecutions, displays of anti-Semitism directed against Jews at any time and by anyone." In a most difficult and complex situation, Cardinal Bea proved himself a supreme strategist and a most committed man. The final vote of the Council on October 28, 1965 was 2,221 yeas and 88 noes, with three not voting, after which Bea observed: "Its beneficial effects will depend on the degree to which it will be understood, assimilated and put into practice."

From the very beginning, American Jewish organizations took a deep interest in the proceedings and were encouraged to do so by Cardinal Bea and American prelates. The Anti-Defamation League sent Dr. Lichten to Rome and he remained there throughout the Council sessions. He later became the permanent representative of the League on Catholic-Jewish relationships in Rome. The American Jewish Committee took a similar interest in church plans for a statement on Jews and the two were soon joined by the World Jewish Congress and the International B'nai B'rith. Subsequently, the Jewish groups formed a coordinating committee for continued liaison with the Vatican, and the Church ultimately evolved a procedure and issued guidelines for implementing the Conciliar declaration. In 1977, the Vatican established a Commission for Religious Relations with the Jews.

The American hierarchy began almost immediately after adoption of the statement to set up its own guidelines. These called for Catholics taking the initiative in fostering Catholic-Jewish understanding, for avoidance of proselytizing, for developing grassroots programs of education, programs at the school and college level and "collaborative scholarly enterprises." The windows of the church were opened wide. Where once no priest could participate in a brotherhood meeting, they now exchanged pulpits with rabbis; where once conferences could become rancorous, there now developed official and permanent Catholic-Jewish community affairs committees. One such was established promptly by Bishop Mugavaro and the League in Brooklyn which has both the largest concentration of Catholics and of Jews in the country.

Change, study, revision of old and the development of new educational material were placed high on the agenda. One spectacular project was the creation of a film series on "The Image of the Jew" as a joint venture of the Archdiocese of New York and the Anti-Defamation League. It was designed as an in-service training course to retrain teachers and ultimately as a parochial school classroom teaching aid. It was ultimately seen by most parochial school teachers

In 1968, the Catholic Archdiocese of New York and the League joined in the production of films on Judaism for parochial schools. At preview left to right: Most Rev. Francis P. Leipzig, chairman of the U.S. Bishops Secretariat on Catholic-Jewish Relations, Dore Schary, Terence, Cardinal Cooke of New York, Henry E. Schultz, Benjamin R. Epstein, Samuel Dalsimer.

throughout the country. Jews and Judaism, studied in the light of the Vatican Council declaration, became a major concern of the American Catholic educational structure.

Whether the "causal chain" that has nurtured anti-Semitism can at last be broken is the unanswered question. The major Christian churches have taken the first step. Catholicism and most Protestant denominations have repudiated the orthodoxy that Jews are responsible for the crucifixion or that they are a rejected people. Can the churches now eradicate the prejudices that have held their communicants in thrall for a millenium? The efforts to reach the minds and to change the perceptions of these millions has now engaged the men of good will—religion's thinkers, leaders and teachers—who have recoiled from the evil that flourishes in the soil of anti-Semitism.

Theirs is an awesome task.

EPILOGUE

Past and Future

Sometime in the 1960's American Jews became suddenly aware that they had lost their identity as a minority. The word had taken on another meaning, and it no longer fitted their status in the American social order. Some felt bereft, like the small boy in the fairy tale who lost his shadow. Many continued to think of themselves in terms of a minority, but somehow the word no longer seemed appropriate. As a group, they were not underprivileged, like the blacks, and certainly they were no longer strangers in the land like the Hispanics and other recent arrivals. Of course, they were only 3 percent of the population and that should have retained for them the designation "minority." But it didn't. In terms of numbers, nearly everyone in this great and populous land was a member of a minority.

What then had been lost? Searching their inner feelings, American Jews found they had lost a sense of siege, a good deal of their psychological insecurities, some of their fears of discrimination and rejection. Some, but not by any means all, felt that Jews continued in an exposed position, targets for attack, if not today then tomorrow, if not in good times, then in some possible and unforseen crisis. But more had become aware that Jews had been swimming in the mainstream of American life for some time. There were poor among them, but also the well-to-do and powerful and great numbers in that middle class which is the backbone of America. Jews had truly merged into the majority; they were in thought, aspirations, commitment, and status part of the majority. They had lost their minority image because something positive had happened over the years, and not because they had been displaced. And what was equally important, the recognized American majority looked upon them no longer as a minority, subject to special treatment, good and bad, but as part of themselves.

Ah, there was the rub. The new, relaxed attitude toward Jews brought its own problems. What had been lost or never understood was the fact that minority status, as currently defined—conditions of poverty and discrimination—was sometimes evidence of anti-Semitism, not its cause. Jews did not have to be a minority in that sense to become objects of anti-Semitism. Anti-Semitism could exist quite independently of its object; it could endure because others found it useful. How could a Jew ever forget that? The new, relaxed attitude therefore brought its measure of menace.

For years, overt expressions of anti-Semitism had been unfashionable. Whatever one's inner attitudes, only the unabashed bigot would give voice to such sentiments publicly. It just was not done; it brought swift condemnation. It was both a matter of morality and manners: public anti-Semitic expression simply was unacceptable from those who valued their respectability. As a matter of fair play, one didn't hit a man who was down. But in the new perception, Jews were no longer a depressed minority. With relaxation, sensitivity toward them also dropped away. The sense of siege, if not of fear, returned. In 1975, so blatant a comment as that of General George Brown, chairman of the Joint Chiefs of Staff, caused anger. It was a shock to hear the head of the armed forces expound publicly the old fabrications that Jews controlled the banks and the media and to warn that Jews have too much influence on Congress. It was a shock, but not as unsettling as it might have been twenty years earlier. He apologized for his *faux pas*, but it wasn't forgotten; it only sank into the collective Jewish subconscious as did the comment a year earlier when Attorney General William Saxbe blurted out that in the days of Joe McCarthy "the Jewish intellectual . . . was . . . very enamored of the Communist party." It was protested, absorbed, and stored away.

It was also noted that even the unprejudiced did not react as sensitively to such violations of the truth as they might have. Indeed, they had lost some of their own sensitivity toward problems of Jews; after all Jews were no longer a depressed minority. Even the depressed minorities—the radicals and the black power groups among them—

could and did spout anti-Semitism, assuming the posture of "giant-killers." Anti-Semitism has its strange uses.

The unease about these matters among American Jews reached the level of anxiety only when faced with attacks upon the security of Israel and the propaganda fallout of Middle East conflict. Arab anti-Semitism was sprayed over Jews everywhere, as if with an aerosol bomb. Most shocking was the emergence of the United Nations as the prestigious forum where the nations of the world would place their stamp of approval on the legitimacy of anti-Semitism. History was made in November 1975 when the General Assembly, in the hands of an Arab—Third-World—Soviet bloc, resolved that Zionism was a "form of racism and racial discrimination." For propaganda purposes, Arabs had long ago eliminated from their lexicon the difference in meaning between Zionism and Judaism. From its inception, American Jews had viewed the United Nations as the hope of the world; now they found it a concert hall for the anti-Semitic chorus. They could console themselves only with the fact that the United States had been vigorous in its opposition. "Infamous" was the word for it, American Ambassador Moynihan told the delegates; they were clearly endorsing anti-Semitism. But the United Nations had become not only a forum, but an instrument of Arab propaganda setting up special operating bodies for the purpose, with the United States refusing to participate and stating its opposition.

To many an observer, there was, in the words of Professor Shlomo Avineri of the Hebrew University of Jerusalem, "a sad irony" here, for the "traditional view of Zionism" saw the emergence of a Jewish state not only as a solution to Jewish homelessness "but also as a therapy to the sickness of anti-Semitism."

"Today . . . it is criticism of Israel . . . which [is] the main target of this new wave of attacks on the Jewish people . . . if [it] starts with Israel, it sometimes very quickly reverts to . . . traditional anti-Semitic patterns."

And American commentator Norman Podhoretz wrote of the same irony:

> . . . it is . . . testimony to the persisting vitality of anti-Semitism which, expelled more or less successfully from domestic society in the countries where once it flourished, now reappears, suitably translated into the current language and modalities of international life, to deal with the phenomenon of a Jewish state among other states as it once dealt with Jewish individuals and communities living in states dominated by other religious and ethnic groups.

Yes, anti-Semitism continues to have its uses. The ultimate unease with which Jews regard the future, even in these, the best of times, and in this the most hospitable of societies, lies in their understanding of history and their long memories. The Holocaust occurred only yesterday; but it was the inevitable result of a millennium of scapegoating. Hitler acted out the hostilities of saints and sinners who through the ages found reason to blame Jews for the shortcomings of mankind. Rome found Hebraic monotheism an attack upon the emperor's claims to divinity and destroyed Judea. Christianity found Judaism's nonacceptance of Jesus as the Messiah reason for centuries of persecution of Jews. In modern times, Jewish liberalism has drawn the fire of reaction on the one hand, and socialism on the other. The Jew has been pictured as the archcapitalist and arch-Bolshevik and chastised for both, whipsawed by contending forces. The Soviet authorities see Jews as a threat to the state and Alexander Solzhenitsyn, who castigates Bolshevik terror, sees Jews as libertarians who brought on socialism, after, of course, rejecting Christ.

What are Jews to make of such a history? In what can they place their confidence? Is America different?

Memory is both the alarm system and the torture chamber of Jewish life. Two dozen powerless ruffians with swastika armbands threatening to march, as in Skokie, Illinois, can set teeth on edge. How far removed are they from the PLO and its murderous raids that recall lives lost through the centuries in persecution and pogrom? The apathy of the majority, even in small things, seems at times as threatening as murder. What awful hostility lies behind some small act of vandalism? A retelling of the events of the Holocaust on television, even though hardly able to record the depths of the evil, evokes remembrance of things past too much for the spirit to bear. And that brooding spirit brings forth, even among the most erudite and sophisticated minds, the nervous question: Can it happen here? It is the wrong question. It should be Mr. Lincoln's question:

Can "a nation conceived in liberty and dedicated to the proposition that all men are created equal...long endure?"

This nation, so conceived, has been tested only in the shattering civil war that called forth Mr. Lincoln's question, not only in cataclysmic world ideological conflicts, but in small ways every day and every year. The nation is a better place today than it was at the turn of the century, before the First World War or the Second; a better place than in the 1930's or 1950's. For all its faults, it is a kinder, more decent society for all its citizens today than yesterday. Will it be so tomorrow? The evidence of 200 years of history would seem to dictate a hopeful answer.

America's poets may sound a truer note than its political pundits. Walt Whitman, moving among the shambles of conflict, could hear America singing its siren song of freedom; an America concerned with mankind, far from a perfect America, but a nation striving for the kinder society. Nearly a century later, on the brink of another war, a world conflagration, Stephen Vincent Benét heard the same siren song, saw the same imperfections, and also the same striving:

> Oh yes, I know the faults and the other side,
> ...All the long shame of our hearts and the long disunion.
> I am merely remarking—as a country we try.
> As a country, I think we try.

And Archibald MacLeish, at yet another crisis, when the nation seemed to have lost its way and gave expression more to its hates than its loves, cried out that "America was a journey toward mankind."

America has continued its journey. The dream and reality of political freedom remain intact. The answer to Mr. Lincoln's question—to his life—is a resounding yes. As long as America values political freedom, there is no need to answer that other nagging question. If the democratic system fails, the answer is obvious, for then the American dream will have faded, the journey toward mankind will have come to an end, and the promise inscribed on the Liberty Bell will not be kept.

Then and only then can it happen here.

Notes

These notes supplement references and sources contained in the text. Books and authors named below are listed in the bibliography.

CHAPTER ONE

American Jewish history has been well served by a considerable number of scholars. Those consulted here include: for Hebraic influence on early American settlers, Oscar Straus, Joseph Gaer and Ben Siegel; for Jews in the Colonial period, Jacob R. Marcus and Lee. M. Friedman; for the Revolutionary War period, Rufus Learsi and Robert St. John; for the Civil War period, Bertram W. Korn and Harry Simonhoff. The well-reasoned interpretations and scholarly studies of Oscar Handlin have been particularly helpful.

For legal history of separation of Church and State, I have consulted the definitive work of Leo Pfeffer, *Church, State and Freedom.*

The George Washington quotation is from his letter to the Newport Hebrew Congregation, 1790.

Thorough-going accounts of the nineteenth-century attacks on Irish immigrants, the Nativist movement and the Know Nothings are included in Gustavus Myers' *History of Bigotry in the U.S.* Another perspective on nativism is to be found in John Higham's *Strangers in the Land.* Lincoln's letter is cited by Myers. The Wolf letter is in the B'nai B'rith archives.

The Beecher sermon and Hilton and Seligman statements are cited in Friedman's *Jewish Pioneers and Patriots.* The material on early American "scientific" racism is drawn from Handlin's essay "The Linnean Web" in *Race and Nationality in American Life.* A related chapter includes his analysis of the Dillingham Commission Report and the Dictionary of Races

CHAPTER TWO

The Burgess quotation is from his *Political and Comparative Constitutional Law* cited by John Roche in *The Quest for the Dream*.

An unpublished manuscript by Hans Adler in the archives of A.D.L. provided data on the life of Sigmund Livingston and the history of the League for the years 1913–1920. The quotation from Gordon Allport appears in his *ABC's of Scapegoating*. Documentation for the discussion on stereotypes in the media and the censorship conflict are in the files of the League and reported in its periodical publications.

CHAPTER THREE

Watson's career has been the subject of several books and many reminiscences; notably C. P. Connolly, *The Truth About the Frank Case*, Judge Arthur G. Powell's *I Can Go Home Again* and C. Vann Woodward's *Tom Watson*. Watson's own publications have been mined intensively by later historians, including Myers. I heard the recollections of Herman Binder directly from him in 1963; the quotation is from an article in the March 1963 issue of the *ADL Bulletin*, "Trial by Prejudice" by Lynn Ianniello. The Boorstin interview with Governor Slaton is in A.D.L. files. The memorial addresses on Watson's death appeared in the *Congressional Record* of January 21, 1923. The Debs quotation is cited by Woodward.

The principal sources of information about the second Klan are to be found in the pages of the *Congressional Record*, the *Federal Register*, court proceedings and the voluminous reporting of the daily press of the period. The Simmons statement was made before the House Rules Committee investigation of the Klan in 1921. The Levinger letter and the Lewis 1926 report are in the files of the A.D.L. Myers treats the second Klan in considerable detail.

For data on Ford's foray into anti-Semitism, I have relied on Allen Nevin's chapter, From Muscle Shoals to Anti-Semitism in his *Ford: Expansion and Challenge* Vol. 2; and the narrative of Keith Sward in *The Legend of Henry Ford*. Myers has an extensive account in his history of bigotry. The Sapiro trial received thorough coverage in *The New York Times*, the *New York World* and the *Detroit Times*. The last named was blamed by the presiding judge for the act leading to the mistrial. Harry Bennett in his 1951 memoir *We Never Called Him Henry* cast doubt that Ford's auto accident ever occurred. Gutstadt's report and Ford's letter to Livingston are in A.D.L.'s files.

CHAPTER FOUR

The Gertrude Atherton quotation appears in her essay "The Alpine School of Fiction," in *The Bookman*, March 1922, Vol. LV No.1. The Harry Starr quotation is from his article "The Affair at Harvard," in the *Menorah Journal*, October 1922, Vol.8 No. 5. E. Digby Baltzell in his *The Protestant Establishment* provides a thoroughgoing account of patrician attitudes and actions in what he calls the "Anglo-Saxon decade." I am much indebted to him. As an aid to my understanding of the Harvard incident, I have had the advantage of a talk with Starr who was a participant in the events as leader of the Jewish students. He is now president of the Lucius N. Littauer Foundation. His 1922 article in the *Menorah Journal* is a classic of its kind. The Conant quotation is cited by Baltzell. Eliot's letter to Adams appears in Henry James' biography of Eliot. The comments from Laski and Ehrmann were reported in *The New York Times*, December 10, 1978 after the ceremonial opening of Lowell's Sacco—Vanzetti papers.

Rubinow's economic analysis appears verbatim in *Jewish Social Service Quarterly*, December 1933, Vol. 9 No. 1. A.D.L. has maintained continuing analyses of trends in social, economic, and educational discrimination since the 1930's. Results have been published in its periodicals, *Rights*, *ADL Bulletin* and *Discrimination Reports*. Among the books in the bibliography reporting these trends are *How Secure These Rights? Barriers, Some of My Best Friends*, and *Discrimination–U.S.A.*

CHAPTER FIVE

For an understanding of the early Roosevelt years, I am indebted to the work of Roche, Schlesinger, Burns and Lubell. The phrase "not so much racial as cultural" is Professor Morton Keller's from his essay included in Stember, *Jews in the Mind of America*.

The McCormack Committee report *Investigation of Nazi and Other Propaganda* was delivered on Feb. 15, 1935 to the 74th Congress. The McNaboe Committee report was titled *History and Organization of the German-American Bund, 1939*. The Dies Committee report, *Investigation of Un-American Activities in the U.S.* was delivered to the 76th Congress, 1941. Donald S. Strong's *Organized Anti-Semitism in America* is a useful compendium for the 1930's.

Sources for the Coughlin story are fully acknowledged in the text. I would add a word of appreciation to my friend Donald Flamm, owner of Station WMCA when it dropped the Coughlin broadcasts. He opened his files to me and shared his personal insights into Coughlin's propaganda methods.

CHAPTER SIX

There has been thoroughgoing research into the agitation against and internment of the Nisei during World War II. I have relied upon the concise accounts in Burns, *Roosevelt: The Soldier of Freedom* and Roche, *The Quest for the Dream*, as well as their accounts of Roosevelt's attitudes towards Negroes.

The statistics on Jewish war service are from the Bureau of War Records of the Jewish Welfare Board, supported by a group of 21 national Jewish agencies. Its work was directed by Dr. Samuel C. Kohs, and guided by a techical committee headed by Dr. Louis I. Dublin, renowned statistician of the Metropolitan Life Insurance Company. The War and Navy Departments cooperated in the interpretation of the accumulated data. The Army and Navy Public Relations Committee was headed by Milton Weill and directed by the author. The data herein are from my files and recollections. A valuable reference is I. Kaufman's *Americans in World War II*

Robert A. Divine offers a scholarly review of events, policy and the contending forces bearing on the admission of refugees and displaced persons in the 1930's and 1940's in his *American Immigration Policy, 1924–1952*. An impassioned account, reflecting the despair and rescue efforts of American Jews, is contained in Arthur D. Morse's *While Six Million Died*. Burns in his biography provides some insights into Roosevelt's reactions and internal conflicts. These together with the *Interpreter Releases* of the Common Council for American Unity, the Congressional hearings and the Jewish relief agencies' reports served as the basis for the narrative here.

The principal testimony on the Immigration Act of 1965 abolishing the national origin quotas appears in the *Congressional Digest,* May 1965; the subsequent debates in the *Congressional Record.*

CHAPTER SEVEN

The data on the media and on restrictive covenants are from A.D.L. files and its 1948 report, *How Secure These Rights?*

The proceedings of the Chicago education conference was published as *Discriminations in Higher Education* (Washington: American Council on Education, 1951). The Roper survey was published by the Council as *Factors Affecting the Admission of High School Seniors to College.* Pamphlet publications included *On Getting into College* by Helen Davis and *Religion and Race: Barriers to College* by A.C.Ivy and Irwin Ross.

Data on the admissions policies at Wisconsin and Purdue will be found in the A.D.L. survey published in *Discrimination Reports,* March 1970; also "Closed Campus," by Harold Braverman, *ADL Bulletin,* April 1970, "Some Things Take a Little Longer," by Robert Gordon, *ADL Bulletin,* June 1972, and "A Campus Controversy," by Saul Sorrin, *ADL Bulletin,* February 1970.

The seven year survey of medical school entering classes appears in *Rights* January 1958 and February 1961, with figures for subsequent years in mimeographed form in A.D.L. files. Articles in *Commentary* by Lawrence Bloomgarden, *Medical School Quotas and National Health* (1953) and *Who Shall Be Our Doctors* (1957) are extremely useful.

A comparison of the DeFunis and Bakke cases and the basic issues is contained in "A Moment of Truth on Racially Based Admissions" by Larry M. Lavinsky, in *Hasting's Constitutional Law Quarterly,* Fall 1976, Vol. 3 No. 4.

CHAPTER EIGHT

Lipset's phrase is from *Politics of Unreason,* his volume in the *Patterns of American Prejudice* series; Schultz's from "Are We a Nation of Againsts?," *ADL Bulletin* November 1953. Buckley's comments on Welch are cited in Forster and Epstein's *Danger on the Right.* The *Union Leader's* comment appeared in an editorial, May 15, 1972.

Socialist Workers' Party statements and articles, unless otherwise noted, are from its official publications, *The Militant, International Press* and the *International Socialist Review.* Whitney Young's letter is cited in the pamphlet *A Black American Looks at Israel,* published by the American Jewish Congress.

Malcolm X's statement appeared in his *Autobiography.* Baldwin's resignation was reported in *The New York Times,* Feb. 28, 1967; Davis' letter in *Reader's Forum,* First Quarter, 1967. Cleaver's comments appeared in a *Reuters* news dispatch. Newton's change of heart and comments on Cleaver appeared in an interview in *The New York Times,* July 17, 1977. Cleaver's article, "Why I Left the U.S. and Why I Am Returning" appeared in *The New York Times,* Nov. 18, 1978.

CHAPTER NINE

For data used in this chapter and related data in Chapter Eight I have had available the voluminous files of A.D.L. and an invaluable guide through the maze in the person of its research director, Jerome Bakst. Included in the massive accumulation are news reports from journals all over the world, research papers, fact-finding surveys and analyses by experienced observers. I am also indebted to his associate Gerald Baumgarten, and to James C. Purcell, who wrote some of the pertinent fact-finding surveys.

The anti-Arab boycott legislative story has been based on a reading of the record of Congressional hearings, official public statements and reports of the various concerned groups. I have had the advantage of interviews with some of the principals in the negotiations leading to passage of the anti-boycott provisions of the Export Administration Act of 1978. Specific dates and sources where pertinent to the narrative have been included in the text.

CHAPTER TEN

Data on the swastika epidemic were gathered by the Civil Rights Division and regional offices of the League and are available in *Swastika – 1960* a report by sociologists David Caplovitz and Candace Rogers. The study team that visited Germany in 1960 included Benjamin R. Epstein and the author.

The statistics, analyses and quotations attributed to the California Survey Research Center are from the series of seven books grouped in the bibliography under the rubric *Patterns of American Prejudice.* Hilberg's thesis is set forth in his *Destruction of European Jews.* Father Hesburgh's comment appears in his foreword to the papers of the 1968 Berkeley symposium published under the title *Prejudice, U.S.A.*

The source material for my discussion of interfaith developments came from memoranda and reports in League files made available by Theodore Freedman, its program director. I have had the good fortune to obtain additional briefings from Rabbi Solomon S. Bernards and Rabbi Leon Klenicki on their work with Protestant and Catholic groups. Dr. Joseph L. Lichten provided me with his personal observations of events in Rome during the Vatican Council sessions. I have also drawn on the work of my old associate, the late Arthur Gilbert. The Vatican Council statement on Jews and subsequent "guidelines" and other data appear in his *The Vatican Council and the Jews.* Father Vincent A. Yzermans devoted a lengthy chapter in his *American Participation in the Vatican Council* to the events surrounding the declaration on Jews. A compendium of church statements and resolutions can be found in the ADL periodical *Christian Friends Bulletin* (December 1965). Rabbi Bernard's article "Jewish-Christian Relationships in America" (*Judaism,* Summer, 1978) is noteworthy. Jules Isaac's thesis is set forth in his book *The Teaching of Contempt.*

Bibliography

Allport, Gordon, *ABC's of Scapegoating* (New York: Anti-Defamation League 1948).
___*The Nature of Prejudice* (New York; Anchor, 1958).
Baltzell, E. Digby, *The Protestant Establishment: Aristocracy and Caste in America* (New York: Random House, 1964).
Belth, Nathan C. (Ed.), *Barriers: Patterns of Discrimination Against Jews* (New York: Friendly House, 1958).
___*Fighting for America* (New York: Jewish Welfare Board, 1943).
Brown, Haywood, and Britt, George, *Christians Only: A Study in Prejudice* (New York: Vanguard Press, 1931).
Burgess, John W., *Political Science and Comparative Constitutional Law* (Boston: Ginn & Co., 1890).
Burns, James M., *Roosevelt: The Soldier of Freedom* (New York: Harcourt Brace Jovanovich, Inc., 1970).
___*Roosevelt: The Lion and the Fox* (New York: Harcourt, Brace, 1956).
Chill, Dan S., *The Arab Boycott: Economic Aggression and World Reaction* (New York: Praeger Publishers, 1976).
Cohen, Naomi W., *Not Free to Desist: A History of the American Jewish Committee* (Philadelphia: Jewish Publication Society, 1972).
Connolly, C.P., *The Truth About the Frank Case* (New York: American News, 1915).
Divine, Robert A., *American Immigration Policy 1924-1952* (New Haven, Connecticut: Yale University Press, 1957).
Epstein, Benjamin R., and Forster, Arnold, *The Radical Right* (New York: Random House, 1967).
___*Some of My Best Friends...* (New York: Farrar, Straus and Cudahy, 1962).
Forster, Arnold, and Epstein, Benjamin R., *Danger on the Right* (New York: Random House, 1964).
___*The New Anti-Semitism* (New York: McGraw-Hill, 1974).
___*The Troublemakers* (Garden City, NY: Doubleday, 1952).
___*Cross Currents* (Garden City, NY: Doubleday, 1956).
Forster, Arnold, *A Measure of Freedom* (New York: Doubleday, 1950).
Fredman, J. George, *Jews in American Wars* (Hoboken, NJ: Terminal Press, 1942).
Friedman, Lee M., *Jewish Pioneers and Patriots* (Philadelphia: Jewish Publication Society, 1955).

___*Pilgrims in a New Land* (Philadelphia: Jewish Publication Society, 1948).

Gaer, Joseph, and Siegel, Ben, *The Puritan Heritage: America's Roots in the Bible* (New York: New American Library, 1964).

Gilbert, Arthur, *A Jew in Christian America* (New York: Sheed and Ward, 1966).

___*The Vatican Council and the Jews* (Cleveland and New York: World Publishing Co., 1968).

Glazer, Nathan, *American Judaism* (Chicago: University of Chicago Press, 1972).

___and Moynihan, Daniel Patrick, *Beyond the Melting Pot* (Cambridge: M.I.T. Press, 1963).

Grusd, Edward E., *B'nai B'rith: The Story of a Covenant* (New York: Appleton-Century, 1966).

Handlin, Oscar, *Race and Nationality in American Life* (Boston: Atlantic-Little Brown, 1957).

___*The Uprooted* (Boston: Atlantic-Little Brown, 1951, 1973).

___*Adventure in Freedom: Three Hundred Years of Jewish Life in America* (New York: McGraw-Hill, 1954).

___, and Handlin, Mary, *Aquisition of Political and Social Rights by the Jews in the U.S.* (Philadelphia: Included in American Jewish Year Book Vol. 56: Jewish Publication Society, 1955).

Hapgood, Hutchins, *The Spirit of the Ghetto: Studies of the Jewish Quarter in New York* (New York: Funk and Wagnalls, 1965; first published in 1902).

Higham, John, *Strangers in the Land: Patterns of American Nativism 1860-1925* (New Brunswick, NJ: Rutgers University Press, 1955).

Higher Education for American Democracy, A Report of the President's Commission on Higher Education. (Washington: U.S. Government Printing Office, 1947).

Hilberg, Raul, *The Destruction of European Jews* (New York: Quadrangle Books, 1961).

Howe, Irving, *World of Our Fathers* (New York: Harcourt Brace Jovanovich, Inc., 1976).

Isaac, Jules, *The Teaching of Contempt: Christian Roots of Anti-Semitism* (Translated by Helen Weaver) (New York: Holt, Rinehart and Winston, 1964).

Javits, Jacob K., *Discrimination—U.S.A.* (New York: Harcourt, Brace 1960).

Kaufman, I., *American Jews in World War II* (New York: The Dial Press, 1947).

Kennedy, John F., *A Nation of Immigrants* (New York: Harper and Row, 1964).

Konvitz, Milton R., *Fundamental Liberties of a Free People* (Ithaca, NY: Cornell University Press, 1957).

___and Leskes, Theodore, *A Century of Civil Rights* (New York: Columbia University Press, 1961).

Korn, Betram W., *American Jewry and the Civil War* (Philadelphia: Jewish Publication Society, 1951. Cleveland: Meridian Books, 1961).

Learsi, Rufus, *The Jews in America: A History* (New York, KTAV, 1972; originally published in 1954).

Lipset, Seymour M., and Reisman, David, *Education and Politics at Harvard* (New York: McGraw-Hill, 1975).

Livingston, Sigmund, *Must Men Hate?* (Chicago: Anti-Defamation League, 1944).

Lubell, Samuel, *The Future of American Politics* (New York: Harper and Bros., 1951).

Marcus, Jacob R., *Early American Jewry* (2 Vols.) (Philadelphia: Jewish Publication Society, 1951, 1953).

___*The Colonial American Jew 1492-1776* (3 Vols.) (Detroit: Wayne State University Press, 1970).

Morse, Arthur D., *While Six Million Died. A Chronicle of American Apathy* (New York: Random House, 1968).

Myers, Gustavus, *History of Bigotry in the U.S.* (New York: Random House, 1943). Revised edition, Henry M. Christman, Ed. (New York: Capricorn Books, 1960).

Nelson, Walter Henry, and Prittie, Terrence, *The Economic War Against the Jews* (New York: Random House, 1977).

Nevins, Allen, and Hill, Frank Ernest, *Ford: Expansion and Challenge 1915-33, Vol. 2* (New York: Charles Scribner's Sons, 1957).

Patterns of Prejudice Series:

Glock, Charles Y., and Stark, Rodney, *Christian Beliefs and Anti-Semitism* (New York: Harper and Row, 1966).

____, Selznick, Gertrude, and Spaeth, Joe L., *Apathetic Majority* (New York: Harper and Row, 1966).

____, Withnow, Robert, Piliavin, Jane A., and Spencer, Metta, *Adolescent Prejudice* (New York: Harper and Row, 1975).

____, and Siegelman, Ellen (Eds.), *Prejudice U.S.A.* (New York: Frederick A. Praeger, 1969).

Lipset, Seymour M. and Raab, Earl, *The Politics of Unreason: Right Wing Extremism in America 1790-1970* (New York: Harper and Row, 1970).

Marx, Gary, *Protest and Prejudice* (New York: Harper and Row, 1968).

Selznick, Gertrude J., and Steinberg, Stephen, *The Tenacity of Prejudice: Anti-Semitism in Contemporary America* (New York: Harper and Row, 1969).

Stark, Rodney, Foster, Bruce D., Glock, Charles Y., and Quinley Harold E., *Wayward Shepherds: Prejudice and the Protestant Clergy* (New York: Harper and Row, 1971).

Pfeffer, Leo, *Church, State and Freedom* (Boston: The Beacon Press, 1967).

Powell, Arthur G., *I Can Go Home Again* (Chapel Hill: Union of North Carolina Press, 1943).

Rischin, Moses, *The Promised City: New York's Jews 1870-1914* (Cambridge: Harvard University Press, 1962).

Roche, John P., *The Quest for the Dream: The Development of Civil Rights and Human Relations in Modern America* (New York: Macmillan, 1963).

____*Courts and Rights* (New York, Random House, 1961),

Schachner, Nathan, *The Price of Liberty* (New York: American Jewish Committee, 1948).

Schlesinger, Arthur M., Jr., *The Crisis of the Old Order* (Boston: Houghton, Mifflin Co. 1957).

Simonhoff, Harry, *Jewish Participants in the Civil War* (New York, Arco Publishing Co., 1963).

Solomon, Barbara Miller, *Ancestors and Immigrants: A Changing New England Tradition* (Cambridge: Harvard University Press, 1956).

Spitz, David, *Patterns of Anti-Democratic Thought* (New York, Macmillan, 1949).

St. John, Robert, *Jews, Justice and Judaism* (New York: Doubleday, 1969).

Stember, Charles, and Others, *Jews in the Mind of America* (New York, Basic Books, 1966).

Straus, Oscar, *The Origin of the Republican Form of Government in the United States of America* (New York: G.P. Putnam's Sons, 1926).

Strong, Donald S., *Organized Anti-Semitism in America: The Rise of Group Prejudice 1930-40* (Washington, DC: American Council on Public Affairs, 1941).

Sward, Keith, *The Legend of Henry Ford* (New York: Rinehardt, 1948).

To Secure These Rights, the Report of the President's Committee on Civil Rights (New York: Simon and Schuster, 1947).

Tumin, Melvin M., *An Inventory and Appraisal of Research in American Anti-Semitism* (New York: Freedom Books, 1961).

Weintraub, Ruth, *How Secure These Rights* (Garden City, NY: Doubleday, 1949).

Wirth, Louis, *The Ghetto* (Chicago: University of Chicago Press, 1928. Chicago: Phoenix Books, 1956).

Woodward, C. Vann, *Tom Watson* (New York: Macmillan, 1936).

Yzermans, Vincent A., *American Participation in the Vatican Council* (New York: Sheed and Ward, 1967).

Index